TWIN DESTINIES

The True Story of the Pappas Twins,
1950s Teen Radio Stars and Broadcasters
in the Classic Hits Era

KATHY PAPPAS ANGELOS

CRAVEN STREET
B O O K S

Fresno, California

Twin Destinies: The True Story of the Pappas Twins,
1950s Teen Radio Stars and Broadcasters in the Classic Hits Era

Copyright © 2023 by Kathy Pappas Angelos. All rights reserved. No part of this publication may be reproduced, stored in a retrieval system, or transmitted in any form by any means, electronic, mechanical, photocopying, recording, or otherwise, without the prior written permission of the author.

Unless otherwise noted, all photos are from the Mike J. and Noula Pappas family archives.

Book design by Carla Green, Clarity Designworks

Published by Craven Street Books, an imprint of Linden Publishing®

2006 South Mary Street, Fresno, California 93721

(559) 233-6633 / (800) 345-4447

CravenStreetBooks.com

Craven Street Books and Colophon are trademarks of Linden Publishing, Inc. Linden Publishing titles may be purchased in quantity at special discounts for educational, business, or promotional use. To inquire about discount pricing, please refer to the contact information above. For permission to use any portion of this book for academic purposes, please contact the Copyright Clearance Center at www.copyright.com.

ISBN 978-1-61035-423-3

135798642

Printed in the United States of America on acid-free paper.

Library of Congress Cataloging-in-Publication Data on file

Good name in man and woman, dear my lord,
Is the immediate jewel of their souls:
Who steals my purse steals trash; 'tis something, nothing;
'twas mine, 'tis his, and has been slave to thousands;
But he that filches from me my good name
Robs me of that which not enriches him,
And makes me poor indeed.

WILLIAM SHAKESPEARE, OTHELLO

For my heroes —
My father, Mike J. Pappas, and my mother, Noula Mehas Pappas,
with love and respect, always

Contents

CHAPTER 1

1946:
Brave Little Warriors

"YOU SEE THE TREE THERE, BOYS? You see the highest branch on that tree? I will hang you from that branch if you ever disgrace the family name!"

As little boys, Pete and Mike stared up into the canopy of the old oak tree where their father pointed, its branches twisting and turning like the arms of a giant octopus waiting to ensnare them should they dishonor the family in any way. Years later as they sat in the school office waiting for their father to arrive, they remembered that tree and those words well, because in a few minutes they would together face the wrath of both the principal and their *baba*, their father, John Pappas, whose words and promised action were chiseled into their memories like hieroglyphs into stone.

With their bruised faces, torn white T-shirts, scratches up and down their arms, and their grass-stained, torn blue jeans, they knew they were in trouble, although they were sure that today's school problems probably wouldn't upset their mother the same way as their father. She would dismiss this problem at school as boyhood mischief, but seeing those tattered blue jeans—the same jeans they begged their mother, Katherine, nicknamed *Titika* (*Tee-tee-kah*), to buy from the five-and-dime store—would be very upsetting to her. The pants were not the name brand of Levi's the boys wanted so terribly, the ones that made them feel just like the other kids, the *Americani,* the American kids who weren't sons of poor immigrants. But their mama, wanting to make them happy so they felt American and prosperous, cut other corners in the family budget so her twin boys, Pete and Mike, could have their treasured *blue jins,* as she would call them in her Greek-tinged English. Their mother understood their need to look nice, to be accepted, to have things *kenooryo,* new, not anything old or used or unattractive. She had that need, too. These two scrappers were her sons, so of course she understood. Pete and Mike's little faces glowed, like brightly lit streetlamps in the middle of a moonless night, when she got them those *pantalonia,* pants. They weren't Levi's, but they would do for now. Their mother had faith they would be successful and own a closet full of *kenooryo blu jins,* all of them Levi's, and she was sure to tell Pete and Mike, and all her friends at church, this fact at every opportunity. Her cubs were not like the other litters born to the average lioness—runts and weaklings. They, like their ancestors, were fighters, and they would win every battle they were forced to fight.

She would make sure they did so.

Both Pete and Mike knew what their mother and father went through every day to survive, with their father toiling in the hot San Joaquin Valley sun as a farmworker and their mother doing all the physical labor required of mothers in the 1940s, so they were thrilled with their new jeans, even if they weren't Levi's.

Now, those jeans were close to ruin and their father was on his way to the principal's office. The major rule of the Pappas family was to not get into trouble in school or anywhere else, especially if it meant that John Pappadojiannis, shortened to "Pappas" at Ellis Island when he landed in New York City in 1914, would come to the school from the fields to attend to his fighting boys. This visit to the twins' school in the middle of the day cost him wages and embarrassment in front of his other immigrant coworkers, especially his fellow Greeks. Bruised and bleeding from their schoolyard brawl, the twins were prepared for whatever punishment the principal, Mrs. Crier, would dole out: after-school detention, extra schoolwork, expulsion, perhaps even paddling. Nothing she could do to them, however, would be as scary as facing their *baba*.

John was a man of strength and old-world virtue. He wouldn't tolerate misbehavior that could cast shame upon the family and its good name, especially after the sacrifices he made in the past to preserve the family honor.

The two of them were of one mind. Destiny had blessed Pete and Mike by placing them in their mother's womb together. They had been gifted with one another, each with the security of knowing that they would be loved by someone forever—best friends, twin brothers. Though they weren't allowed to speak to each other, they knew what needed to be said. It had always been that way for Pete and Mike—knowing what the other felt and thought—and they were hopeful that *baba* would understand.

They were shaken from the silent dialogue of their thoughts the moment their father walked into the principal's office. Standing big as an old olive tree, his white hair set starkly against the sunbaked brown of his skin, he commanded their love, respect, devotion, and, yes, there was a bit of fear there, too. He stood before the principal's desk, not looking at the pictures of past winning athletic teams and spelling bee champs that lined the institutional-green walls of the office. Instead, he glared at Pete and Mike, the unmistakable look of a questioning parent.

"Why you boys here? What you do to get in trouble?"

They both stared up at him, expecting the worst but believing that how they had acted on the playground was right, regardless of the consequences. At the same time, Mrs. Crier sat behind her desk, smug in the knowledge that she was doing her job as school disciplinarian and that she was in the right. Before either of the boys could respond, Mrs. Crier spoke for them.

"Mr. Pappas, your sons started a fight in the schoolyard. We simply cannot have physical altercations…"

John looked at her quizzically.

"…fights between the children. I have no choice but to punish them. They will be expelled for one day."

John looked at her again, not fully understanding what "expelled" meant.

"Mr. Pappas, I know you are new to our country and how we do things here." She hesitated, not knowing how much he would understand. "They will be punished by not coming to school for one day."

John worked long hours, leaving his family before sunrise and not returning until late in the day. He didn't have the time modern-day fathers had to take his children to parks or throw baseballs in the backyard. First, he didn't understand American sports. More important, though, he had to work for his family to eat, to keep a roof over their heads, to clothe them, and to pay the bills. As it was, it took the efforts of both John and his wife to do so. Consequently, what few words he shared with them were what a good Greek father from Crete taught his sons: respect for the family name and reputation, the value of a hard day's work, honesty, and integrity.

Being young boys in their little house, Pete and Mike felt so different from everyone else. Inside the walls of their home was "Little Greece" and outside was America. Children of immigrants, like Pete and Mike, were in school playing sports like football, basketball, and baseball, but at all times, Greek youths remembered not to disgrace their parents or, in turn, their forefathers. Pete and Mike were mischievous, and yes,

4

sometimes too questioning, but they were not bullies. He turned and looked at them again.

"Why you boys here? What you do?" he asked again, this time in his native Greek. *"Yah tee eese etho? Tee ekaness?"*

Pete jumped out of his chair to his feet and excitedly answered for the twins. *"Baba,* Daddy, we had to fight! They called us dirty Greeks!"

John paused. He took two steps toward the twins, pointing at them, his face reddening with rage. "Anybody call you 'dirty Greek,' you fight them!"

As he turned to leave the office, his business done, he motioned his sons to follow his lead. As they stood to follow their father out of the office and out of the clutches of Mrs. Crier, they heard her slam her hands on her desk as she stood defiant, angry at this immigrant father for encouraging his sons to fight, usurping both her authority and the rules of the school.

"Mr. Pappas! It is that attitude that has kept Greece at war for hundreds of years!"

"Yes," he answered, as he turned once again to face her. "And that is why we are free!"

John turned back and the boys followed him out the door. Mrs. Crier sat down, frustrated at not receiving parental support for her rules but determined that, come the next school day, they were suspended from school, regardless of whether or not their father supported her authority or her rules. For her, this was just another disciplinary problem to be addressed, merely one of her many daily duties as an elementary school principal, made more difficult by these foreigners who didn't understand American ways.

For Pete and Mike, though, the scene was one they never forgot. With one sentence, their father summarized the belief of every Greek, one born from hundreds of years of oppression and slavery at the hands of Persians, Venetians, Romans, and Ottoman Turks, rooted in the philosophy of Socrates—that freedom was valued above all else, and came with a price. Perhaps as an American who lives in a free land, Mrs. Crier had become comfortable and forgotten this fact. For John to expect his children to endure name-calling, especially "dirty Greek," was to spit upon Greece itself and the people who had created the very idea of democracy, who fought and died for freedom and against tyranny for centuries. John Pappas's children came from a rich heritage and a proud culture. If they fought to defend all that was Greek, he must defend them.

Their fight was just!

Walking out of the office that day, Pete and Mike looked up at their *baba's* white hair (they never remembered ever seeing their dad without white hair), and they thought how brave a man he was, what honor he had—this old soldier who held their little hands in his weathered, brown, big ones; hands that had fought in the Balkan War and later tilled the soil; hands that held his children's hearts. How tough it must be to face the unknown as he had in a new country, adjusting to it, living in it with seemingly everything and everyone against you, and still to stand up for your beliefs and your family.

The three of them walked down the newly painted industrial-green hall toward the family's old Dodge, and even though the twins had been suspended, they had never felt happier. A battle had been won that day by their father, and somehow, the two boys knew it. In coming years, Pete and Mike fought anyone who called them "dirty Greek" and were never again afraid that their father would be angry if they did so. If anyone called Pete and Mike "dirty Greek," the two boys went back-to-back as twin brothers and slugged it out with the kid calling them that name. If one brother was attacked, the other brother came to his defense. They were defending both their culture *and* each other, with every punch.

Pete and Mike felt so much love for one another. Like invisible chains, their love bound them tightly together. With each sunrise and sunset, they always knew every day how lucky they were to have each other—for Pete to have Mike, and Mike to have Pete, and to face all of life's battles, sadness and loneliness, with the other brother standing by steadfastly, like an extra backbone whenever needed. Pete knew he could never live without Mike, and Mike knew he could never live without Pete. It was unimaginable! How lonely it must be to not have a twin, to go through life all alone. They never thought, for one moment, that they could ever be separated from one another.

As the Dodge, with its passenger door firmly attached by rope salvaged from scrap thrown out from the farm, made its way toward home, Pete and Mike sat in the back seat quietly, only the sound of their thoughts rising above the car's motor and the cacophony of sounds heard through the open windows. The hot air blowing in on them, mussing their hair and toasting their skin like a giant blow-dryer, felt good as John drove past wood-framed houses scattered between rows of orchards and vineyards that lined the road, seemingly far into the distance.

Modesto, California, was a rural place, with people whose lives, whether they worked the soil or were merchants, revolved around the thousands of acres of farmland surrounding the little town, with corn and cotton; orchards of peaches, nectarines, oranges, and lemons; trees heavy with walnuts, almonds, and pistachios; and grapevines whose crops were eventually eaten at the table, either fermented into wine or laid out in the fields, drying under the scorching sun, being transformed into raisins. The San Joaquin Valley was the goddess of this agricultural Olympus, and every new immigrant who came here to work saw the opportunities in every piece of produce birthed from her soil.

The trip home took just a few minutes but seemed longer to the twins, anxious as they always were to go home. Their skinny, olive-colored legs stuck to the seat, the sweat acting as glue between their flesh and the seat's vinyl. Each boy took turns raising one thigh, then the other, as the intensity of the valley's late spring heat was trapped in the car's interior, the cracked window barely ventilating the oven-like space.

Mike leaned over to whisper in Pete's ear: "What do you think is gonna' happen when we get home?"

Pete's smirk turned into a smug smile as he thought for a moment. "What's gonna' happen? Nothin'! You saw! *Baba* stood up for us. They called us 'dirty Greeks' and we fought back like Greeks, so what's gonna' happen to us? *Teepohtah*—nothin'—that's what!"

Mike turned away from his brother and stared at his father, who was focused on his driving, unaware of the whispers between his sons. Mike looked back again at Pete.

"But what about Mama? Look at our *pantalonia!!* She's gonna' be mad!"

"Ah," Pete answered, knowing how important it was that they not get into trouble with their parents or hurt their mother's feelings. Mike was so much like their mother, too—his feelings easily got hurt and he was always concerned about what people thought of him.

"For how long? She's not gonna' like that they called us 'dirty Greek' either! *Titika* Minerakis, the colonel's daughter? She'll probably reward us for what we did!" laughed Pete. "Maybe we'll even get some extra sweets!"

Always the more serious of the two, Mike wasn't so sure. "But what about the holes in our new jeans, Pete, *panayioti?* What about the holes!"

Pete shook his head. "You worry too much. She can sew, right?"

"Yeah."

"Then, she'll fix 'em right up." Pete put his hand on his brother's shoulder. Mike was such a worrier, always anxious. He wished that

Mike would take things as they came and let problems, like leaves in a late-fall wind, blow away if they weren't important. Pete could do that automatically—deal with a problem and move on—but somehow Mike held onto everything with the tight grip of a baseball player clutching a bat. It was as if, when God was handing out genes and dividing them up between the two of them nestled in their mother's womb, he gave Mike the "worry gene" and Pete the "happy-go-lucky gene," if there were such things. He smiled at the face that looked exactly like his.

"Don't worry, *Manoli*, Mike, it'll be okay, you'll see. She'll be proud of us. She won't be mad at all."

Always, every day, the best of the twins' school day was going home, running through the front door to the smells of their mother's cooking, of garlic and lemon, of basil and oregano, and hearing the constant song of clanking pots and pans in her kitchen. As Pete and Mike burst through the door, the smells and sounds of their mama's cooking wrapped around them like a soft blanket. They saw their beloved mother coming out of the kitchen in her once-pure-white apron, now colored with age and the remnants of a hundred love-laced meals on its cloth, her arms open and her smile wide to greet them—her two boys, her twin blessings sent to her by God.

"*Pethakia mou, agoria mou, pos ese?*" she asked. "My children, my sons, how are you?" They ran into her arms, waiting for the warmth and love that enveloped them, predictably and reliably, returning her love with equal fervor, holding her as they held each other. While she embraced them tightly, she looked up at John, her vibrant dark eyes questioning him without words.

"*Olee eene kala, Titika,*" John said. "Everything is fine."

After hearing the events in the school office and being told the twins wouldn't be going to school for one day as punishment, Titika, upset and indignant, didn't understand the reason for it. How could children—especially *her* children, the children and grandchildren of freedom fighters—be expected to endure such cruelty and humiliation and do nothing about it? To not defend themselves? To not stand for what is right? It was one of many things she didn't understand about Americans. This was a country founded on democracy—a concept created in Greece—yet her boys were being punished for defending Greece and their heritage? No, she didn't understand this at all. Since she couldn't do anything about their punishment, she accepted it, and took them, still clinging to her skirts with her arms about them, into her kitchen.

"Ella, palikaria mou, na fahme kati—ella stee couzina," she said. "Come, my pride and joy, my brave little warriors, let us eat something—come to the kitchen."

Hanging on her, swaying like ornaments precariously dangling from the heavy boughs of a tree, Pete and Mike obediently and glee-fully followed their mama into her realm, her kitchen, running to the table and taking their seats, squirming and giggling with the energy that pulsates through the veins of twin nine-year-old boys.

Besides their games of pretending to be ancient Cretan warriors, defending their village from the ever-marauding, ever-evil invaders—the hated Turks—or playing army or cowboys and Indians, eating their mother's food was the twins' most favorite thing to do. Titika's cooking talents were legendary, even among the local Greeks, and they were always happy to sample her Cretan *pilafi*, rice, cooked in chicken broth and dripping with butter, or her desserts like *baklava*, so good, bathed in honey and walnuts. Her food beckoned them like the sweet songs of the sirens, calling Pete and Mike to partake of the richness and decadence of every dish, with their mother's love present in every bite. Getting expelled from school wasn't so bad when they could come home and eat their mother's delicacies earlier than usual.

The boys spent the afternoon playing outside then running in and out through the back door, taking breaks from their games of war (where the boys battled the dreaded Nazis) and hide and seek. After filling their bellies with their mother's dinner meal (which she spent most of the afternoon preparing and cooking) in the early evening, and since there was no school the next day thanks to their suspension, Pete and Mike crept into their room, where the warm glimmer of the setting sun shone on the walls and bathed them with the fading rays of light. The heat added to the sweat cascading off their brows, and their eyes soon became heavy with sleep.

Because the family was too poor for the traditional separate twin beds, Pete and Mike slept together on a double bed pushed up against the wall, useful for hiding under when one of Titika's slippers came sailing after them as they ran from her. Running, screaming, and laughing, their thin, lean bodies hit the shiny wood floor with their white T-shirts becoming toboggans, sliding under the bed, crashing into the wall and into each other at the same time. They didn't like getting into *real* trouble, like at school, but on occasion, aggravating Titika on purpose made for great fun. As a young girl, she had been nicknamed "Titika" for her feistiness. Her sons inherited that spirit-edness from her. Nobody could hurl a slipper or use a broomstick for reaching under the bed like their mother.

Pete and Mike lay on the bed together, staring up at the texture on the white ceiling, its pattern making swirls like whirlpools, round and round, with no beginning or end. The circles seemed to go on forever, and, as with all boys who liked to pretend, at night the ceiling became the sky, always moving and changing. It was the focal point for their eyes and imaginations, when their minds wandered and they shared their thoughts and dreams with one another.

"Pete, are you still awake?"

"*Mahlasela,* yeah, I'm awake. I ate the whole rest of the garlic and onions at the bottom of the pot of *bammyes me kota* (chicken with okra). I'll be awake for hours and so will you!" They both giggled under the covers.

"What!—oh no, Pete!—please no! You know what onions and garlic do to your stomach!" Mike couldn't help but laugh. Pete always found a way to make his brother laugh. Pete was naturally funny, and Mike loved it. Pete was a comedian with a built-in, lifelong audience. Life could be serious, but Pete could make anything fun. He found laughter in everything, in every moment.

"You want my belly to sing a special song for you?" asked Pete, lying on his right side close to the wall, so his back was facing Mike. Bitten by the bug of silliness that finds children at bedtime, the twins giggled until hearing the soft steps of their mother down the hall.

"*Panayioti! Manoli! Kale Neekta tora! Prepees nah keemeetheete tora! Soappee!*"

"Pete and Mike," their mama said, "good night now! You must go to sleep now! Quiet!"

They both knew there wouldn't be a second warning from their mother. If they wanted to talk as they always did before falling asleep, they needed to be quieter about it. Pete turned back toward Mike and they huddled together in a little ball, arms and legs wrapped around each other, shutting out the rest of the world as they whispered.

"Pete?"

"What?"

"Why are we so different?" Pete held Mike close, staring into his eyes. Pete didn't need the light from the sun or a lamp to do this. He could see into Mike's heart, even in the dark.

"We just are."

"How come? 'Cause we're Greek? 'Cause Mom and Dad are from the old country?"

Pete yawned. They talked about this all the time: in the schoolyard, in the backyard, every night before going to sleep.

"Yeah. Maybe. We look different from everybody else. Dark-skinned. Brown eyes. We're different from everybody else," said Pete.

"How? 'Cause there's two of us?" Mike knew the answer to this question. They were identical twins. Pete and Mike dressed alike and they looked exactly alike. People whispered and stared when they walked into a room or a store, "Quick—look—twins!" They were used to it—sort of. But at school, it was tough. When the kids weren't calling them "dirty Greek,'" they were social outcasts for being twins, not included in the little cliques that dominated the schoolyard. In some cultures, twins were considered evil or a curse. Plus, Pete and Mike liked being in charge, thinking for themselves. They didn't like being told what to do by the other kids, so that didn't make them popular, either.

"We don't need 'em anyhow, right, Pete? It's just you and me, the brothers—right? Who needs 'em!?"

"Yeah, brother, who needs 'em!" answered Pete. Their cuddle turned into a deep bear hug as they lay intertwined on the bed, losing their battle with Mr. Sandman to stay awake.

"Still," Mike said dreamily, "it sure would be good if kids liked us more."

"Yeah," nodded Pete. "*Kale neekta*, Mike."

"*Kale neekta*, Pete. Good night."

CHAPTER 2

1946:
The Blue-Eyed Gang

AFTER PETE AND MIKE'S RETURN TO SCHOOL, the remaining days of the academic year disappeared into one another other like a Chinese fan folding in upon itself, melding one day with the next, their classroom work a secondary concern over the playground skirmishes the twins faced together daily. They had a common connection with the other immigrant kids in school whose parents came from places like Assyria, Italy, Mexico, and Portugal, the children of dust bowlers from southern states like Oklahoma, along with Black kids whose families had been in this country since the days of slavery. And even though all the children were culturally different from one another, their differences from the kids everyone called the *blue-eyed's*—those considered traditionally white—were enough to bind them tightly together, a band of brothers joined against a common enemy.

What the immigrant kids like Pete and Mike didn't understand was *why?* Why couldn't the blue-eyed's accept them into their cliques just because they, or their parents, weren't born in the United States? Was it because these newly arrived Americans were poor? Because they had brown eyes or darker skin than the pasty-white, fair skin they were used to? Or because these children of immigrants wanted a good life, too? As children, they didn't have the answers to these questions. Youngsters like Pete and Mike didn't know what prejudice was, or what it meant, just that the blue-eyed's didn't like them, didn't pick them for teams, didn't want them in their games, didn't want them at their table in the cafeteria, and certainly didn't want to be their friends.

At first, it hurt. It hurt *a lot,* and the boys took it personally.

But after a while, Pete and Mike developed a shield against all the hate. They were naturally independent, and their fellow immigrant, dust bowl, and minority friends turned to the Pappas twins for camaraderie, friendship, and even leadership, which the twins knew was the key. In order for them to truly stand their ground (Pete and Mike knew there was power in numbers, since as twins they always had the advantage of two against one), they needed to have a lot of kids stand with them, to face down the blue-eyed's, who were always very good at intimidation and picking on the weakest kids, usually the quiet ones who just wanted to fade into the background and be left alone.

But Pete and Mike were never the type to fade into the background.

They decided to organize and lead a group of kids who would defend themselves and each other against the constant harassment and attack of the blue-eyed's. So they made a pact with their friends—all the outcasts and misfits and shy ones and poor ones and anyone who didn't fit in with the blue-eyed's—to one night meet after school in the alley near the Pappas house and form a club: a *gang,* 1940s style.

Pete and Mike never went looking for a fight. But, growing up with the stories of classical heroes like Achilles and hearing tales about freedom fighters like their grandfather Colonel Hariton Minerakis, they wouldn't endure endless name-calling, and they told the other kids they shouldn't, either. If someone called them "dirty Greek," they fought them. They also fought anyone who called their Italian friends "wops," their Portuguese friends "portagees," their Black friends "ni---rs," or their Mexican friends "wetbacks." The kids all fought elbow-to-elbow united, for each other, against the blue-eyed's. All the kids had been in trouble enough at school, so they tried to keep the conflicts out of the schoolyard. None of them wanted their parents called, especially Pete and Mike. So, they stayed together as a group. The largeness of it kept the blue-eyed's at bay.

After school was when they planned their tactics. They lived in a tough neighborhood, but still, the schoolyard gangs weren't really organized crime. The kids' school gangs fought over turf—areas of the neighborhood where they were free to play, have fun with their friends, and collect empty soda bottles. Bottles equaled money. If the bottle was on your turf, it was *your* bottle and *your* money. They didn't have weapons. If they did get into a fight, they fought with their fists. It was all more for show than inflicting any real damage to anybody. Looking tough helped them survive.

What did they do with the big bucks they made from recycling soda bottles? Pete and Mike and their friends might have enough money by Saturday afternoon to watch a Roy Rogers or Gene Autry movie at the matinee. Being more industrious than some of the other kids, Pete and Mike also solicited work in the neighborhood mowing people's lawns or doing odd jobs for whatever the neighbors wanted to pay them. If it was the right time of year, they might use the money to go down to the county fair or visit a carnival that was passing through town.

Over the course of a few years, the twins and their friends had minor run-ins with the blue-eyed's, though with no one ending up with more than bumps and bruises. Pete and Mike had a black-and-white McNab sheepdog left over from their dad's sheep ranching days that acted as their guard dog on their turf whenever they were threatened by the blue-eyed's. He was naturally protective of the two boys, and they used it to their advantage. But one year, Pete and Mike had finished taking abuse from the blue-eyed's. It seemed like nothing was changing. The blue-eyed's ran the game, always on the offense, with Pete and Mike and their friends on the defense. The twins talked about it and decided it was time to change their strategy, to put the blue-eyed's on the defense. They gathered their friends after school and told them of their plan. It took Pete and Mike weeks (in later years Mike couldn't remember how long, but at the time, it seemed as if they would be all grown up before they raised enough money), but they finally had enough money to buy two BB guns, the one weapon they could buy that might actually defend them against the blue-eyeds' preferred weapon—pocket knives.

So one day, Pete and Mike placed their dog on one side of the alleyway, their own personal sentry, after they got word to the blue-eyed's through a little kid in the neighborhood that there were a bunch of soda bottles dumped in the alley just waiting there to be taken. The alley was some 500 yards long, and the boys knew their rivals were afraid of their dog, so if they posted him on one end, Pete and Mike knew their enemy would be trapped. They had seen plenty of cowboy movies to know the best way to beat your enemy was to ambush them.

Lining each side of the alley were about ten garages. They sent their friends up onto the rooftops with rocks, their slingshots handy, with Pete and Mike positioned with their BB guns pointed and ready. When the blue-eyed's ended up in the center, cut off on one end by their dog, Pete and Mike ran to the opposite end of the alley, boxing them in, and opened fire with their BB guns. That was the cue for the cavalry on the garage rooftops, which let fire with slingshots, shooting down all the rocks they could muster.

"Take that, you blue-eyed's!" the boys yelled and, as expected, the blue-eyed gang fought back. One of the neighbors heard the noise and shouting. The boys heard the ensuing sirens and told their friends to scatter before the police arrived. Before Pete and Mike could get away, though, the leader of the blue-eyed gang ran toward Mike, threw his opened pocketknife, and hit him in the right arm. The twins ran over to the side of the alley and hid their BB guns behind some tall hedges in front of the neighbor's fence that bordered the alley.

Pete and Mike and their dog were the only ones in the alley when the squad car approached, the passenger window slowly rolling down. Mike grabbed his wounded, bleeding arm, swaying, the tears flowing on cue, and he began talking as fast as he could with Pete standing beside him, wide-eyed and wondering what they were going to do if the two of them were taken home by the police.

"What's going on here, boys? We got calls there's a problem," said the officer, staring at Mike's arm, as the boy greatly exaggerated his pain.

"Officer, officer, we don't know *what's* goin' on, we heard a noise, and we came to see what was goin' on, and then someone threw somethin' at me, and now I'm bleedin', and…well, they went thataway." Mike pointed down toward the other end of the alley, breathlessly, with tears rolling down his cheeks.

"I see your arm's bleeding there, boy. How're you involved with this?" asked the officer, not believing Mike's story.

"Honest injun', officer, we were playin' over there," Mike said, pointing to their yard, "on the other side of the fence, and then, *bam!* we heard all this yellin' and shoutin' and we came to see what was goin' on, and then *bam!* My arm gets hit with somethin' sharp, like a knife or somethin'. I don't know what it was but it was sharp and it hurts and it's bleedin' and…"

"All right, all right, son, all right now—calm down. You two boys go on home and let your mommy look at that arm," said the officer as Mike's tears made his face muddy and he was playing as if the cut was a mortal war injury. "Get on home and stay there. We may need to talk to you some more."

The officer asked for their names and address, just before speeding away. Pete looked at Mike askance. "What are we gonna' do now, Manoli? Baba won't like the police comin' round, you know that. What are we gonna' tell him?"

Mike wiped his dirty, wet face with his sleeve, the one that wasn't covered with drying blood. "We'll tell him the truth—that some boys from school that's been pickin' on us stabbed me with a knife, and we fought back, that's all. We defended ourselves." Pete looked at his brother doubtfully. "Anyhow, maybe he won't be home from work yet, and Mama doesn't understand English, so it'll probably be okay."

They grabbed their BB guns and ran back through the gate into their backyard. Pete and Mike felt tired and bruised, and in Mike's case also bleeding, but they had won the battle. The twins, still young and innocent, had no idea that it was the first of many battles to come.

Pete and Mike tried getting past their mother without being seen, but of course, that was impossible: the back door, with its squeaky screen door, opened right into the middle of the kitchen, the headquarters of their mother's daily work. She was always there unless she was cleaning another room in the house or taking care of little Mary or newborn baby Hariton (whom they always called "Harry"), born in March of that year, named after Titika's brother, Hariton, who came from a long line of Cretan warriors. Like many other young Greek men of his generation, he had valiantly fought in World War II, ending up in a Nazi concentration camp until freed by Allied forces.

"Oh, *panagheea mou, tee epethes?* My virgin Mary, what happened to you!" the twins' mother cried. She noticed Mike's bleeding arm immediately, and their dirty, smudged faces just added to her worries. Busy peeling potatoes, she quickly wiped her hands on the towel hanging around her apron at her waist as she ran over to them.

"*Manoli, ya tee to herri sou eghee emmaa?* Why is your arm bleeding?" Titika pulled him into her arms, then took him over to the sink, running cool tap water over the wound to better assess the damage. The bleeding was slowing down, with blood drying around the wound, although it had not yet stopped entirely. She finished washing it, talking quickly, in her typical style, rat-a-tat-tat, like a machine gun, all exclamations. Pete and Mike loved to listen to their mother when she dramatically reacted to something minor, *so Greek,* like an actress upon an ancient stage, uttering the words of Euripides or Aeschylus. As she spoke, Mike cranked his head over his left shoulder, looking at his brother, who was covering his mouth with both hands, trying not to laugh as she fussed over Mike.

"*Manoli, tee epethes! Pethi mou! Ese komati mou! Pyos ekane afto? Pyos thyalo ekane afto! Matakia mou!* What happened to you?! My little child! You are a piece of me! Who did this to you! What devil did this to you? My little sweet-eyes!"

She washed and dried the wound gently and had him hold his arm over the sink as she went into the utility porch and came back with a clean white rag to wrap the battle wound. She then took the two of them into the bathroom, where she began running the bath water and helped them both to undress, making sure that Mike sat so that his right arm was dangling over the top of the tub. She poured bubble bath into the water as it flowed from the tap, and the two boys sank into a thousand frothy bubbles as their bodies slid into the slippery porcelain of the tub. Pete gave Mike that look of his—a look only his twin understood, mischievous and victorious at the same time. Their mother left them for a moment to check on their crying baby brother, and they both began laughing.

"You're good at cryin' and gettin' Mama's attention!" Pete said. "You...you get away without even telling her what happened! Good thing, too, with the police and all! You're so lucky that blue-eyed stabbed you! Wounded and everything! Like a *palikari*, a hero, like *Venizelos!*"

Pete was right. They were lucky that they weren't caught. The police hadn't come to their house yet, and Titika…well, she wouldn't understand even if they explained it to her. She didn't understand Americans—she didn't even *try* to understand them. They were so foreign to her, not like Greeks at all.

"Whaddya' want me to do?" Mike responded. "I was bleeding! She needed to take care of me. You see how happy it makes her!"

The boys laughed again, knowing full well that Mike was the happy one, with his mother fawning over him, and she was the one worried and upset.

"Ahh, it was a good fight, eh' Pete? We beat 'em good. I don't think we have to worry about the blue-eyed's anymore. Whaddya' think?"

Pete looked at his brother and smiled. "Nah, they'll leave us alone now that we stood up to 'em once and for all. Except for…"

"What?"

"What if they save up their money and buy BB guns, too?" They both fell silent, staring at each other across the bubbles, wondering what the blue-eyed's might do next. As Mike opened his mouth to speak, they both heard the telephone ring. The twins slid down under the surface, hoping they could stay under the bubbles long enough to avoid the police they were sure were waiting outside on the front porch.

They held their breaths for a half-minute or so, came to the surface, and sat facing each other, bracing for the worst. They could only hear the conversation of their mother, but it was hard to tell who was talking on the other end of the phone line or what was said, with the sturdy, thick walls of their 1920s house acting as a buffer, muffling the words into faint mumbles. They tried to act uninterested, pushing a toy boat, which they had fashioned out of popsicle sticks, back and forth between them. Their mother came back into the bathroom and pulled the metal stool she kept under the sink over to the side of the tub and sat down, bringing a white washcloth with her. She spoke to them as she always did, in her native Greek.

"It was Mrs. Tazides on the phone." She took the washcloth and began rubbing Mike's back and Pete's back, alternately. "She says she talked to the police and she saw everything." What exactly had the neighborhood busybody seen? "She says she heard noises, kids screaming, and breaking glass, and she ran to her back fence, and looked into the alley, and saw those *Americani pethya,* those American kids, attacking you boys and your friends, and yelling bad words at you, and she saw the blond boy throw the knife at you and cut your arm. Then, she fell off the rock she was standing on, and when she climbed back on the rock, she saw the police come in the car, and she saw them talk to you, and she saw your arm bleeding and she saw them drive away, and she saw them again a few minutes later driving in the street in front of her house, and she runs outside and she waves, and they stop, and she tells them what she saw, and then they drive away. She says I should not worry, *this time,* that it's not your boys' fault. I tell her *it's not my boys' fault ever!* You are good boys and you don't cause trouble. And she says to me, 'Titika, this time you are lucky. This time I see they don't start the troubles. But next time, maybe you won't be so lucky, and *they* won't be so lucky, and maybe next time, they are going to get caught and go to jail.'

"And I tell her, 'Thank you, Mrs. Tazides, for your help, but I know my boys will never go to jail. They will be the most successful Greek boys, Cretan boys, to ever come out of Modesto and maybe in all of America! You will see,' I tell her."

She began washing Pete's hair, and as they listened to their mother, their greatest cheerleader talked some more, her Greek rapid and her thoughts flowing, her love and faith in them filling every tear that streaked down the front of her powdered, rosy cheeks.

"Panayioti and Manoli, you are my *kalee agoria,* my good sons. You will do many great things in your life here in America! You will be great men. You will be successful men."

She turned her head away, wiping her eyes with the back of her wrists, quickly blinking, the tears disappearing back into her eyes, so dark brown they looked black. She looked down at them again, smiling with an abundance of love. Mike saw the goose bumps on the flesh of his brother's arms, the same sort that covered his own body.

"You will live in big, beautiful houses and drive big, beautiful cars, and marry nice Greek girls and have nice families, and all these others...." Her voice cracked, and she paused. "These others, these jealous Greeks—they see what good boys you are, what smart boys you are, and they are jealous, because they don't know if their children will grow up to be successful like you. They don't know, but *I* know. They put you down and say you make trouble and you will go to jail, but they will see, and they will come to admire you and wish that their children would be as successful as you."

She looked up and straight ahead, like a gypsy gazing into a crystal ball and seeing the future, and she sighed wistfully.

"They will regret their poison words, these small-minded *horyati,* these village peasants! They say you are *kakomiri,* bad fate, but they are wrong! You will be *aristocratia!* They will see that I am right and they are wrong!"

In just a few moments, Pete and Mike saw their mother go from angry to sad and back again to cheerfully optimistic. She helped them out of the tub, dried them off, and tucked them into their pajamas, and the twins went into their room and sat on the bed. After she left them alone, Pete and Mike reached out at the same time and took each other's hand.

"Brother…" said Pete.

"I know, brother," Mike said. "When we grow up, we have to be successful."

"And make a lot of money…"

"And marry nice Greek girls…"

"And prove to all these people that we're gonna' be somebody someday!"

The tears came, along with the big lumps that made them both feel that each had a giant boulder in their throats.

"And we gotta' do it for Mama and Baba…."

Pete and Mike shook hands on it, their secret promise to each other, vowing that their mother's tears and father's toils wouldn't go without reward.

———————

Titika never let Pete and Mike forget the sacrifices made by their ancestors and their parents, but especially by their father, for their lives to be better. *To onoma sou, to onoma sou, nah mee ksehases toh thoro pou o pateras sas ethohse.* "Your name, your name—do not forget the gift your father has given you," their mother often said. Although not educated in America, Titika was an inherently bright woman who saw the success of other immigrants who came to the United States before her, and saw no reason for her children to not become successful and prosperous as well.

"If they can do it, you can do it, too. Use your brains—you are Greeks, you are smart boys—you can do anything! Make me proud!"

In the Pappas household, nothing was considered "mine" or "yours," but rather "ours"; the family members were one unit going through life, together. Their mother toiled at home, their father out in the fields. He rose before the sun, along with their *Theo,* Uncle Manoli (actually, their father's cousin), who lived with them, and the two men had their breakfast of coffee, homemade bread and cheese, eggs cooked in olive oil, and then would leave for the farms, working through the midday and afternoon heat, up high on ladders, picking fruit. In winter, they pulled oranges, grapefruit, and persimmons from heavy branches. In the spring and summer, they picked from orchards whose branches arched with the weight of ripened apricots, nectarines, peaches, and plums. Cascading clusters of grapes barely clung to their vines, waiting to be plucked by gentle hands. Fall took them into orchards where they worked the last of the fig harvest and the beginning of the lemon and orange harvest.

Greek immigrant parents worked long hours and struggled to support their families, but they knew the work they did and sacrifices they made would be the keys that unlocked and opened doors of opportunity for their children, like Pete and Mike, so they could leave that miserable world of poverty and prejudice behind.

CHAPTER 3

1948:
Destiny Takes a Field Trip

IT WAS LATE APRIL, the school year was winding down, and Pete and Mike were looking forward to summer's warm days spent at home and with friends. The end of this school year would be especially fun because the boys discovered they would go on field trips. They were blessed that year with a teacher who thought field trips were an integral part of education for children, taking them out of the classroom, with its usual rigid environment and textbooks, into the real world.

Pete and Mike hungered for and craved the world outside of school, like two children staring into a candy store full of chocolate, their faces pressed against the glass, wondering how long before they could get a taste of it. When their teacher announced that the class would visit a radio station, a place that played music by Hollywood stars like their movie heroes, the boys were thrilled. They felt like their cowboy heroes, itching to head out into the prairie with all its adventure. Pete looked over at Mike, his brown eyes bigger than usual, and winked. When the bell rang and they went to recess, the two ran to the corner of the schoolyard to talk.

"Mike—a radio station! Hey, maybe we'll meet our favorite singing cowboy!"

"Yeah, like what we hear on the radio at home—Gene Autry, Roy Rogers, all those guys! You 'spose they'll come to Modesto?" Mike didn't doubt that the biggest stars in the world played in their little valley town.

"Hey, maybe we'll see 'em," said Mike. "Maybe we'll get to go on the radio, too!"

Pete put his arm around his brother's shoulder. "Yeah, we'll be like those guys that talk on the radio and interview the stars. That would be somethin', huh? That would give the old ladies reason to gossip! The Pappas twins on the radio—big stars!"

Pete and Mike laughed at the thought of ancient, chatty Greek ladies at church seething with jealousy: the Pappas twins as radio personalities and local celebrities.

"I can't wait until Friday!" said Pete.

"Me neither!" said his twin.

———————

For children, time passes slowly, and the week seemed endless for Pete and Mike until Friday, the day of the field trip to radio station KTRB. They had no thought of what to expect because they actually had no concept of what a radio station was, or how it operated. They knew it played country-and-Western music. The few times their father put the radio on in their home, they heard all the great country-and-Western stars of the 1940s, like their heroes "the singing cowboys." The station was known for promoting San Joaquin Valley talent as well, with shows featuring locally known stars like the *Maddox Brothers and Rose*.

The bus ride took about twenty minutes from the south side of town where Pete and Mike lived, to the north, newer side of town, way out in the country, through rows of orchards until the bus reached the radio station on Norwegian Avenue, the only building in the middle of farmland. It was a big white building, with the station's logo spelled out vertically on a sign down the front of its chimney. The twins, along with the others in their class, followed the teacher's instructions and lined up, walking into the building single file, "keeping your hands to yourselves and looking, not touching" as they walked into the main lobby.

The twins' first breath of radio station air was a mix of cigarette smoke, musty carpets, and dust blended with the static electricity they felt by being in that magical place. The twins overheard the conversations of different people talking fast in rooms whose doors were all ajar to let the smoke out (even chain smokers needed a little fresh air). Although they couldn't hear any of it clearly, or understand any of the conversations even if they could, the words intermingled with the sounds coming from the overhead speakers, broadcasting what was being aired that very moment from the KTRB studio. It was 1948, so what went out on the radio was live, spilling out into the homes of everyone in Modesto and the surrounding farm communities, at the instant it happened—no audio delays, no editing, no rehearsals—just live, every moment.

As they made their way through the station, they met some of the KTRB staff. The sales manager, the program director, the news director, and even the announcer took a break from being on the air to talk with the class and answer questions. The children knew he wasn't actually on the air from the big red neon sign hanging over the doorway, going into the studio, that only flashed *ON THE AIR* in red when he was talking. After leaving the studio, they watched him through a window and while the rest of the building was buzzing with activity, the announcer's booth was silent. Nothing of the station's office noise could be heard through the speakers. Pete and Mike and their classmates only heard the announcer speaking, and they saw his lips move to match the words they heard.

Mike, John, Harry, Pete, Katherine and Mary in front of the family's vineyard, circa 1940s.

Through another window the twins could see the big, main studio that had microphones on stands positioned in different groupings, ready for the next group of live entertainers to perform. One set of microphones was gathered around a beautiful brown Wurlitzer piano, the color of walnuts, with sparkling black and white keys. The second group of mics was positioned around a brown upright piano, the type in Western movies that were played by crusty old men in saloons.

On this tour, for the first time in their lives, Pete and Mike didn't say a word to each other. They didn't speak at all.

They didn't need to. All they had to do was look at each other to see, to feel, the pulsating life of this special place, where people got up every day, dressed in clean, white, crisply starched shirts with neatly pressed ties and trousers, and went to work at a job people admired. How could they even call this "work"? This was not like the work their father did, climbing up and down ladders in the hot sun, coming home exhausted each day with dirt and spider webs caked on his arms.

Radio station work wasn't work at all. As far as they could tell, it was paradise.

The tour ended too quickly for Pete and Mike. The teacher coached the students to say their final "goodbye and thank you for having us" speech before they had to leave the building and board the bus for school. As they left the main studio and began making their way out, the boys and their classmates stopped for a minute to hear the announcer on the radio.

"Well, folks, we here at KTRB are saying a fond farewell to our little friends from Roosevelt Elementary school, who came to visit us today on their school field trip. So as our final salute, we'd like to play this song for them, wishing them a happy and safe journey back to school and home."

With that, Pete and Mike heaved a collective sigh, while a song by one of their favorite singing cowboys, Roy Rogers, played on the radio as they walked out of the building.

Pete and Mike absorbed the energy of live radio the minute they entered the KTRB studio—the excitement, the spontaneity, the radio program's ability to transform them with just few minutes of a song or a news bulletin. It could take them out of their little life in their small town, into the big, wide world where everyone else lived, where exciting things happened to other people, in faraway places.

They wanted to share in that world, not just dream about it when they lay awake at night.

Radio was part of that glamorous world, and they could see that it might be a way out of their poor immigrants' life in the farmlands surrounding their little town of Modesto.

Pete and Mike boarded the bus, while all the other kids were talking and laughing, and still didn't say a word. Radio invaded their souls and psyche, and from that day on, radio broadcasting became the great driving force of their lives. They didn't know how they would make the journey from their immigrants' world of poverty, wrapped like a budget Christmas package with beautiful ribbons of hope and faith, into this new world of talking voices in booming boxes. Still, they took their first steps into the world of radio that day, shown down that road unknowingly by a teacher taking poor students on a field trip to KTRB-AM 860.

The mystical world of radio cast a spell upon their hearts, infusing them with a desire and passion that enveloped their lives.

Like their Cretan forebears crossing the ancient Mediterranean, merely travelers on a ship going through life, Pete and Mike worked hard to be as American as their friends but were profoundly influenced by their Greek heritage, down to the marrow of their bones, into the sparking center of their cells.

In coming years, the twins instinctively dug deep into themselves for the strength of warriors past and mythic tales of old, to deal with the problems of everyday life they encountered. Their bloodlines linked them with ancestral kin who survived occupation and slavery. As they grew, they were uniquely shaped by their mother's and father's old-world Greek ways in a nervous dance—like a seasoned teacher and her clumsy students—with the American world in which they lived. This dance between the old and new worlds, which began in youth as a slow and deliberate *zembekiko* (a dance of contemplation done by men in Greek tavernas after a long day's work), ultimately became a fast and powerful *pentozali*, the Cretan dance of war done before going into battle, as Pete and Mike lived through their blissful boyhood days and approached the trials of manhood, bracing for the wars in their lives yet to come.

CHAPTER 4

1914–1927:
A Greek Immigrant's Journey Begins

As PETE AND MIKE GREW, they pressed their father for stories of his early life and days as a young Greek man coming to America. They learned that memories of laughter and happy times with his parents, siblings, and extended family in his early youth, together with his Orthodox Christian faith, were the loving foundation that kept John strong through all the hard times and struggles that awaited him in America, beginning with his arrival in New York City in 1914. After disembarking on Ellis Island, going through the immigration checkpoints, and meeting the cousin who sponsored him, John Pappas's first task was to find work.

Ads for laborers ran in ethnic newspapers all over the country, but especially in New York, which was full of nearly starving, newly arrived immigrants from Greece like John and hundreds of thousands of others from Austria-Hungary, Russia, Italy, Greece, Romania, and Turkey—all part of the new wave of immigration that began in the late 1800s and continued into the new century.

After battling in the Balkan War, young men like John faced poverty and starvation. Becoming indentured to American labor contractors was usually the only way for them to escape their lives in Greece where, in addition to postwar misery, one's family economic station stayed the same for generations. America became the only hope for creating that new life with a better future for the next generation.

Word of work traveled from neighbor to neighbor in the bitterly cold or excruciatingly hot tenement slums that stank of rotten food, human sweat, and excrement in New York City. With new railroad jobs in places like Ohio or Wyoming or jobs in the coal mines of Colorado and Utah, men like John found work aplenty, though wages were barely above starvation. One day he was in a *kafenion,* a coffee-house with other Greeks, when a labor contractor arrived and asked the men if any of them were interested in working for the Pennsylvania Railroad. Through that contractor, John and his friends found work for a time on chain gangs in Ohio and Pennsylvania. Not knowing English, he was taught to say the words "yes, sir!" whenever the fore-man barked his orders to the gang. Another Greek in the crew told him privately that, in truth, the foreman was really yelling racist and derogatory epithets at him each time he thought the foreman was giv-ing orders. John might have been a poor man but he had dignity and a sense of his own self-worth. He wouldn't work for anyone who hurled abuse at him when he was just trying to make an honest day's wages. After having shed blood for Greece in the Balkan War, listening pas-sively as his heritage was attacked was not something he could tolerate. When John discovered what was happening, he quit.

Without work again, he talked with his new friends from the old country and heard of work in the coal mines of Sunnyside, Utah, near Price, about 120 miles south of Salt Lake City. Just as he did upon arriving in Ellis Island, John pinned the names of his relatives on his lapel and took the six-day train trip to Sunnyside, Utah. In the dark, gassy pits of the coal mines, John Pappas found his first steady work in America.

John worked as a miner for a short time, fearing the black dust and cave-ins of the mines, working from sunup to sundown with all the other Greek immigrants struggling to survive. When his English language skills improved, John found that that his polite "thank-you's" and "yes, sir's" had again been preceded by the foreman shouting, "Get to work, you S.O.B. Greeks!" This verbal abuse confirmed what he learned as he worked longer at the mines: that the immigrant was valued for his strong back and little else. The mining company had a rule: in the event of cave-in, fire, or explosion, the mules were to be evacuated first, *before* the miners, because "mules cost money and Greeks don't." John endured the abuse for a short time until he found a way out of the mines for good.

He managed to attend nineteen classes of night school when he first arrived in Utah. He was determined to finish his education in his new country, since he was not able to do so in Greece. He read about the different states and studied their history and geography. He fell in love with the image of California, which the book called the "garden of America." In his mind, it was settled: he would move to America's garden, California! After two years of working at the Sunnyside Mines, he only made $16 a month, but it was enough for him to leave coal mining at last and make a living doing something else, all the while keeping in mind the goals he had for himself.

John heard that the Ute Indian Reservation was leasing land to ranchers. He went to the Indian Affairs office and arranged to lease a parcel. Then he returned to what he knew and loved from his days in Crete: sheep ranching. Within a few years, and for the first time since his arrival in America, he was making enough money to provide for himself, to send a little money to what was left of his family on Crete, and to save money to eventually bring a bride to America. This new country would be the womb that nurtured the rebirth of the Pappadojiannis family. The only way to achieve this goal was to find a good Cretan wife, bring her to America, and create a new family with her.

———

As the seasons came and went, the years passed with each spring's newborn lambs tumbling from their mother's bellies, populating his little ranch. The days went quickly, with much work to do: he tended to the pasturelands so that he could safely graze his sheep, and he kept a keen eye out for predators like coyotes, wolves, and human poachers, who found it easier to steal another man's property than work to raise their own flocks. Keeping his animals healthy and free from disease was paramount. One nasty illness could wipe out his whole ranch.

His farm grew, so he employed friends and relatives to do the extra work he didn't have time to do himself, having grown the ranch from a small, one-man enterprise to an eventual flock of some 4,000 sheep.

When he had time, John studied the written materials detailing all the knowledge necessary to pass his citizenship exam. With his keen mind and thirst for knowledge, learning the information needed for citizenship was not so daunting a task. When the day finally came and he went to court to take his citizenship test, he didn't expect that the correct answer to a question posed by the presiding judge would be the one that determined whether he became an American citizen, or stayed in the U.S. as a legal, working immigrant with just a green card.

He stood quietly and respectfully before the judge.

"Mr. Pappas, if Greece and America were to go to war, which country would you defend?" the judge asked.

John was not prepared for this question, which asked him in one moment to define his loyalty to both his birth country, Greece, and his adopted country, America. How could he answer this question honestly and with integrity, when there was no right answer? John stood before the judge and thought about the question.

Having prepared himself for the examination, which was conducted orally in those days, due to the myriad of languages spoken by the immigrants, John answered all questions accurately, but he couldn't answer the judge's question in the way he expected.

John, standing up straight, shoulders back, his sun-darkened skin a stark contrast to the neatly starched white dress shirt he had borrowed from a fellow Greek, took a deep breath.

"Your Honor, I cannot answer that question."

John could see the exasperation on the judge's face. The day had already been long. Why couldn't this immigrant just answer this question like all the others? The judge asked him again while John stood politely and firmly.

"Mr. Pappas, you must answer this last, most important question."

"I love my old country, Greece, your Honor. But I could never fight against America."

John looked at the American flag with tears welling in his eyes. He looked back up at the judge.

"I would kill myself first."

The judge looked upon this immigrant and understood that sometimes, living each day with honor was the only treasure a poor man might ever possess.

"I understand that you are a true patriot, and a man of honor, so I am willing to grant your citizenship today. Welcome to your new country, Mr. Pappadojiannis."

"Thank you, Judge…sir…your Honor, I thank you very much," he said, quietly exhaling the breath he had been unconsciously holding in his lungs.

The day's date was June 6, 1927. John Pappas was finally an American.

John Pappadojiannis is at last an American. Photo Courtesy: Harry J. and Stella A. Pappas family archives.

CHAPTER 5

1929:
Love Flourishes While Betrayal Looms

JOHN WAS DOING WELL ENOUGH in his sheep business to send for a wife from Crete. He remembered a woman he had fallen in love with as a child. Maria was the most beautiful young woman in his village and the pride of everyone in it, and he was as enamored of her as any youth of today might be of a movie goddess or rock star. As a boy, he attended the young woman's wedding. His little heart ached when she married a handsome Greek army officer named Panayiotis Minerakis from a neighboring village. He vowed to get even with the groom by one day marrying one of Maria and Panayiotis's daughters.

During his sheep ranching days in Price, Utah, whenever he met new arrivals in from near his village in Crete, he asked about the Minerakis family. Did they have any daughters of marrying age? He also sent inquiries to Greece through the famous "Greek grapevine"—a vital source of hearsay, gossip, and vital information that linked all immigrants with the news back home via letters and visits to the home village by friends and family. His hopes skyrocketed when he discovered that the Minerakis family did indeed have several daughters of marrying age, and they were interested in a marriage proposal from Yanni Pappadojiannis of esteemed reputation, from the village of Katamitsi, Crete.

John, having only one photograph of himself, enclosed it with a letter to the patriarch of the family, Panayiotis, who was a colonel and highly regarded by Cretans for his service to the island. John wrote and asked for the hand of the eldest daughter, which was the custom and tradition of the period, and enclosed the photo of himself. He wrote, "If you like what you see and wish to accept my proposal of marriage, you may keep the photograph until we are married. If you do not like what you see and wish to decline my proposal, please return it to me, because it's the only one I own."

Back in Crete, John's letter was received with much excitement by Panayiotis and his daughters. The matte-finish and wrinkled black-and-white photo enclosed showed a young man with short hair and a narrow mustache. Well-built and handsome, he looked to be a romantic vision of manhood for a young girl in Crete. After Colonel Minerakis did some checking into the name and reputation of Yanni Pappadojiannis and discovered his heroic and honorable deeds in both Crete and the Balkan War, one night he gathered his daughters around the table with their mother after dinner. He read them the letter, passing the photo around for each girl to see.

The eldest daughter, Nina, was the first to be offered Yanni's hand in America. Panayiotis watched Nina take a quick but respectful look at the picture of the young man in America. He knew what her answer would be—for she had her heart set on a boy in the village who was already betrothed to another girl, one selected for him by his parents. Nina didn't notice how her father saw the stolen, longing glances that she and the young man exchanged when seeing each other in the village plaza as the families passed each other on their evening strolls.

"Titika?" Panayiotis asked next. He wasn't surprised that Nina didn't want to go to America. He wasn't certain that Titika would want to go, either. In fact, he wasn't sure he wanted any of his daughters to go so far away, when he might never see that daughter again. He wanted each of his daughters to be happy and provided for, so if going to America might accomplish that, he would agree to it. His wife, their mother, Maria, sat at the table quietly, her eyes still swollen from the tears she had shed into her pillow the night before and most of the afternoon. She thought he didn't hear or notice her heart-wrenching sobs, but the couple later discussed it and he had decided that if one of the girls agreed, she would go to America. Since he was the head of the family, it was ultimately his decision regarding such family matters, especially since three daughters required three substantial dowries.

Titika hesitated, but she had heard such fantastic stories about America from other villagers whose family members wrote letters from that faraway place. Titika reached for the picture her father held in his hand. She looked at the photo and the face staring back at her. The man in the photo had striking features, though he was a bit older (this was not unusual). And, how she longed for some adventure in her life! Being Colonel Minerakis's daughter had its advantages, but she loved the stories of ancient Greek goddesses and heroes and wished that her life might have some interesting twists and turns, like all those characters in stories and history. Even so, this would be a big step. She ran her finger across the front of the picture, hoping that, like a magical looking glass, doing so would give her some indication of the man in the image. She looked up at her father and mother.

"*Paterra, meeterra*, father and mother, I accept the proposal of this man, Pappadojiannis, and I will go to America."

Her father nodded his head, then took her hand across the table, squeezing it.

"It is settled then. I will write him at once."

Her mother took Titika's hand as Panayiotis left the table, and smiled reassuringly at her daughter, holding back the tears she was sure would flow any moment.

Titika saw the pain in her mother's eyes.

"Don't worry, everything will be fine, you will see. My life in America will be grand, and you, Father, and my sisters will come to America to see me with my husband and children! After all, it is America, and every man who goes to America becomes rich, so there is nothing to worry about." Back in Utah, a few months went by before John received a response from the village. Now, here in his hand, he held the letter that would tell him whether his boyhood dream might come true.

He began to tear the envelope open, then stopped. He closed his eyes and prayed for strength. Whatever Minerakis decided, he would accept. The matter was out of his hands, as had been so much of his life. Whatever happened was God's will.

He tore open the envelope and began to read. It began with the usual pleasantries, which seemed to go on forever, but truthfully only went on for a paragraph or so.

His heart swelled and the air left his lungs. His eyes blurred.

His bride-to-be's name was Katherine; her nickname was Titika (*Tee-tee-kah*).

A short time later, they became engaged by proxy. The year was 1929.

With his future bride waiting for him in Crete, he needed to get his citizenship certificate so he could start the process of bringing his fiancée to America. After telling his friends and relatives of the good news, the always methodical and organized John went to the place in his house where he kept his most valuable documents. He removed the lid to the wooden box where he kept his important papers for safe-keeping and sifted through the documents. Every document of his life was there, except the one he needed the most—where was his citizenship certificate? It was missing from the box. He looked again. Was he mistaken? Perhaps he put it somewhere else. No, he remembered putting it in this box with all his other important documents. It *had* to be there. His face grew hot and he was losing patience. He knew he didn't lose it. Someone must have taken it. For what purpose would someone take his citizenship certificate?

The thought that one of his ranch hands had stolen from him made him angry. How could this be? He felt like a piece on a vast game board, with every decision of his life being made by a roll of the dice from the hand of some evil god, like Zeus, who toyed with him for amusement. He knew all his hired hands, most of them Greeks, and he couldn't believe that one of them had stolen from him. His citizenship document was gone, and perhaps, too, the young woman waiting for him on an island on the other side of the world.

Regardless of his planning, hard work, and finally finding some success in America, he had to sit down and write another letter to Colonel Minerakis, telling him of his plight. He hoped that Titika would wait for him to clear up this mess and to send for her. But, for how long? He thought of her waiting in Crete for perhaps months or even years and wondered if he was being fair to her. Why should she wait for him when it was possible for her to marry someone else and get on with her life? He decided not to write the letter to Colonel Minerakis just yet. Perhaps the citizenship document would turn up in short order and this problem would solve itself. He set pencil and paper aside for now.

The weather was turning cold in Utah and the dark skies reflected the gloom in John's heart.

———

Winter, the nemesis of every farmer, was on its way, and word among his Greek farming friends had it that this winter would be harsh.

Not long after the cold season set in, a series of storms swept through the region. Hail rained down over random areas of the reservation, leaving some parcels of land virtually covered in ice and others left untouched. As the storm moved swiftly and ominously across the horizon, John watched helplessly as the black sky opened and tennis ball–sized hail bombarded his land, burying and killing crops he planted that would have provided a profitable harvest, *and* the money needed to bring Titika to America.

He rode his horse to his property and assessed the damage after the storm. He hoped he could salvage some of his crop. He rode from east to west, north to south, and couldn't believe what he saw: none of the land bordering his ranch had been hit by the storm. Nature's fury had devastated only his farmland. He bowed his head, closed his eyes, and prayed. Only a prayer could help him deal with one more defeat, the last in a long line of setbacks for him.

When the storms wiped out his crops, he was nearly ruined. Shortly thereafter, the market for his sheep disappeared with the stock market crash of 1929. All the money he had good-heartedly lent to family and friends during the late-1920s was lost with the Depression, too. Some people

Katherine Minerakis, left, poses with her sister Stella in Crete, circa 1920s.

made promises of paying him back, even with interest, but the money never materialized. His money, along with everyone else's, was gone.

His hopes of bringing Titika to America were crushed.

He wrote to Colonel Minerakis and told his fiancée's father that he would have to obtain a copy of his citizenship certificate and that his finances were a shambles. He had faith he would rebuild his farming business again, but releasing Titika from the engagement was the only honorable thing left to do. It was unfair to have her wait for him when she could marry another. Her life should progress with happiness, even if it meant that she would do it in Crete, without him.

After several months, Colonel Minerakis responded to John's letter. He assured him that they still wanted John for Titika's husband. John was an honorable man, and they approved of him as a husband for their daughter. These circumstances, he wrote, were a simple setback and would pass. Katherine, their treasured daughter Titika, agreed to wait for him faithfully, for as long as necessary. He should rebuild his business and rest assured that his fiancée would join him when he was ready to send for her. And so, with her father's blessings, Titika continued to wait for her betrothed.

It would be seven long years before John traveled to New York City to meet his lovely, eager, and hopeful fiancée, Katherine.

During that time, he discovered it was indeed several of his workers who had stolen his citizenship document, fearing that John's marriage would result in them losing their free living arrangements, which were included in their pay. Their duplicity cost precious time, along with the storm, long delaying his marriage to his cherished fiancée.

So he fired every treacherous Judas who had betrayed him.

CHAPTER 6

1936–1943:
Babes on the Reservation

AFTER BARELY SURVIVING the storm's obliteration and financial losses from the Depression, John rebuilt his ranch with one goal in mind: to raise enough money to bring his patient fiancée, Titika, to America. Finally, he sent another letter to Colonel Minerakis with money for Titika to make the long voyage by ship to Ellis Island, in New York harbor.

After the trip east by bus and train, he waited with hundreds of other Greek immigrants, also at the docks of Ellis Island, to greet their fiancées-by-proxy, with only photographs to guide them to the faces of their future brides.

John and Katherine were married in New York via a civil ceremony and later celebrated with a traditional Greek Orthodox Church wedding in Price, Utah. The year was 1936, and the new bride and groom made their way back to Utah.

The Pappas farm on the barren flatlands of Fort Duchesne was desolate and primitive, a little shack of two rooms without plumbing or electricity. All their water—for drinking, cooking, and bathing—was brought into the house with little barrels. As with most immigrants, the Greeks in Utah lived within segregated communities composed of other fellow Greek immigrants, which made the process of assimilation a little easier to manage. Greek immigrants who had been in America longer were available to help their newly arrived friends and relatives.

In Utah, the immigrant Greeks settled in Salt Lake City or Price, or in mining towns and other smaller towns, as they rapidly emerged to service local farming and industry. Most of the Greeks who made the trip across the Atlantic settled in cities across the country where they found the camaraderie and solace of their fellow Greeks, in places like New York City and Chicago's Greektowns or Florida's Tarpon Springs. They also settled in other typical American towns and cities where Greeks gathered and formed communities, which became the seeds from which new Greek Orthodox churches sprang, like the church nearest to John and Titika, in Price.

Living within a community of Greeks was not what awaited Titika, who found herself completely alone at Fort Duchesne, for long periods without her husband, who left for weeks at a time to graze his sheep.

Four months after her marriage, she found herself pregnant.

The support and care she would have received as a pregnant woman back in Crete with her mother and sisters didn't exist for Titika. She spent much of her pregnancy alone, with only the company of her husband, John, when he returned home. She felt homesick and missed her family terribly. However, she rejoiced in watching her belly grow rapidly, thrilled that she would soon have her own child to love, nurture, and grow. Life in America was not as she expected, but she was young and robust and her new husband had given her a babe to fill her days and years. Her pregnancy was a blessing, and she thanked God every day as the baby grew quickly in her womb, active and copious.

Thirteen months after their marriage, John and Titika's firstborn children, a set of twin boys, arrived on September 2, 1937. Her enormous belly had housed two babies, not one. The first twins ever born in the newly constructed hospital in nearby Price, Utah, the babies were named Panayiotis (Pete, after Titika's father) and Emanuel (Mike, after John's father). They were beautiful—with Titika's enormous brown eyes (which she inherited from her father) and John's classic Greek profile. She had delivered two vibrant, healthy babies and survived herself at a time when infants and their mothers frequently died in childbirth. She was as resilient as any of her Cretan ancestors, and she wore that strength as a shield. Titika was a young, pioneering woman with her youth, fortitude, and faith the only pillars on which to lean in very hard times. She was without community, family, or friends nearby for what seemed to be a very long time at Fort Duchesne, with only her husband and two little sons for company.

When she looked at the angelic faces of her twin boys, Pete and Mike, her heart softened and her tears of disappointment or loneliness swiftly changed into ones of joy the moment she gazed upon them. Pete and Mike were Pappadojiannis, but they were also Minerakis, a part of her—the best part of her—and she would live for them. Her dreams would be fulfilled by them and through them. They were her reason for waking each day, for working so hard, for weeping and for smiling. They were everything wonderful in the world, and no matter how hard her life might be or whatever struggles she and John endured, she vowed that their lives would be better, special, full of adventures, the kind of life she had longed for a young girl. Still, living in that little shack at Fort Duchesne with her husband, both working so hard to survive, she realized that her dreams for her own life may not come to fruition.

Little Pete and little Mike would be the ones to live her hopes and dreams.

She worked and prayed every day of her life that the twins would shine, like the brightest stars on the bleakest, darkest nights. And like those black nights, when her world seemed dreary and dismal, they would be the fire in her heart and the lights of her life.

Titika imbued her twin boys' hearts with love, kindness, and deter-mination, while John shared his keen mind with them through stories told as poems, called *mandinathes*. As they grew into toddlers, they were curious and mischievous. Pete and Mike habitually got into child-hood mayhem, the kind Mark Twain wrote about in *Tom Sawyer* or *Huckleberry Finn*. The boys tried to catch fish with their bare hands in the creek that ran near the house. They stuffed frogs in their pockets and took them to their mother to cook for dinner (and fell on the ground, laughing hysterically at her screams and laughter), and they liked to roll around in the mud with the animals after a hard rain.

Despite John's reassurances that his friends the Ute Indians were harmless, Titika had a great fear of them and was vigilantly watchful of the boys. One afternoon while John was out on the ranch with his sheep, she had lost sight of Pete and Mike for just a moment as she hauled water into the house. When she came back outside, they didn't respond when she called. Her heart raced as she searched. Where could they be? They were in the middle of open land, desolate and untamed. What if wild animals had gotten to them?

"Oh my God, oh my *panayia*, my Virgin Mary, what if the Indi-ans have taken them?" she prayed as she ran, calling out frantically, *"Panayioti, Manoli! Panayioti, Manoli!* Pete and Mike, Pete and Mike, where *are* you?"

Her tears gushed as she prayed desperately.

"Oh, *panayia mou,* my Virgin Mary, please protect them, please keep them safe!"

She searched the surrounding land for hours and couldn't find them anywhere. Her heart breaking, she returned home without her young sons. Titika sat down, cried, and prayed some more. How could this have happened? How could she have let something terrible happen to her angels, her precious twin sons?

After a short time, John returned home. Walking through the door, he found Titika sobbing. She leaped to her feet and spoke to her husband in their native Greek.

"Yanni, Panayioti and Manoli are gone! The boys are missing! I've looked everywhere and they are gone!" John looked at her, his brows furrowed.

"They are gone? What do you mean they are gone? I leave you here with only one job to do—to watch two little boys—and you lose them?"

Titika could barely speak through her tears. "I've looked everywhere and I can't find them. Please go and look for them. I'm so afraid, Yanni! What if something has happened to them? What if the Indians have them? Oh *panayia mou*, my Virgin Mary, my babies—they are so small!"

She fell into her chair, crying, her mind thinking of every bad accident that could befall two little boys all alone in the prairie. John grabbed his rifle and started out the door as Titika's sobs filled the room. As he reached the door, his heart melted when he looked back at his beloved Titika, suffering with a mother's fear.

"Titika, don't worry, I will find them." The door slammed behind him.

While John walked over much the same area as Titika, the knot in his stomach wound tighter and tighter. He couldn't find his boys either. He thought back to his own days of mischief as a young boy in Crete and remembered wandering through the fields and hills, throwing twigs from trees as if they were the swords of ancient warriors, picking up fallen figs from the ground and hurling them as high and far as possible, and lying underneath an old orange tree, letting the fragrance of its blossoms fill his lungs.

A young boy could find much adventure in the tiny valleys and rolling hills of this reservation. Two boys could find twice as much. He just had to remember what it was like to be a small boy in a gigantic world. As he walked from fencepost to fencepost, he searched with the eyes of his two young boys, and not as a middle-aged man, who felt tired and not prone to view everyday as a grand adventure. For Pete and Mike, every day was a new chance to discover their little world. Leaving the watchful eyes of their mother afforded them greater opportunities to do just that.

As he rounded a corner, John looked up to the top of a slight hill, which descended gradually on the other side into a soft slope. He noticed that one of his empty wine barrels—the ones he used for aging and fermenting his homemade red wine—was missing. He remembered with much clarity that there had been five barrels on that hill. Looking at it, he could only see four, all toppled. Since he was already within a short distance, he walked over to set them upright. When he arrived and stood the barrels up, he looked down to the bottom of the slope.

Lying on its side at the base of the slope was the missing wine barrel.

He walked to the bottom of the hill. As he leaned over to pick up the barrel, he grabbed it across the middle and noticed that the lid was missing and the barrel was heavier than it should be. Perhaps a fox or similar creature had crawled inside for cover. He very slowly looked inside, ready to knock the barrel in the opposite direction so the animal could escape. As his eyes lowered, a slow smile crept across his face.

Inside his empty wine barrel were two little creatures named Pete and Mike, curled up into a ball, arms and legs wrapped around one another, sound asleep.

John gently woke the boys, who immediately jumped into their father's arms. When he asked them what they were doing in the barrel, and they explained their game, he laughed out loud.

"Baba, we had so much fun!" Pete said.

John and Katherine on their wedding day in 1936, Price, Utah.

"Baba, we were rolling down the hill, over and over, and then we saw the barrel, and we looked inside and it was empty, so Panayioti and I had the same idea to get inside and roll down the hill! Baba, it was so fun, *so much fun!*" Little Mike bubbled over with excitement.

The two boys laughed as John carried them, one boy slung over each of his shoulders, back to their worried mother.

Through a fountain of her tears, Titika hugged and kissed her twin boys until their faces were red and they felt crushed by her embrace. Afterward, they did receive the expected warnings about wandering too far from the house without their mother and father, in Titika's typically dramatic way. ("There are wild animals! And Indians! We would die without you! You are everything to us! A part of us!") When she heard the story of their roller-coaster ride in the wine barrel, her tears turned to laughter. Titika and John looked at one another for a moment, with the look that loving parents share, when they realize their treasured children are home safe.

Later that night, Titika tearfully prayed a lifetime of thanks to the Virgin Mary for bringing her boys back to her safe and unharmed. Next time, she promised Jesus Christ and the Virgin Mary she would never let them out of her sight, not for one moment. Little Pete and Mike were her life, and without them, she had no reason to live.

———

After church on Sundays when visiting friends' homes in Price, John heard stories about California from other Greeks whose relatives visited California, returned to Utah, and eventually moved with their families to the Golden State.

He weathered the 1930s as best he could, but after the birth of Pete and Mike in 1937 and sweet baby Mary in 1941 (John called her "the flower of our family" when he first saw her), John knew he had to do something to make his life and that of his family better. California was called the Golden State. After all, in olden times, miners had discovered gold there. Perhaps it was the place for John and his family to find their gold, too.

Also, Utes began canceling the land leases that many Greeks, like John, had signed with them. A sad incident occurred when a drunk Greek tenant farmer killed a friend who was a member of the Ute tribe. Even though the Greek had no memory of the event, his Ute friend was dead. Prior to the incident, there were Utes who wanted tenant farmers evicted from their reservation land. The killing of one of their fellow Utes by a tenant farmer expedited the process. John and other Greeks were soon to be evicted. He sent his flock to a friend's ranch out-of-state while he made plans to visit California.

He told Titika his thoughts and said that he would leave her and the children for a few weeks to visit some of his Greek relatives and friends who had moved to San Francisco and to a nearby valley. She was not happy to be left alone again, but the possibility of leaving Utah excited her. It would be a blessing to leave that cold, desolate place. Perhaps God was listening to her prayers after all.

The bus trip to California was long. When John arrived in San Francisco, he was met by his friend Louie. When John asked if there was room for him to stay a night with his friend's family, his old friend threw his arms around him.

Pete and Mike as toddlers in Utah with Katherine, circa 1939.

"Welcome, John, welcome! If I don't have a bed for you, I will have you sleep in my bed!"

Louie made sure that John was comfortable and at home. Greeks were known for their hospitality, their *philoxenia*. The two men stayed up late, talking over glasses of homemade Greek wine (always red), homemade feta cheese, and tart, home-cured Kalamata olives, dandelion greens (known as *horta* in the old country), and Grecian chicken.

John had traveled from Crete by ship to New York City, then by train to Toledo, Ohio, and finally to Utah, by bus to San Francisco. As a passenger in his friend Louie's car the next day, they drove to his family's new *horio*, village, of Modesto, in the San Joaquin Valley of California.

CHAPTER 7

1952:
Twins Rock 'n' Roll in the '50s

To support his family, John worked before sunrise to the late afternoon in the Central San Joaquin Valley's fields, harvesting crops for local farmers. The drive to work became easier when he rented 15 acres of land (so he could grow food and raise livestock while Titika could make cheese from the family's sheep and tend to their garden), and he moved the family there during Pete and Mike's teen years. The twins helped him support the family in the summer when school was finished. They were the oldest sons and, as such, it was their duty to help ease their father's burden. Since age restrictions in California prohibiting teens from working until age 16 didn't come about until the 1960s, if young people wanted to work in the previous decade, they could be hired. So the twins went to work in area farms.

Pete and Mike got up around 4:00 a.m. each day, joining their father and Theo Manoli, their father's cousin who lived with them, for a hot, homemade breakfast made by Titika. They helped slap together their Greek sandwiches for lunch, with fresh feta cheese made by their mother and tomatoes picked from their garden. The twins hitchhiked to work and home again.

The work was hard and filthy. Pete and Mike picked grapes with a Greek crew in the intensely hot San Joaquin Valley summers, getting thick dust all over them. They climbed ladders and picked peaches that resulted in peach fuzz coating their clothes and skin, causing rashes on their arms and neck. They plucked apricots off branches and even worked on a goat dairy, where they milked goats, fed them hay, and cleaned the barn. They hoed beans at 25 cents an hour for a neighbor in the hot sun, clearing away the weeds from the beans and stocks. They drove tractors mowing hay and worked on turkey ranches while keeping a keen eye on the turkeys, who sometimes ran up from behind and bit them.

Working in sweltering hot sheds, they cut the pits out of stone fruit like apricots and peaches so that the fruit could dry in the sun. When the foreman gave his workers a short break, Pete and Mike sometimes jumped into a nearby canal to cool off.

When the twins returned home each day, they helped around their family's farm. Their father raised chickens, rabbits, goats, and sheep and also maintained fruit trees, a small grape vineyard, and his own garden. The boys took care of the animals, pruned trees, tilled the soil, and hoed weeds in the vineyard because their father wanted to have the cleanest grape vineyard in the valley. When it came time to harvest the grapes, Pete and Mike picked them, loaded them into boxes, and put the boxes heavy with grapes onto the back of the trailer hitched to their father's tractor, which they drove alongside the vineyard until the harvest was complete. They even worked in the garden as needed, helping to hoe weeds and pick vegetables for Titika's homecooked family meals.

In the Pappas home, everyone worked together for the family's survival. In their family, as was the case for most Greek immigrant families, work was valued, honorable, and an important way to teach the children a work ethic. It was expected that children would help the family and in turn learn to work and support themselves. John told his children that "no Greek goes on public assistance." He thought charity was for widows, orphans, the ill, and the disabled.

A man's duty, he firmly believed, was to support his family, and he would teach his children how to do so.

No job was thought too hard or dirty for Pete and Mike. They were young, energetic, and industrious. They gave the bulk of the money they earned all summer to their father for the family and kept a few dollars to buy clothes for school from a little department store on Crows Landing Road. Their father never asked the boys for money or financial help, but they saw how hard he worked and how little money the family had, regardless of his long hours. All of that miserably hard work primed Pete and Mike for a clean job indoors, away from the toil of the fields. They dreamed of the day they could wear clean white shirts with dress slacks and sit at a desk and work like *Americani*, in a clean office job, like the people they saw at the KTRB radio station.

Over the summer, Pete and Mike got tired of hitchhiking and decided they needed a car. They worked more days and hours to buy and support a vehicle. They asked their father over dinner one evening if they could buy a car, knowing they would need a cosigner for their first major purchase.

John finished chewing, wiped his mouth with his napkin, and looked at his twins. He marveled at how quickly they were growing up. They were still boys but becoming men. In many ways, they were men already.

"I will cosign for the car, but you will have to pay for it—make the payments and support the car and buy gas." He looked at Titika and back at the twins, who were sitting next to each other at the table, like they always did. "It is your responsibility."

Pete and Mike, thrilled, ran to their room after dinner, counted the money they had saved, and figured out how much they still needed to earn, then made their plans.

By summer's end, they had saved enough money to buy a vehicle. At 15, Pete and Mike each already had a driver's license to drive on the farm so with a car, they could finally stop hitchhiking. The car they chose, a 1939 Buick, represented freedom and became their first refuge outside of home. They drove around together and talked of their dreams or aired their frustrations. They used the time alone to pep each other up and keep the other one going, when one brother had the blues, or when their troubles seemed insurmountable. "Brother, let's take a drive" became the secret, lifelong signal one twin sent to the other when he needed to dream, talk, or unwind.

A car became their cocoon, beginning in high school, with that Buick.

Time traveled swiftly for Pete and Mike, who found themselves freshmen at the local high school in the nearby farming town of Ceres, just south of Modesto. At Ceres High, just as in elementary school, Pete and Mike stood out: mirror-image twins with their dark, almost black hair, each greased with hair gel, one ringlet falling onto their foreheads, dressed identically. They finished each other's sentences and laughed at each other's jokes. They shared private thoughts with one another from across the classroom with a glance.

Always gregarious, Pete and Mike made friends quickly and were instantaneously popular, elected early in their freshman year to be class cheerleaders, a dual-identity pep squad all by themselves. At the same time, they also went out for football, and made the 'B' team (now known as junior varsity). During that year, even though both the 'A' and 'B' teams lost all their games, the boys loved the camaraderie and competitiveness of sports, school spirit, and pride, and, for once, enjoyed being part of the in-crowd. It was a fun time for them, but one that was not shared by their parents, who didn't understand the whole concept of team sports and, especially, football. They didn't know anything about the habit of going to football games to root for their sons. John was in his mid-60s and too tired at night from working to attend sporting events, even if he understood them. Though younger than her husband by a decade, Titika didn't drive. Thus, neither John or Titika ever attended one of their sons' football games. Pete and Mike took this in stride, knowing that their immigrant parents simply didn't understand the high school football obsession that gripped every small town in 1950s America. What they *did* understand was sharing their hospitality, so the Pappas house became the go-to hangout after practices for good Greek food while sharing gossip and laughs.

After football practice, five or six of Pete and Mike's friends from the team crawled over and on top of each other getting into the twins' car for the ride over to the Pappas house. At any of their teammates' homes, that snack might consist of chips and a sandwich, or maybe leftovers from the family's dinner the night before. However, at Pete and Mike's house, the snack was a freshly prepared meal cooked by Titika that day.

Pete and Mike's friends loved her food, and as they made their way home from practice, the talk centered on the team they were going to play the upcoming Saturday night, who was dating whom, the girls they wanted to date, any parties they knew of on the weekend, and school happenings. Carl, Tommy, Butch, and Tony—all kids like them from the poor side of town—bonded with the friendly and charismatic Pappas twins. Pete and Mike's popularity spilled over onto anyone nearby, so those who craved being attached to it, like their football friends, formed a 1950s version of a celebrity posse. These boys, all scrunched together in their friends' car, in wrinkled jeans, torn shoes, and mussed plaid cotton shirts, with the breeze from the open windows blowing cool air into the car (a welcome break from that unique body odor that came from running football drills for two hours), made the drive to Pete and Mike's house a short one.

When the gang finally arrived, everyone, talking and laughing all at once, ran for the kitchen, with shouts of "Hey, Mrs. Pappas!" and "How are *you*, Mrs. P.?" aimed at Titika, while a few like Tony, whom Titika identified as "your Italian friend," and who came from similarly ethnic backgrounds, gave her a polite kiss on the cheek. One of the boys, an African-American lad named Carl, took his place at the table along with his friends and Pete and Mike, never once glancing over his shoulder and worrying about having a meal with a white family. When Carl first visited Pete and Mike's, he had paused outside their home, hesitating. But Mike just threw his arm around his friend's shoulders.

"Don't worry, Carl, this is a Greek house and the Pappas house, so everyone is welcome."

Once inside, Carl found Mike was right. It was 1952, and even if the rest of America was a photo viewed in black-and-white, the picture of the people sitting around Titika's kitchen table was in vivid Technicolor.

Titika, with her hair and makeup just so, stood ready with her crisp, clean apron on to serve the boys whatever they desired and as much as they desired. "Hello, boys," she answered. "Whatta' you say today, we hava soupa'?" Knowing her twins would be home from practice with their friends soon, she had set the table with utensils, napkins, bowls, and glasses for each place. The boys made their way to the stove where she stood ready to ladle plenty of *avgolemono*, egg lemon soup, into their bowls. Pete and Mike acted as translators for their mother, who nevertheless tried to make each boy comfortable and at ease with lots of nods and smiles.

"Good boysa, you wanna' more, I gotta' more, hava' some *psomaki?*"

She looked at Pete, who was slurping his soup, and said in Greek, "Panayioti, how do you say 'bread' in English?"

Pete shouted over the cacophony of voices in the room, "Bread! She wants to know if you want some homemade bread, and there's homemade butter, too."

Carl and Butch, who were already seated, looked up from their soup bowls, eyes wide, as if someone had called out their lucky numbers in the weekly church bingo game.

"I'll take some of that, Pete," Carl said, and he slathered the homemade bread with warm butter and wolfed it down. Mike looked at his brother, Pete, as he translated and they both grinned. Titika brought out more of her Greek bread and butter she had made from goat's milk. After the third round of soup and bread, the teenagers fell silent, their mouths and bellies full with the sumptuousness of the meal Titika had lovingly prepared for them. While the twin's teammates were enthusiastic and excited to eat this delicious, homecooked meal from scratch, the twins were enthralled to share it with their friends.

As the school year progressed, Pete and Mike were busier than ever, though they did manage to find time for dating, which usually began by attending one of their high school's sporting events on Saturday night. With the football season over, they could relax on the gym's bleachers and watch a basketball game like any of the other kids, except that, try as they might, they just *weren't* like other kids, and the other kids made sure they knew that fact.

At one home game, Pete and Mike climbed the steps of the bleachers, making their way through the crowd, with their dates in tow, saying hello to friends they knew in the stands. Mostly, though, they focused on the two pretty girls with them, who were dressed like twins—identically, down to the imitation pearls around their necks

61

and the ribbons in their hair—who had spent the entire week planning their outfits to match each other's, just as Pete and Mike matched with one another. The practice of dressing alike by their dates became the norm, and each time the boys went out, a new set of girls tried to outdo the previous set of girls in the elaborateness of their outfits. The lower bleachers were full, so that night the foursome made their way toward the top.

As the game ended, the bleachers emptied quickly, with families headed home and teenagers ready to get into their cars and spend the rest of the night out. Mike saw someone at the bottom of the bleachers he knew and went down with his date to talk to the guy. Still at the top of the bleachers but making his way down were Pete and his date.

"Yeah, there's Mr. Big Stuff, the mother-f-r of the football team, who's one of the Pappas twins but should be called 'Pappas mother-f-r twin.'"

The guy yelling at Pete was an upper classman who had been sitting on the opposite end of the bleachers but was now walking toward Pete. Like Mike, Pete was used to name-calling and kids trying to pick fights, and usually he tried to ignore them, but this time the insult had the word "mother" in it. And nobody, even by slight implication, could insult their mother without paying for it. Pete moved quickly, barreling shoulder and headfirst into the kid's gut, quickly dragging him down by his shirt collar, punching and jabbing as they landed in the middle of the gymnasium floor. In between blows, Pete yelled as he punched.

"Don't you *ever* call me that, 'cause when you call me that you're using the word 'mother' and nobody calls me any name like that with my mom's name attached to it!"

With a bloodied nose and bruises after falling from the blows, the guy scurried away as soon as Pete let him up for air. Mike had seen his brother get entangled on the floor so he broke away from his girl and ran over to him.

"What happened, brother?"

Putting his hand on his twin's shoulder, he listened as Pete told him, and Mike's face and mood turned somber.

"That s-o-b, mentioning Mom. He deserved it!"

Pete and Mike and their dates left the game, with the girls more shaken than either of the twins. For the boys, this was just another case of jealous rage directed at them and their family. They had fought to defend themselves all their lives, with this being the latest case. For that kid, Pete's blows were simply an appetizer before the full-course meal that he'd receive the next day.

Word spread through all the teen hangouts that night and by Monday, the school was buzzing with gossip, the story of the fight made more dramatic and even life-threatening as it passed from ear to ear. When news of the fight and the insult that caused it reached their friend Carl, who had been repeatedly and warmly welcomed into the Pappas home by the twins' mother, Titika, and had enjoyed her good food and hospitality at a time when black youth weren't always welcomed into the homes of their white friends (if they had any, with racism being what it was in the 1950s), he cornered the offender and gave him another beating.

"Nobody—*nobody*—ever, *ever* insults Mrs. Pappas, or they're gonna' hear from me, you got that?" said Carl. "You gonna' hear from me again if you ever say a bad thing about Mrs. Pappas ever again!"

Word traveled within Ceres High—that you might not like Pete and Mike, but insulting their family was off-limits.

Regardless of jealous troublemakers, the twins were determined to pursue their dreams and have some 1950s teenage fun as well.

Modesto was the quintessential drag town. Tenth Street was the drag strip and teens drove a big circle around downtown, ending up at Burge's Drive-In, where they'd park, roll a window down halfway, and wait for the waitress on roller skates to take their order. Teens might also take the longer route, cruising up and down the newest boulevard, McHenry Avenue, ending up at Webb's Drive-In. While they waited for their food (usually a cheeseburger, fries, and soda, or maybe a milkshake), they'd blast tunes on the radio, from groups like the Clovers, the Del Vikings, the Drifters, and singers like Fats Domino, Chuck Berry, Elvis Presley, Frankie Laine, Nat King Cole, Patti Page, and Rosemary Clooney as they talked with their dates and kids they knew in neighboring cars.

The teeming social life desired by every teenager required two things: great music on the radio, and a car. The car was key. Teens routinely had transistor radios (usually in those popular colors of the period, lime green and iridescent orange) with ear buds connected to a wire connected to the radio, which was great for listening to Jerry Lee Lewis, Bill Haley and the Comets, Kay Starr, or Teresa Brewer, but not so great for cruising Tenth Street. Pete and Mike's car gave them the freedom and social life that all American teenagers craved.

CHAPTER 8

1953–1955:
Twin Star Power

IN THEIR SOPHOMORE YEAR, the boys got involved with student affairs when they became unofficial spokesmen for the teens at Ceres High. Pete and Mike, known collectively in high school as "the Pappas Twins," were invited to go to the number one local radio station in Modesto to talk about the need for a newly proposed youth center in their city. Parents, concerned with their offspring spending their free time cruising, drinking beer, smoking, and the like, wanted a youth center built in their town at the Fourth Street Park. As teenagers, though, the twins didn't share those concerns. Instead, they and their friends wanted the youth center built mostly because they were bored with small-town life. In 1950s Modesto, as in many working-class American towns, there was nothing to do but cruise the boulevard, so Pete and Mike did everything possible as teen leaders to get the youth center built.

Visiting a radio station for only the second time in their lives, it was the airwaves of KTRB-860 AM, the same station they had visited in elementary school, that first carried the voices of the Pappas twins.

After their short interview, Pete and Mike's aspirations to be in the radio business, born on that first field trip in the fifth grade, went from schoolboy dreams to a possible reality. Convinced their future was in the radio business, the boys visited several radio stations in the area and pitched the idea for a teen radio program they would host for an hour a week. Just because the city was slow to recognize that teens needed a venue for socializing with other teens didn't mean Pete and Mike weren't hip to the idea. The show would feature the newest popular music, along with the news of local high schools, teens, and events around Modesto. KTRB was the most popular radio station in town, so the twins approached the station first with their idea. They managed to get a meeting with the program director (P.D.) who made the programming decisions for the station.

KTRB was the radio equivalent of a sports dynasty—the winner of every game, number one in every season, the one to beat. With its schedule established and its audience loyal, it didn't really need a teen show to attract attention, publicity, or advertising dollars. Thus, the twins were turned down by KTRB.

KBOX-AM had recently hit the airwaves in Modesto. Having been interviewed on KTRB, the twins were the talk of the town, so getting in to see that station's general manager, a kindly man named Milt Hibdon, along with KBOX's P.D., wasn't difficult. With their charm, polite demeanor, and natural talents of persuasion, Pete and Mike presented their idea for a teen radio program.

Hibdon listened to their idea and then, admiring their enthusiasm, threw some blank contracts on the desk toward them. "Look, kids, I'm real busy today, and this is a brand-new station, but I'll make you a deal: if you can go out and sell advertisers for one hour every Saturday night, I'll let you do your own show." The general manager smiled at the boys as he watched the twins leave his office, convinced he'd never see them again.

Pete and Mike, determined to succeed, left the station, parked their car on the side of the road, and divided the town into two lists of businesses. They were young and didn't know this would be an arduous task, but they felt full of energy and optimism, so they just went out and did it. They called on merchants and sold advertising to sponsor their teen radio show.

Two weeks later, Pete and Mike returned to KBOX and Hibdon's office with the blank contract forms he gave them, now signed by local merchants. They had no sales training or experience selling anything to anyone, but they accomplished it nonetheless.

When the boys gave Hibdon the signed contracts, he was both incredulous and pleased at the same time by the twins' determination. He told Pete and Mike they had earned their chance to do their first radio program.

Pete and Mike's Dance Time was born.

The twins drove home and ran into their mother's kitchen, the screen door slamming behind them.

"Mama, baba, we got our show! *We got our show!*" Pete was talking so fast that even though using his parents' native Greek, they didn't quite understand. Mike saw their perplexed looks and took them over to sit on the family's sofa.

"Mama, baba, we're going to have our own show on the radio!" cried Mike. "Remember the radio station we visited on the field trip? We are going to have our own radio show for teenagers on KBOX-AM!"

His mother stood up and smothered them with hugs and kisses while speaking in her native Greek. "My *agoria!* My sons! I am going to tell everyone in Modesto that my twins will be on the radio! My Pete and Mike will be radio stars!"

Their father got to his feet and shook their hands.

"Bravo, bravo, *Panayioti* and *Manoli*, bravo! You are going to make some money with this radio show?" Pete and Mike nodded their heads.

"Baba, this is for the family too," said Mike. "For all of us, baba, for all of us," said Pete.

Their future began in one week.

The show started with one hour every Saturday night at 10:00—not considered prime radio listening time even in 1954, though it was the time when teenagers were out in force, cruising the main drag, lying on their beds at home, or talking to their friends on the phone. It was the perfect time for a radio show aimed at teens. After the first few Saturdays of *Pete and Mike's Dance Time*, news of the show spread from teen to teen between high schools. In terms of today's social media world, Pete and Mike were *trending*. They sparked more talk by airing recorded announcements promoting the show during KBOX's regular daytime programming. The twins frequently talked to their classmates at Ceres High about the show. They designed a poster and walked door to door in Modesto's downtown, asking their merchant sponsors if they could place a *Pete and Mike's Dance Time* poster in their window touting the show. Soon, *Pete and Mike's Dance Time* became every teenager's show, regardless of which high school they attended in Ceres, Modesto, or even Turlock. Audience requests for special songs dedicated to their teenage sweethearts were a big attraction of the show. Listeners called into *Pete and Mike's Dance Time* and the twins announced the dedications within a short period, allowing enough time for listeners to let their friends know to listen for the dedication on-air. The dedications personalized the show, making everyone a celebrity-of-the-moment. *Pete and Mike's Dance Time* became a big deal in the community, especially to its teenage audience. Each of them felt they knew Pete and Mike personally.

AM radio stations like KTRB had been the kings of media but in the 1950s, a new, young medium hit the airwaves, changing the landscape for both news and programming.

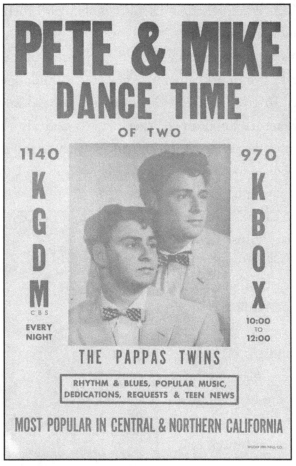

Poster of Pete and Mike's Dance Time, circa 1950s.

In the late 1940s and 1950s, television proliferated. Radio variety programs like those of Roy Rogers and Bob Hope successfully transitioned to television. Radio's loss of national shows resulted in a new programming focus for radio stations—to better service their communities with more local entertainment, news, and information. It was during that transitional time in the radio industry that *Pete and Mike's Dance Time* thrived. Radio in their 1950s small town eagerly embraced

Pete and Mike's entrepreneurial talent, coupled with their innate gift for self-promotion.

The twins' success eventually led to the expansion of the show to six nights a week, five hours a night, from 7:00 to midnight. Pete and Mike wanted to give teenagers something to do besides listen to the radio. They needed to promote their show—and also make more money—so they began hosting teen dances. They found a venue and hooked up with a local band, called Otis Morrow and the Foxes of Morrow, to make it happen.

The band had about eleven members with horns, drums, guitar, and piano with Otis Morrow himself singing lead with back-up vocalists, and it wasn't long before they were attracting hundreds of teenagers every Friday night to their dances. Pete and Mike dressed identically with handsome light-gray suits and black bow ties. They emceed the dances together, taking turns with introductions to various numbers, talked to their audience, and made special note of the latest hits that the Otis Morrow band was going to "cover." The dances became the go-to spot for Friday night entertainment in the Modesto area.

Young Harry with his mother, Katherine, circa 1954.

The whole Pappas family worked together to help *Pete and Mike's Dance Time* dances succeed. Pete and Mike arrived hours earlier at the

California Ballroom on Sixth Street to do microphone checks and get everything on stage set up for the show. John and Titika arrived a short time later, with Mary, aged 12, and Harry, then 8, in tow, all dressed in their finest to help at the dance. Mary sold tickets in the box office (her maturity and grasp of mathematics made her perfect for the role), while Harry did his best to run the concession stand. Pete and Mike befriended the local Pepsi distributor, who delivered a working soda fountain and buckets of ice to the dance each week. Harry sold each glass of Pepsi for 10 cents. Not the typical 8-year-old, Harry would later skip two grades at Westport Union Elementary School, receive a science award, and get paired with a scientist at the local Shell Laboratories for mentorship.

Neither Mary nor Harry was paid to work for the twins, but the tradition of the family working together continued throughout their adult lives.

Pete and Mike promoted their teenage dances, printed their own *Pete and Mike's Dance Time* business cards, fliers, letterhead, checkbook covers, and posters, all featuring pictures plugging the program. They promoted the dances despite not having any money to pay for the stage, bartender, security, and even the hall itself, hoping that they'd make enough money to pay for all of it at the end of the night.

They never failed once. Their show, and their dances, were big moneymakers.

Pete and Mike usually made $100 to $150 profit from each dance. Along with the commissions they made by selling advertising for their radio show, they took in enough money for them to make their car payment. They made spending money for dating and going to the movies. They bought their own clothes, and the money they earned helped ease the financial burden of their parents.

Pete and Mike's Dance Time became a phenomenon in the Modesto area, yet the twins' ambitions weren't limited to doing their show only in their small hometown. Their audience was large and reached to the north and south of Modesto. Advertisers were clamoring to get a spot on the show. For the first time in their lives, Pete and Mike had some regular money coming in, and they racked their brains to find a way to make *more* money: say, by expanding the show into neighboring cities, the closest and largest being Stockton, some thirty miles north. So one

Some horseplay between the twins, circa 1950s.

day Mike took the boys' Buick and drove to Stockton, talking his way into meeting the two women who owned KGDM-AM radio.

Mike convinced the station's owners to give the twins' show a chance, provided that they find their own sponsors. Mike didn't know his way around Stockton, but he went downtown, parked his car, and walked from business to business to sell sponsors for *Pete and Mike's Dance Time*. Soon, Mike did the program on KGDM-AM in Stockton every night while Pete did it on KBOX-AM in Modesto. *Pete and Mike's Dance Time* played on two radio stations concurrently, and they often called each other by phone to chat on each other's shows.

By their senior year in high school, the twins' radio show was making so much money that Pete and Mike bought their first new car: a 1956 Mercury Montclair. With a white exterior, red hard top, alternating red and white pleated seats, and a state-of-the-art AM radio, the Montclair replaced the old Buick they bought by working on valley farms. It symbolized their very first success in the broadcasting business.

CHAPTER 9

1955–1956:
First Foray into Television

PETE AND MIKE DECIDED that television would be the next outlet for *Pete and Mike's Dance Time.* The big three television network affiliates serving the Modesto-Stockton-Sacramento television markets, just as KTRB radio in Modesto, didn't need programming. But a new independent television station, KTVU UHF channel 36, without the benefit of network programming, had plenty of airtime to fill.

Pete and Mike's Variety Show, a half-hour program airing every Friday night, featured local talent—singers in duets, trios, and quartets, as well as dance groups from the local area. However, producing two radio programs and a television show, selling advertisers to keep them on the air, while trying to keep up with school, homework, and dance hosting, soon became too much for the twins. They gave up their television show after only six months. However, their introduction to the independent television business was fortuitous and foreshadowed the Pappas brothers' venture into the independent television business later in their lives.

While the show aired, Pete and Mike became television stars and with that distinction came even more local fame. When the twins took their dates to football and basketball games and other public events, the eyes of local teenagers were on them. They heard murmurs of "there's Pete and Mike—there go the Pappas twins!" as they walked by.

Pete and Mike were everywhere: on two radios stations, on television, and at their weekly dances. Their opinions on teen issues were aired on their radio programs as editorials, and they even made an appearance before the Modesto City Council to speak on behalf of the proposed teen recreation center. Moreover, jealous teens weren't the only listeners irritated by Pete and Mike's opinions. Some adults found disfavor with them as well. They were considered controversial as teenage disc jockeys for defending teenagers when the twins said there was more adult delinquency than juvenile delinquency.

Pete and Mike wanted and enjoyed success but didn't foresee the problems they'd experience in high school, putting them on the defensive.

The ugly side of teenage fame was that jealousy arose among the teenagers who weren't fans, both at their high school and at surrounding high schools. That hatred turned to pervasive threats of violence that required calls to the Sheriff's Department. Deputies were dispatched to the radio stations to escort the twins safely home after each show. Pete and Mike couldn't understand how people could dislike them or why eight or ten teenage high school students at a time picked fights with them when they didn't personally know the twins. As juniors, they left Ceres High and spent the last two years of high school at Modesto High but found they had to deal with resentful students there, as well.

During the first few weeks the twins were at Modesto High, the halls were thick with hate, like the blinding fog that blanketed the valley in the middle of winter. During one ten-minute break between classes, as students scurried about, Pete and Mike scrambled to their lockers. After grabbing their books, they turned to find themselves surrounded by a gang, all clad in black leather jackets, in white short-sleeved T-shirts, packs of smokes tucked into their back pockets.

"Oh, I'm a big disc jockey! I'm a big TV star!" yelled one.

"You guys think you're big shots!" shouted another. The circle tightened around them. Pete and Mike dropped their books, standing back-to-back, just as they did in elementary school, fists ready. A crowd had already gathered around the group. "Fight, fight, fight!" the spectators chanted. They were drowned out by the gang's leader.

"You think can just show up here, and we're gonna' treat you like big stars? That's what you think, isn't it?" he shouted. "Well, that ain't how it's gonna' be, you get me?"

Pete and Mike didn't waver. They were surrounded by at least ten guys. But numbers didn't matter.

They would never surrender.

"Let's see if you can fight as good as you talk, big mouth," said Pete. He nudged Mike, who understood his brother's prompt.

"I dunno', Pete!" Mike shouted. "I think all these guys do is look tough and talk tough. I don't think they can actually fight!"

Just as the boys were about to come to blows, the vice principal intervened. Sending the gang to the office, he escorted Pete and Mike to class. The aggression forced the twins to meet with the Dean of Men and the principal, to request that they be allowed to finish their senior year of high school at Modesto Junior College (MJC). Wisely, the two men agreed and arranged for Pete and Mike to attend that college.

Even with all the hours they worked and attended school, the twins still tried to be normal teenagers and managed to get into some mischief.

Prior to buying their new Montclair, one afternoon they drove around town in their 1939 Buick with their Greek friend Bill (the son of immigrants, like them), and a beautiful girl in a swimming suit walked by on the sidewalk as they were rounding a curve. The three rolled down the windows and whistled at her. Even though he was driving, Mike was focused on the pretty girl instead of the road.

He drove their prized Buick into a telephone pole.

Because they were traveling at a very slow speed, both the car and the boys were fine. Since they were local celebrities, the incident was featured on KTRB's evening newscast. Mike called the news director at the station to make a statement on the twins' behalf but was declined the opportunity.

Embarrassed, they vowed there'd never be any more news stories about Pete and Mike Pappas unless they were flattering ones. Fortunately, when Mike was later involved in a terrible accident (the car he was driving rolled over three times and was demolished), he survived without a scratch and the story never made the news. It was his second brush with death.

Titika and John didn't understand their sons' fame or the effect of it on them at school or in the community. They were proud of Pete and Mike's accomplishments even though they didn't understand how the twins' radio and television teen career helped them establish careers in the future. Broadcasting was not a profession they comprehended.

"What are you doing playing phonograph records?" asked John. "You should work with your hands to make money and not play records. How are you going to support your family someday?" Pete and Mike repeatedly reassured their parents that playing records was just the start of their career in broadcasting and they would use their teen radio and television experience to launch their careers. *Pete and Mike's Dance Time* was just the beginning.

Due to Pete and Mike's teen radio and television programs, their lives were certainly not typical for teenagers in the 1950s. The resulting hostility from many of their fellow classmates forged an even stronger bond between the twins. It fortified their resolve to successfully focus on building a broadcasting career.

Despite the jealous backlash from male teens, Pete and Mike, still immensely popular, double-dated regularly with steady girlfriends. One evening, after they drove up to the home of Pete's girlfriend Georgia, her American-born father blocked Pete's entrance to the front door.

"I don't want a dirty Greek dating my daughter!"

The date was over before it began.

On another night, Mike's girlfriend Gayle walked a block from her house to meet him, because her father had forbidden her to see Mike.

"We're God-fearing Christians," her father told her. "We don't want you to date a Greek, or even a southern European. Those people aren't Christian."

The man, ignorant of history, didn't realize the boys' Orthodox faith was over a millennium old and originated in the Holy Land.

One day in the previous summer, Pete and Mike finished working in the fields, emerging hot, smelly, and with dirt caked on their arms and clothes. They decided to visit another of Pete's girlfriends (despite her parents' disapproval, the two had been secretly dating). His girlfriend's folks owned a drive-in restaurant off McHenry Avenue, so they drove over for some burgers, fries, and sodas. After they drove in and parked, the owner of the restaurant told the waitress on skates to go back inside, while he confronted the boys, red-faced, with fists waving.

"I want you *g-d black Greeks* off my property, out of my parking lot! And I don't want you talking to my daughter anymore!"

Both boys felt insulted and angry. Pete tried to jump out of the car, but Mike grabbed his arm.

"Don't, brother!" he cried, pulling him back into the car. "Let's leave here and talk about it. I have an idea."

Later that night, the boys sneaked into the local National Guard Armory, took some smoke bombs, and went by the drive-in a few nights later after it closed. The car sped into the lot in front of the restaurant. Mike rolled down the passenger window, and both boys yelled, "Remember the Greeks!" as they lobbed the smoke canisters out the window and through the back door, which was open for end-of-day cleaning. No harm was done, but as sons of immigrant Greeks, Pete and Mike felt avenged. They had long heard of the hateful verbal abuse and treatment their father and other Greeks had endured in Utah, and they weren't going to take it in their hometown or anyplace else.

The inner resolve that drove their ancestors to survive, fight, and free themselves from nearly 400 years of enslavement under the Ottomans was bred into them like the color of their eyes or the wave in their hair. They would never tolerate discrimination against the Greek culture or its people.

CHAPTER 10

1955–1956:
Dreams Drive Achievement

NOT ONLY DID MANY NON-GREEKS, *Americani,* disapprove of Pete and Mike—their successful programs, their local fame, and their independent, outspoken candor—some Greeks from the local Greek community condemned them, as well. Tongues wagged incessantly about them, especially when some older Greek folks saw Pete and Mike with their *Americani* girlfriends walking down the street.

Pete and Mike didn't care if people gossiped about the girls they were dating. They would walk calmly down the street, addressing the Greek person they ran into as *theo,* uncle, or *thea,* aunt (as a sign of respect), and would say, "Hello, *theo"* or "Hello, *thea*—this is my girlfriend, Helen" or "my girlfriend, Sally." Before they arrived home, the Greek grapevine had already delivered the news home to their mother, via telephone calls from multiple Greek women, whom Titika knew socially.

"Your twins will be failures, they won't marry Greeks, they will get into trouble and go to jail," they told her. "Twins are a curse. Pete and Mike are a curse!"

Often in tears, Titika passionately defended her sons. What hateful and jealous women! How could they *say* such horrible things about her twin boys? She had been blessed twice the day they were born. These women were *horyateethes*, village women, ignorant and superstitious.

All her children illuminated her life.

Pete and Mike's accomplishments as teen radio stars proved they were on the road to success already.

Their future would light up the skies.

The twins weathered the hostility and malevolent slurs but hated that their mother sobbed so much when she heard them from others.

The boys' bluntness, independence, and individualism fed the green monster, in both adults and teens, *Americani* as well as some Greek immigrants.

Pete and Mike's almost otherworldly attachment, beginning with their love for one another in the womb, protected them like a steel bastion from the moment they emerged into this world. Pete and Mike stood alone on their own mountaintop, and whatever jealousy and resentment they faced just made them resilient and tenacious. They didn't go home each day to parents that were raised in the United States and knew American ways, so they had to rely on each other for consolation and motivation, and on people like Milt Hibdon, the radio station general manager, who gave them advice, guidance, and their first opportunity in radio.

Ambitious, creative, and hard-working, Pete and Mike developed a clear vision of their future together. Radio, as an industry and its people, welcomed them, nurtured their dreams, and gave them an opportunity to earn their way out of poverty and into a glorious, prosperous future.

Unfortunately, except for that fifth-grade teacher of their youth, some of their teachers in high school and community college were anything but encouraging.

An instructor at Modesto Junior College who taught a radio station class in communications went to the radio station and tried to get the twins fired and *Pete and Mike's Dance Time* canceled. He alleged that they were nonprofessionals, not college educated, and played this corrupt new music, rock 'n' roll, which was not beneficial to teenagers. Of course, the general manager didn't listen to that teacher or anyone else. He was firmly in Pete and Mike's corner. He admired the twins' chutzpah. He also kept them on the air because of the popularity of the program, not to mention the resulting revenues from all the advertising Pete and Mike sold sponsoring the show.

Besides the money they made, the affection from their fans was gratifying and made the jealous tirades of fellow students, teachers, and others worth the work and worry to Pete and Mike.

Pete and Mike's Dance Time fans even created floats that appeared in July 4th Independence Day Parades—an annual event in Modesto. Despite their bad experiences with jealous teens and naysaying adults, they had splendid fun. They still lived the lives of regular teenagers, dragging the boulevard, going to dances, and taking their dates to the Ceres Drive-In.

Pete and Mike's Dance Time was the vehicle that drove their success. The show demonstrated to *Americani*, to cynics in the Greek immigrant community, and even to fellow teens that the twins could succeed. When their parents heard that "someday your sons will grow up to be failures," and the twins heard it too, they worked harder to prove that one day, *their sons and daughters may become failures* but not the Pappas twins—not Pete and Mike. That tenacity was characteristic of their younger siblings, Mary and Harry, as well.

The twins presented an exterior of bravado, but down deep, their feelings were hurt. They were, despite their young success, just teenage boys who wanted to be admired, popular, and to fit in with the other kids. While they were proud of their rebel spirit, which was born of their culture, but also was strengthened from their grammar school years, when as the children of immigrants they were treated as outsiders, they craved acceptance. In the cocoon of their car, the boys let all those hurt feelings out, sharing them only with one another.

There was much torment in their hearts. Many times, together in the privacy of their car, they wondered why some people felt so negative about them. Why was there so much criticism and jealousy?

In the end, Pete and Mike turned the negative into the positive. The abusive and derogatory things people said inspired them to aim high—to set firm goals and to make plans for achieving them.

Regardless of the trials the twins faced, who could pick a better, more peachy-keen time to be a teenager than the 1950s? Could there be anything more fun than being Pete and Mike Pappas, stars of *Pete and Mike's Dance Time?* Not likely. There were no parallels in their later, adult lives that surpassed the glamour and local fame the twins experienced as teenagers, though that life reappeared when they aired editorials on their radio stations or when Mike wrote his column for local weekly newspapers. The twins were local celebrities once again. The teenage years spent by most kids rebelling or wondering what their place was in the world were not the same sort of years for Pete and Mike. While in high school, they already decided what to do with their lives. They just needed to make it happen, and they weren't going to waste time waiting to grow up. Life was in the here-and-now, and they refused to let the opportunity slip by wasting too much time living "regular" teenaged lives.

Their feelings of being outsiders were the flash to the flames in their collective gut that drove them to relentlessly pursue their future, and to start making that future happen when all the other teenagers their age were worried about being popular or fitting in. Pete and Mike couldn't focus merely on fitting in or being popular (though they loved their fame as local radio stars), because they weren't trend followers, they were *trendsetters*. That's what they believed and that's what they lived. And, with faith and fervor, the twins held onto their dreams, no matter what destiny the fates wove for them. Pete and Mike planned and worked 12 to 18 hours a day, beginning as high school students, so that their dreams could became reality.

The day they visited radio station KTRB-AM 860 as schoolboys was the opening sentence in the first chapter of the book of their lives.

If their father could suffer through a transatlantic crossing at the bottom of a ship in steerage; come safely to America; survive soup kitchens, coal mines, betrayal, the Depression, and the bitter-cold winter storms of Utah; save money for years to bring a bride from Greece; and then manage to raise a family with Titika, as poor as they were, then the twins could do anything! They just had to figure out how. They were rich in spirit and love from their family and each other. If they could dream of their future success, then they could achieve it. They didn't believe *anybody's* doomsday predictions about their futures. The warped reality of skeptics was never Pete and Mike's. The twins envisioned their future success in their minds and were determined that no people and no circumstances would change that future world. They held onto their dreams as they worked so that those dreams, despite anyone or anything, would come true.

The future was theirs to create. For Pete and Mike, there was no other way to go but up.

CHAPTER 11

1956–1957:
Twin Teens Become Men

PETE AND MIKE DECIDED they needed to get out into the world beyond their small hometown to find the excitement they had experienced with *Pete and Mike's Dance Time* on a larger scale. They were two sons of poor immigrants, so their options were few. As they prepared for high school graduation, Pete and Mike talked with one another about where they were at that moment in time and where they needed to be in the future.

College was out of the question, since they didn't have the money for tuition or expenses. And besides, they wanted to live adventurously, not read about it in a book.

There was only one option.

Pete and Mike enlisted in the military after high school.

They knew that military training would hone their natural leadership abilities, teach them management skills, and provide them with the opportunity to travel. They also sensed that their preternatural closeness, having been an asset throughout their lives, could become a liability as they grew into adulthood. They needed to learn how to function and think independently of one another—at least for a while. Upon graduation in June of 1956, they enlisted in separate branches of the armed services. Pete went into the Navy and Mike joined the Marines.

After tearful farewells from their mother and hugs from their father, sister, and brother, Pete and Mike took a bus to San Francisco and transferred to another bus bound for San Diego. Upon arrival there, the brothers said a quick goodbye (with lumps in their throats, since they had never been apart from one another, even for a day) and boarded separate buses for their respective boot camps. Pete was headed to the U.S. Navy Recruit Training Center (RTC) and Mike to the Marine Corps Recruiting Depot (MCRD).

At MCRD, the transition for Mike from civilian to Marine swiftly happened after everyone got off the bus. The recruits formed a line, as commanded by a shouting drill instructor (DI), and walked in single file to an intake hut. Heads were unceremoniously shaved, the rookies were given Marine Corps denims and regulation shirts to wear, and they were assigned to various platoons.

Mike's training in the Marines was particularly brutal—calisthenics at 4:00 a.m. after reveille (a wake-up call via a loud and annoying bugle), then a quick breakfast of regulation slop, a number of obstacle courses, and hikes with 30-pound packs on the backs of recruits.

And bloody, blistered feet each night from not-quite-broken-in feet in boots.

All their *Pete and Mike's Dance Time* experiences, even working in the sweltering San Joaquin Valley sun on farms, hadn't prepared them for boot camp.

On the last night of broadcasting their *Pete and Mike's Dance Time* show, the twins announced they were going into the Navy and the Marines, and they gave the addresses of both RTC and MCRD, asking their female fans in the audience to send them letters.

And they did so.

Pete and Mike, elated, became the envy of their fellow trainees.

During mail call a few weeks after his arrival at MCRD, Mike's Marine Corps drill instructor grimly noticed the girlie letters sealed with lipstick kisses from love-struck fans.

Mike received boxes of letters.

"Private Pappas, front and center!"

Mike stepped forward and stood at attention.

"Private Pappas is quite the lover boy in the civilian world. In fact, he is quite the Romeo, a big star!" growled the DI.

Mike immediately regretted having given his military address over-the-air.

"He's a real Casanova—lots of pink and red kisses on these envelopes just for him," the instructor snarled. "How sweet! The problem is: Marines aren't sweet lover boys! We're soldiers—*warriors!* What the hell is this sh–t, Private Pappas? Do you think the Corps is your personal love-letter mail messenger service?!"

The DI was inches away from Mike's face now and he was afraid of what might happen next.

"Sir, no sir, the United States Marine Corp is *not* my personal love-letter messenger service!" Sweat was pouring down Mike's face, his cheeks flushed.

"Very well, Private Pappas. I'm glad you're aware that the United States Marines, the greatest fighting force ever in the history of mankind, is not here to serve your needs and that you're here to serve the Corps' needs!"

"Sir, yes sir!"

"Private Pappas, I have a very important service I need performed by you. Would you like to know what it is?" The DI was still shouting.

"Sir, yes sir!"

"Private Pappas will now perform a service for me by doing his Marine Corps best by eating the flap of this envelope," the DI said, picking one envelope out of Mike's mail, "with the bright red lipstick kiss on it! Right now! You will enjoy this snack, Private Pappas! This is your special snack this afternoon, Private Pappas! And you will eat it slowly, savoring every bite!"

Mike accepted the envelope thrust at him by the DI, took a bite, and ate it.

He ate the whole flap as instructed, one bite at a time.

At the next day's mail call, he read his fan mail quickly and hid the letters before his DI returned, with his fellow recruits laughing and shaking their heads, remembering Mike's special snack from the day before.

———————

After graduating from about 13 weeks of training at MCRD, Mike was sent to Camp Pendleton, located just up the coast from San Diego on some of the most picturesque and expensive beachfront property in the world. During his first few days at Pendleton, Mike stood at attention and tried to focus on the directions he and his platoon mates heard from their DI. The sapphire-blue sky and puffy, marshmallow clouds, along with the cool, early-morning breeze from the trade winds blowing through the camp, made paying attention difficult, especially when all the young recruit could think about was relaxing at the beach. Pete's Naval training continued after his graduation from RTC, during Mike's time at Pendleton.

"Relaxing" was not in the vocabulary of a Marine Corps DI, and Mike didn't hear the word for some time.

At Camp Pendleton, Mike participated in advanced combat training, was taught to use various weapons, and attended classes to learn battle strategy and tactics. He was assigned to the 11th Marine

Regiment, the heavy-artillery section of the 1st Marine Division, with which he trained for five months.

One morning, their DI gave the raw recruits in the division their orders. They were to fight in a mock battle against trained Marines from the base that day.

They were ordered to take a hill from the Marines defending it and, as one would expect, the newbies were losing the "battle" as it progressed. Many of the recruits were getting hit with the equivalent of paint balls, and for the purposes of the day, died.

Mike, though, was not a man who accepted losing, even if it was at a practice battle drill.

He charged the hill alone during the advanced combat training, going around the hill by himself with a Brownie automatic rifle, shooting the fake ammunition and taking out most of the Marines guarding the hill. Then the "attack!" horn blast sounded and the rest of his platoon took the hill.

The battle was won by the recruits, although at a price unnoticed by Mike.

He felt a surge of pride at how heroic he had been, and enjoyed all the pats on the back from his platoon mates. He was instrumental in winning the battle.

Mike later stood proudly in line with his fellow Marine trainees and waited for what he was sure would be awarded to him: a mock "medal of honor."

"Private Pappas, front and center!" He stepped forward.

"Private Pappas receives a special award today."

Mike's heart raced as he stifled a grin.

"Private Pappas believes he is the entire United States Marine Corps," bellowed the drill instructor, "and he believes that he can win a battle entirely on his own!"

It was dusk and the cool breeze blowing in from the ocean cooled all of San Diego County, including Camp Pendleton, but Mike's face was getting hot. His chest tightened.

"Now, had this been a real battle, well, Private Pappas here would have been a hero since he took the hill, but since he was hit, he would've been killed. He wouldn't have lived to see a medal or his mother's tears."

Mike knew something bad was coming and clenched his jaw.

"So, in honor of Private Pappas's valor and his inability to follow orders, he is awarded this special medal."

The drill instructor pinned the medal on his chest, and Mike could smell it.

It was a large piece of dried feces, wrapped in red, white, and blue ribbon.

He was required to wear it pinned on his chest for a week.

He learned an important lesson that day: A dead Marine is no good to his platoon, his family, or his country. Battles and wars are won because every single Marine works as one unit, all advancing toward the same goal. The Marines teaches its soldiers to think critically and, at the same time, to follow orders. If a thousand Marines decide to fight a battle or a war their own way, they won't achieve the objective of conquering enemy troops or surviving to go home again.

Since Pete and Mike were both still in San Diego (missing each other immensely and desperately homesick), on some weekends when they had liberty (also called R&R, "rest and relaxation"), they met and spent their time off with each other along with their new buddies from their respective bases. They bought a Willys sedan in San Diego (Willys being an automotive line manufactured by Willys-Overland Motors from 1937 to 1942), purchased with their *Pete and Mike's Dance Time* earnings plus proceeds from the sale of their Mercury Montclair before leaving Modesto, and they put it to good use on their moments of liberty.

The twins, always outgoing and witty, made friends easily, and their new buddies often needed transportation around San Diego and over the Mexican border to Tijuana during R&R. Pete and Mike, forever inventive, made their free time both frivolous and entrepreneurial.

They would drive by MCRD and RTC and charge 25 cents per passenger (about $3.00 in today's dollars) and give four or five Marines and Navy sailors rides into town. Essentially, they formed their own private cab service (*Lyft* and *Uber* drivers before there was such a thing), and did that for two or three hours a day. Between their weekly pay from the Marines and Navy and their driving gig, they took in enough spending money for the weekend: to date girls, to go to U.S.O. dances (a private, nonprofit organization that provided hospitality and entertainment venues for service members while in uniform), and trips to Tijuana.

The trips across the border weren't nearly as complicated in 1957 as they are today, and GI's like Pete and Mike routinely went into Tijuana looking for booze and broads. The twins piled into the Willys, picked up their regular buddies from both bases (charging more than their usual 25 cents for the trip out of town), rolled down the windows, and hit the road. The banter was fast and sometimes profane but laced with laughter and the energy of red-blooded boys heading out for a night on the town.

After arriving in Tijuana, they drove directly to a gin joint that both Marines and sailors had been talking about. A ramshackle two-story structure, the building had pink walls with peeling paint, its doors flung open, and someone barked orders in Spanish as workers washed tables and finished mopping. The sun was setting and *La Señiorita Roja*, the Red Lady, was opening soon. Its business was both funny business and monkey business, and *La Señiorita Roja* was famous for providing a good time to their all-male customers. Mike and his buddies had planned a big night for Pete there—a famous night, or an *infamous* night, a night that Pete never allowed anyone to speak of, publicly or privately, ever again.

Naturally, of course, that edict was not obeyed by Mike.

The twins were fiercely loyal and protective of one another, except when it came to something embarrassing, which translated into something funny. Only with humor did loyalty melt away, replaced by repeated and energetic rounds of teasing and laughter.

The young men, full of bravado, hormones, and thirst, parked their car around the corner and walked to the bar. Night had fallen and the bar was dimly lit, with multicolored lights, the type that decorated houses on the nice side of town back home, strung across the walls, around the stage at the front of the room, and across the center of the room, from one side to the other. The room was a rectangle with the stage on one end and bars lining the other three walls. Wooden chairs were strewn about haphazardly, with most of its patrons, all young GIs, standing. The show was beginning soon. Mike and his friends had heard about the show and were going to do everything possible to make sure Pete was at the center of it.

The lights dimmed, the announcer introduced the dancing girls, and the boys got more excited, more drunk, and more willing to do things that would have gotten them into big trouble back home. But not there—not in Tijuana of 1957. A band was playing and the booze was flowing. Finally, the climax of the show commenced. The music faded and the drum rolled. The emcee introduced the prize for the evening—and out sauntered a tall, long-legged beauty with black eyes and flowing black hair.

"Ah, you see, *mi amigos,* this beauty. This beauty, she will go home with a man tonight, for no charge, for free!"

Marines and Navy men in the room roared—a deafening cacophony of shouts, whistles, catcalls, and laughter.

The prize walked the perimeter of the stage, hiking her skirt just high enough to give her audience a tantalizing tease of the prize that could be had that night for free.

"The man who can shout the loudest, 'I want her!' will have this prize tonight for free—for free, my friends, for *free!* Which of you can shout loud enough?!"

The crowd became even more unruly, but one man's voice was the loudest and the deepest and could be heard above all others.

That voice was Pete's.

Mike and his friends knew that Pete would be the loudest because he was *always* the loudest, most boisterous, most girl-crazy of any man, in any room, anytime, anywhere.

Mike knew Pete and he knew about the prize.

The emcee, as Mike planned, called Pete up onto the stage. The prize was standing on one side of the announcer.

And Pete was on the other.

"What is your name, my friend?"

"Pete. Pete Pappas."

"Ah, Pete. You must tell me again—do you want her?"

Pete, staring at the prize, said huskily, "Yes, I want her."

"You are *sure* you want her?"

Asking a sailor if he wanted to spend the night with a woman for free, no strings attached, was like asking a parched man if he wanted water.

"Then," said the emcee to the woman, "you will go tonight with this American, Pete Pappas."

The emcee looked at Pete.

"Would you like to see her naked first?"

Pete nodded "yes."

Mike stood in front of the stage, crossed his arms, and looked down. Pete mustn't see his brother's Cheshire cat grin, or all would be lost.

The woman began disrobing slowly. The crowd got louder with each article of clothing tossed onto the stage. Shoes. Stockings— one leg at a time. Garter. Finally—the dress, slowly, slipped over her head.

Dead, stunned silence filled the room.

There were no breasts.

There was a bulge in a place where there shouldn't be a bulge.

The color drained from Pete's face and the crowd went wild as the black lace panties came off. The crowd laughed uncontrollably, and Pete wanted to both cry and shout.

His free prize was a man dressed as a woman.

A man, dressed as a woman, given to a sailor as a free gift in 1957.

Mike could barely stand, paralyzed by his own laughter, as he watched his brother sheepishly leave the stage.

The gag was worth every penny he and the guys had paid for the prank to be played on Pete.

As they drove back to their respective bases in San Diego, and when they were finally alone, Pete made Mike promise that their tale of hijinks in Tijuana must never be told.

Ever.

To anyone.

Mike promised, with one caveat.

Pete had to let Mike tell the story to their dad and Theo Manoli when they went home for their first visit since enlisting.

Pete agreed.

The incident made a good opening story (with much loud laughter from their father and uncle) when the twins returned home for their first three-day break from the service. Both Pete and Mike wore their uniforms home after their initial four months away. Greeting them with tears and smiles, their family looked on proudly while their mother felt concerned.

"Tee epathes? What happened to you?"

Pete and Mike had gained much life experience in the military but lost girth. Each lost about thirty pounds over their first thirty days of training, and they were in the best physical condition of their young lives.

Titika had no knowledge of the physical conditioning that recruits went through in boot camp. She did, however, know how to cook every day of the week before their arrival, making their favorite foods and pastries for their visit home. They didn't gain back thirty pounds each that long weekend, but they enjoyed trying.

CHAPTER 12

1957–1958:
Pete and Mike's Dance Time
on Land and Sea

AFTER COMPLETING BASIC TRAINING AT CAMP PENDLETON, Mike found himself on a ship bound for the Marine Corps Air Station at Kaneohe Bay, in the territory of Hawaii. Pete was posted to the USS *Roanoke*, a destroyer on its way to complete three Western Pacific cruises through the end of 1958. The fourth Navy vessel to be named after the City of Roanoke, Virginia, it was one of two Worcester-class ships built after World War II.

The 1st Marine Division had some 22,000 Marines, along with its own jets, tank corps, light artillery, and infantry. It was designed to go to trouble spots anywhere in the world in 24 hours. Mike was assigned to Squadron 232, the Fighting Red Devil Squadron, and assigned to S-2: Marine Corps tactical intelligence.

He felt thrilled with his assignment. The Fighting Red Devils was one of the most decorated squadrons in American military aviation history. To be attached to the Red Devils was an honor, and he drove himself relentlessly to prove that he was worthy of the assignment. Due to an incomparable work ethic and his innovative thinking on the job, he was promoted from Private, to Private First Class, then to

Corporal and to Buck Sergeant in less than two years. Meritoriously promoted for two of those ranks (he didn't have to take the usual test) for his exemplary performance, he wore those three stripes on his sleeve proudly. As a member of the division's tactical intelligence unit, he had plenty to do. Still, he missed his time behind the microphone and on stage, and with the full blessings of his commanding officer (after convincing him that a radio show for the troops would provide a much-needed boost to morale), he revived his radio show on the island.

Mike soon began hosting two radio shows on two different radio stations in Honolulu.

He hosted a morning program on KANI-AM, located in the windward city of Oahu, which was close to the Marine Corps base at Kaneohe Bay. That show was called *Wake Up Right with Pete and Mike.* He played the hits of the day along with standards of five or six years earlier. He called the evening show on KIKI-AM *Pete and Mike's Dance Time,* in honor of the show he had with his twin brother, Pete. While he enjoyed being in radio again, he missed Pete terribly. Keeping busy helped eased his loneliness. Loving the attention of a live audience and the adulation that comes with being on stage, he also acted as an announcer at a number of local events.

He emceed the assemblies of local high schools while also organizing entertainment for Tripler Army Hospital, on the slopes of the Moanalua Ridge, overlooking Honolulu. He arranged for hula dancers and high school performers from the various Honolulu junior high and high schools to entertain military patients. He accomplished what no Marine probably had ever attempted: he was a master of ceremonies for live, local shows; sold advertising for his radio programs; and produced two radio shows all while he was an active-duty Marine in Oahu.

While Mike was busy in Hawaii, Pete approached his commanding officer on the USS *Roanoke* and convinced him that having a radio show broadcast on the destroyer would be good for the morale of the large crew (the same argument his twin had used in Oahu), all of whom were lonely and far from home. Despite his commanding officer's initial doubts, Pete tenaciously prevailed and reclaimed his radio fame on the *Roanoke*. As it made its way across the Pacific, Pete discovered the ship was docking in Hawaii. Getting word to Mike by mail, Pete and Mike were overjoyed at the prospect of seeing each other.

As the *Roanoke* approached Oahu, Pete tuned into KIKI-AM, hoping he might catch Mike on the air while he was doing *Pete and Mike's Dance Time* on that station. Pete smiled when he found the station and heard his brother's voice over the air, broadcasting on the show named the same as the one they did back home.

He immediately asked permission of his commanding officer and proceeded to broadcast *Pete and Mike's Dance Time*, Mike's version from Hawaii, throughout the ship.

Pete, the sailor, and Mike, the Marine, reunite after the USS Roanoke *makes port in Honolulu, Hawaii, circa 1957.*

When Pete disembarked and the twins saw each other, hugs and tears overcame any macho, 1950s prohibition of public displays of affection between men. Their bliss couldn't be contained by the scruples of the time.

Pete and Mike had missed each other tremendously during the months they were separated. The three days they spent together on Oahu were days of joy as well as verve. The brothers talked and yearned for the day they would be discharged from the Navy and Marines so they could take a swing at a full-time career in broadcasting. Fervently, they held onto their dreams, co-pitchers in the World Series of their lives that they played, together.

Their time in the service was just Game One.

Mike showed Pete the sights around the gorgeous island, a place he loved. With its tropical foliage, exotic flowers in bloom everywhere, colorful birds, and sunny, breezy weather, he thought it was the most mystically beautiful place on Earth.

The time was too short for the twins. When duty called, as always, they answered. Pete went back to the USS *Roanoke,* and this young man from a poor family of Greek immigrants, who had never traveled anywhere outside of California, eventually saw Australia, Japan, and the Philippines. In the meantime, Mike remained stationed in Hawaii until the division was called to duty.

During what little time off he had, between his Marine Corps duties and his radio programs, Mike headed into Honolulu and to the Waikiki beach area with buddies from his unit. Never one to look for skirmishes, they nevertheless found him, just as they had in Modesto as a teenager with his twin. British warships had docked in the harbor and their sailors, like American sailors, flooded into Honolulu bars and clubs. Feeling especially melancholy after Pete's departure, Mike with his Marine buddies did the same. When the two groups arrived at a bar, after their initial hellos, drinks flowed for hours, and inevitably talk with the Brits turned to sports and politics.

At the time, Great Britain was occupying Cyprus (a Crown colony), something that many Greeks opposed. Mike talked with a British sailor who backed his government's occupation of Cyprus patriotically and enthusiastically. Mike, being a Greek-American, stood up for Cyprus and considered it his patriotic duty to defend Greeks anywhere in the world. Thus, he told the Brit his country should not be in Cyprus at all. Pete wasn't there, but Mike was always a scrapper and now a Marine, so he didn't hesitate to express his opinions. Leaning onto the bar, one elbow supporting his weight and the other hand holding his glass of Kentucky bourbon, Mike turned toward the British sailors.

"You, you sons of bitches, should get your asses out of Cyprus," Mike said, taking a swig of bourbon and smiling crookedly at the British sailors.

"Oh, really, Yank—and who are you to tell the British Empire to do anything? You're an American—what business is it of yours?"

The Brit looked at Mike head on.

"Who are you to have any opinion at all? Those islanders should be bloody thankful we're there to save them from their petty nonsense."

The Brit stood up with his buddies, who formed a tight circle around Mike. He looked Mike right in the eye and poked him in the chest.

"I think it's best you leave now, Yank."

Neither Pete or Mike ever ran from a fight, and this late, blustery night in a Hawaiian bar was no exception.

"Who am *I*?" Mike kicked the bar stool aside as his Marine buddies circled around him.

"I'm a Greek Yank and I'm going to wipe your ass with the bar."

The Brit took the first swing. Mike ducked and swung back, hitting him square in the jaw. In minutes, people were running for cover, and the barkeep called for the military police. As soon as the MPs arrived, everyone dispersed, running as fast as possible. They had opposing politics, but the Brits and Yanks did have one thing in common—neither side wanted to spend the weekend in the brig or, worse, lose liberty privileges for a weekend.

The next day, there was a big article in one the Honolulu paper that Greek-Americans who were United States Marines had attacked

Mike (right), with Naval officers, at an entertainment event he organized for his fellow Marines at the Marine Corps Air Station Kaneohe Bay, Hawaii, where he was stationed, circa 1957. Photo Courtesy: United States Navy.

British sailors in a Honolulu bar. Although his buddies weren't Greek-Americans, Mike felt thrilled. He had stood up for fellow Greeks, and it was acknowledged in the local press. The publicity he and his brother Pete always craved and enjoyed had followed him to Hawaii!

He bought three copies of the paper—one for himself and a copy for his parents and siblings, which was mailed home. He sent the third paper to Pete on the USS *Roanoke.*

Though he was extroverted, at times he just wasn't in the mood to go out. Mike without Pete was like a surgeon operating with one arm. He spent many late nights alone in his Marine Corps office, typing away on his battered Underwood typewriter, its keys sticking, with the ink from the ribbon that needed constant untangling, staining his fingertips. Homesick for his brother Pete, his parents, his sister Mary, and brother Harry, he typed long letters to Pete and his family and also wrote poetry to express his melancholy feelings.

One of the poems was about the *Fighting Red Devils*, the squadron to which he was honored to be assigned. He wrote poems about his love for his parents and family, and one about Pete, titled *"My brother whose life is like mine."*

Mike's poetry would have to wait for duty, though.

A short time later during the Formosa (Taiwan) crisis, when the United States government responded in defense of the Republic of China (Taiwan) against the aggression of the People's Republic of China, Mike's division was called up.

He found himself on a ship bound to the South China Sea.

Because of the division's reputation and President Dwight Eisenhower's show of military might by deploying them along with Naval warships, the Communist Chinese government decided not to pursue a war with Formosa.

So, what was to be done with some 22,000 Marines sent to a crisis that's averted?

Practice military maneuvers.

Mike was put into counterintelligence two-man teams, with only single men selected. Married men weren't permitted. They were taken on maneuvers with helicopters. On command, the teams jumped into the water off the Formosa Strait. The purpose was to practice invading Communist China if the next crisis turned to war.

Mike never felt so terrified.

The teams dropped into the frigid water, swimming and then wading onto shore with packs on their backs containing hand grenades and a rifle. The maneuver's goal: to not get captured by the enemy, in this case played by allied nationalist Chinese troops from Formosa who acted as enemy infiltrators. Mike and the Marine teams went in advance of the division to recon (get reconnaissance information) and radioed messages back to the commanding officers.

Once the practice was over, the Red Devils squadron and the First Marine Division traveled by ship to Atsugi Naval Base in Japan, close to the city of Yamato.

Mike grew to appreciate his time in Japan. He loved history, and Japan was a land of ancient history with an abundance of historic sites. He was impressed by the country's storied past and its people. As a young man from the rural farmlands of California, he valued the opportunity to visit Japan and meet its people, something he never could have done had he not enlisted in the Marine Corps.

His official duties as a Marine aside, Mike's commanding officer assigned him an additional responsibility: entertaining the troops, since he had become so successful in Hawaii. Familiar American entertainment boosted the troops' morale. He was happy to help ease the homesickness of his fellow Marines in Japan.

CHAPTER 13

1957–1959:
A Nice Greek Girl

AFTER HIS FIRST TWO YEARS IN THE MARINES, Mike had three weeks of leave. He learned much in the Marines but wanted a breather from military life. The twins missed one another terribly and hated being so far away from family while in the service. The visit to Modesto, for Mike, was bittersweet. Pete served two years in the Navy while Mike had committed to three years in the Marines. Honorably discharged in 1958, a year before Mike, Pete came home and found no radio jobs available in either Modesto or Stockton. He instead found a job in Juneau, Alaska. By the time Mike came home on leave, Pete had already moved to Juneau.

The years Pete and Mike were in the service forced them to leave boyhood behind and face manhood alone with the most mentally and physically grueling days each underwent without their twin's companionship and support. Living without his twin was something neither brother wanted to experience again, even for a brief time.

Still, for the short term, enlisting in the Navy and the Marines had been good decisions. The twins polished their natural leadership skills while learning organization, planning, self-discipline, combat tactics, and strategy. Both Pete and Mike's minds and bodies were in the best condition of their lives, sharper than before entering the service. The twins were ready to tackle the future, like exceptionally trained running backs ready to shred the defensive line of any opposing team they faced in life. The twins made big plans for their future. Their careers in broadcasting and their lives with their own future families—wives, children—would be shared, as their lives had always been, since before they were born.

For Mike, there was always Pete, and for Pete there was always Mike, and it would always be so.

There was never any thought that even one day of their lives would be lived without the other.

While home, Mike relaxed and enjoyed his mother hovering over him while she cooked all his favorite Greek foods. His father, John, never spoke of the battles he fought or the atrocities he witnessed in the Balkan War. Nevertheless, he asked Mike questions about Marine Corps training, weapons, and strategy. John was impressed at the knowledge his son gained.

He saw a profound change in Mike, just as he saw in Pete.

The twins left home as boys but returned as men.

This was not surprising to their father, as he too was transformed as a young man, his innocence lost forever on the battlefield. A soldier returning from military duty is never the same man as the one who left home.

Titika told friends that one of her dear twins was home, so the family hosted guests virtually daily. She was determined that Mike attend every social function happening within the Greek community, and her son was happy to comply. There was an ice cream social, sponsored by the Arcadians (local Greeks whose families hailed from the area of Tripoli, Greece) held in Lodi, about 40 miles north of Modesto, and also a dance at the Modesto Greek Orthodox Church, sponsored by the local chapter of the Pancretan Association of America (for families from the island of Crete), happening two Saturdays in a row.

A Greek immigrant girl named Noula Mehas and her friend Effie from St. Basil's Greek Orthodox Church in Stockton were attending the ice cream social. The rented banquet room was on the second floor of a building owned by a local ice cream company and was plain, with light gray walls. Chairs and tables were scattered throughout, and decorations added a festive touch to the otherwise drab surroundings. The live band played Greek music while groups of young men and women talked with their friends and danced as they eyed the opposite sex across the room and on the dance floor.

Noula noticed a young man.

"Who is that cute soldier boy?" Noula asked Effie.

"Which one?" Effie knew most every boy in the place.

"The cute one, with the black curly hair. The soldier boy. That one in the uniform."

Noula didn't know what branch of the service he was in, since she was still new to America, but, having grown up during two wars in Greece, she knew what a soldier looked like.

Mike was the only young man wearing a uniform in the room, so he was easy to spot.

"Uh, oh no, Noula, not him." Effie knew Mike dated extensively, and even though she was friends with him, Noula was innocent, just a young girl from Greece. Her friend wanted to protect her from the big bad wolf dressed as a Marine.

"Not him, not now—let's go over there." Effie put Noula's arm through hers and took her in the opposite direction, away from Mike's side of the room. "I know some nice fellows over there. Let's go over there and say hello."

Noula looked back over her shoulder at the cute soldier boy and sighed. She had never seen any boy that looked like that, so dashing and handsome.

Perhaps it was not meant to be.

Since arriving in the states from her village in 1956, she endured never-ending setups and blind dates with countless young Greek men that her aunt and uncle arranged. In those days, nice young Greek girls, preferably in their early twenties (lest the girls develop an immoral reputation or were deemed defective in some way), were often introduced to young, eligible Greek men. Those introductions were usually made by friends and family at appropriately public and social venues. Noula respectfully met each young man introduced to her by her aunt, uncle, and well-meaning yentas in the Greek community. Each didn't pass muster, for different reasons.

One was so tall (she was 5'2"), Noula thought she would need a ladder to kiss him. Another was too old. Yet another—well, the spark just wasn't there for her, and she wasn't going to get married if she didn't fall madly in love with the young man. The life-altering decision to leave Greece as well as her entire family at age eighteen happened partially because Noula decided she wouldn't be forced into an arranged marriage, unhappy and loveless. She aimed to accomplish more in her life and she couldn't do it in Greece, especially since she was forced to quit school at age ten. Her father needed the money he had set aside for Noula's schooling to pay for her sisters' dowries. Although she was the smartest student in the village school and had great dreams and hopes for herself and her future, she would never escape the socioeconomic system foisted upon her by tradition. Noula was a poor village girl who would likely be forced into an arranged marriage with a poor village boy, and she would spend the rest of her life in the village, poor and unhappy.

Noula survived Nazis invading her village in World War II as well as Greece's civil war that immediately followed between Communists and non-Communists (like those in her village, including her father and brothers, for whom she dodged bullets to bring water and ammunition). She survived the postwar famine and poverty that racked Greece, due to the destruction brought by the Communists. She wanted to live someplace where she could live in freedom and never see war in the streets again.

She chose to emigrate to the United States where freedom lived.

At age 16, she submitted applications with the Greek and American governments to go to America, against her family's wishes. They felt devastated at the idea that they would likely never see their youngest child, their *Noulaki* (little Noula) ever again.

Patiently, Noula waited for her name to come up for immigration approval from both Greece and the United States. Once she received approval at age 18, she boarded a ship, never to look back at the life she left behind. She gazed into the sun as she walked up the gangplank of the *Queen Frederica* and traveled across the Atlantic, alone. In America, she would live her dream: go back to school and become the nickname her father had called her—*thaskalaki*, little teacher.

After she arrived (via Portland, Oregon, where she had an uncle and stayed with his family for a time) in Stockton and met her aunt and uncle's friends and girls her own age, like her friend Effie, she sweetly endured the blind dates and met all the people her family in America wanted her to meet, with one caveat: she would ultimately decide if, and with whom, she fell in love. There hadn't been one young man she met in her new country who interested her until she saw the cute little soldier boy at the Arcadians dance in Lodi.

The following Saturday night began with Effie driving Noula to Modesto for the Cretan dance at the church's hall. Effie had a cousin visiting from Crete who would be at the dance and she wanted to introduce her to him. Noula's aunt happily approved of her attending the Modesto dance.

"I'm so glad you're going to the dance with Effie," said her Aunt Katina in their native Greek. She stood behind the dressing table where Noula sat on the bench, putting final touches on her hair. She looked at her aunt's reflection in the mirror.

"I'm not going for *him*," said Noula. "I'm going to have fun."

Noula's aunt sighed. The girl was so much more independent than other local Greek girls, and certainly much more so than the usual Greek immigrant girl arriving from her native land. She hoped that Noula would find someone to marry soon. She and her husband were old and they wanted to see Noula settled with a good Greek husband sooner rather than later.

Mike and two of his Greek buddies, both home on leave from the service, had gone to the dance with the intention of checking out the girls and having a good time. The hall behind the Annunciation Greek Orthodox Church in Modesto, where all the celebrations and gatherings for the Greeks took place, soon filled with adults sitting and talking and young people dancing and staring at each other across the dance floor. What made this dance and the Arcadians dance in Lodi different from the typical high school dance (with the boys on one end of the room and the girls on the other, all filled with dread, angst, and fear of rejection) was that this was a Greek dance—so everyone would get up and dance as a group, so a dance partner was not necessary. Folks could join the dance by taking someone's hand in the circle and then dancing. It didn't matter if a dancer had friends, was beautiful or homely or handsome or nerdy—everyone could dance. And people *did*—the young, the old, the feeble, the nimble—everyone got up and danced to music from the island of Crete played by a live band.

Noula and Effie themselves got up and danced. Mike and his friends didn't dance, but they noticed the girls who did, and Mike was intrigued by one lovely girl dancing elegantly. He watched her stroll gracefully across the room as the music stopped and she walked over to talk with her friends.

Mike's two Navy buddies noticed that Mike couldn't stop staring at this one pretty girl across the room. The three had been drinking and inhibitions dwindled with each bourbon and beer.

"Hey, Pappas, bet you don't go up to that girl and talk to her," one said.

Mike shook his head and laughed.

His friends were teasing, but Mike's heart burst the moment he saw her. He was in a good mood and naturally convivial, but this Greek girl made his heart race and gave him butterflies.

He had dated a lot of girls both in high school and in the Marines, but no female had flabbergasted him like this one.

What was he going to say to her? Conveniently, she was hanging around with a girl he knew. Maybe he could just walk up and start a conversation with Effie? But this new girl was just so stunning—like a movie star. So what if he tried to start talking and nothing came out? His buddies, full of themselves, laughed at him and said there was no way he'd walk across the room, without an introduction, and say the perfect opening line. Mike pointed at her with the hand that held his drink.

"See that beautiful brunette, boys? That's the girl of my dreams. I'm gonna' marry her."

His two friends shook their heads.

"You're so full of sh-t, Pappas. You're gonna' marry her!"

With his cheeks blushing, he laughed. "You watch me!"

"Oh, really," said one. "Go ahead. I dare you! Walk over there and ask her—ask her to marry you!"

"Yeah, I'll just come out and ask her to marry me! No hellos, no 'how are you's?' just, *hello, my name is Mike Pappas, and I'd like to marry you.*"

Mike's glistening brown eyes widened as he laughed. It was crazy enough to work, and anyway, he was leaving for the base in a week, so even if she thought he was an idiot, he might never see her again, so what the hell? Might as well give it a shot.

Mike set his drink down and made his way across the room, glancing over his shoulder to see his two buddies huddled in laughter.

He walked directly to where Noula and Effie were standing and extended his hand to Noula. He spoke to her in her native Greek.

"Hello, my name is Mike Pappas. Will you marry me?"

Effie rolled her eyes and laughed. Despite his reputation as a lady's man, she liked Mike and couldn't believe that he had just proposed marriage. Noula smiled curiously at the cute little soldier boy she had seen the week before for the first time. She looked directly into those big, sparkling brown eyes framed by long, dark eyelashes, and shook his hand delicately.

"Hello, my name is Noula Mehalopoulos and, yes, I will marry you."

Mike and Noula shared their first laugh that night. It was the first of what later became a lifetime of shared laughter. They spoke for a few minutes, sharing their families' roots. Mike's family, like most everyone in the Annunciation parish in Modesto, hailed from the island of Crete, while Noula was from Mistras, near ancient Sparta, not from Crete. They engaged in the usual small talk that a couple share when meeting for the first time.

Mike asked Noula if she had a job, and he found out that she worked at Dunlop's, a high-end department store chain with outlets in both Stockton and Modesto. She labored in the ladies' department on the third floor at the Stockton store as a seamstress. The department was mostly composed of Greek immigrant women whose old-world dressmaking talents were unmatched by most local women. As with many immigrants, the Greek women assisted other newly arrived Greek immigrant women by helping them get a job in their department. Women like Noula could work around fellow Greek immigrants, earn a wage, acclimate to the American way of life, and learn a little English as well.

As Mike spoke with Noula, he felt more charmed and was falling in love with each passing tick-tock of the big old black clock that hung in the hall.

An hour or so had passed. That was enough time. He decided it was time to introduce Noula to his mother, Titika.

Mike took Noula by the hand to where his mother sat with her friends in the corner of the church hall. He interrupted her conversation abruptly.

Mike and Noula's engagement photo, 1957. Both were just 19 years old.

"Mama, you've wanted me to marry a Greek girl. You've told me this my whole life. I found one. I'm going to marry this girl. Her name is Noula Mehas and she is from Sparta. I met her tonight and she will be your first daughter-in-law."

Titika looked up from her coffee and pastries, as her friends quickly stopped their multiple conversations. She answered him directly.

"What? She's not Cretan?" Mike laughed at his mother's response.

"Mama, you said to marry a Greek girl. Noula *is* a Greek girl. You didn't say she had to be Cretan too!"

Noula didn't understand the exchange but it didn't really matter. She was one hundred percent Spartan, and that made her one hundred percent Greek. Moreover, she was one hundred percent the girl Mike loved and wanted to be his wife. The fact that she was not from the island of Crete was inconsequential.

Later in the evening, before Noula left with Effie, Mike asked her out on a date for the next Saturday night and she agreed.

Instead of waiting to see her the following Saturday, Mike showed up at Dunlop's department store Monday morning and headed straight for the floor where Noula worked.

When he enthusiastically greeted her, Noula was surprised.

"Mike, you shouldn't have come here! This is the women's wear floor. Men don't come to this floor."

Mike seemed undeterred.

"I can go wherever I want to go! This is America!" Mike laughed as he told her goodbye and left the store. She looked at her friend, who sat next to her and had got her the job at Dunlop's.

"Who *is* this guy," she asked, in her native Greek. "Is he okay?"

Her friend smiled. "Yeah, he's okay, just kind of a wild boy."

Mike began a very quick courtship the next day, when he drove his mother and sister to Dunlop's Department Store to pick up Noula from work. This impromptu trip marked the first time she met Mike's sister, Mary. Noula got into the car and Mike drove all of them to her aunt and uncle's home, where he and his family met them for the first time. Prior to their visit, he had purchased a woman's ring from the Marine Corps exchange (bearing the Marine Corps emblem) to give to Noula. When they had a few moments alone, Mike suggested that while he was away in the Marines, they would go steady, which he explained to her meant "almost engaged, but not quite engaged," and the ring he was giving her symbolized their exclusive relationship. He also told her that it meant she couldn't date anyone else and that she had to wait for him to return in under two years, and at that time, they would become engaged. Noula didn't understand what "going steady" was all about, but she decided that she would wait for Mike to complete his stint in the Marines nonetheless. Noula planned to continue her English language and citizenship classes and to attend school, so she wasn't in any hurry to get married. Both trusting and smitten, she accepted his explanation of the ring and what it symbolized. She would wait for him and date no one else.

That night at home, Mike tossed and turned in bed. What was he *doing*? Someone was bound to tell her that going steady wasn't close to being almost engaged, and he might lose her to someone else. She was an honorable girl with high moral standards rooted in her Greek Orthodox faith. He needed to treat her respectfully and propose marriage.

The next morning, he told his mother and father of his intentions and received their blessing. After borrowing money from his father to buy an engagement ring, he drove to Noula's aunt and uncle's home in Stockton and asked her if he could come into the house. Walking into the little family room, Mike dropped to one knee and, as he held Noula's hand, placed the ring on her finger and proposed marriage. With the blessing of her aunt and uncle who were witnessing the scene, Mike and Noula became engaged.

―――――

Mike was to return to the Marines on the weekend, so with the help of family and friends, John and Titika hosted a first-class, all-homemade Greek engagement party for Mike and Noula in their backyard on Thursday night. John, with his cousins and friends, set up borrowed tables and chairs under the *crevatina* (or pergola) and in the yard. Titika and her friends cooked and baked Greek food and pastries

Mike and Noula's wedding at St. Basil's Greek Orthodox Church in Stockton, California, in July 1959.

and set out their finest linens. The party was filled with Greek *kefi* (love of life), joy and laughter, Greek dancing, and the happiness that comes with celebrating the love and upcoming nuptials of a young couple. Mike was John and Titika's first child to marry. So they determined that the engagement party to celebrate his betrothal to the Greek girl they quickly came to adore, Noula, would be the best possible. The buffet table burst with *moussaka* (eggplant and meat casserole), Cretan *pilafi*, Greek salad, *spanakopita* (spinach pie topped with filo dough), *tiropites* (cheese turnovers in filo dough), *pasticho* (meat and macaroni casserole covered in béchamel sauce), *karydopita* (honey walnut cake), *kourambyethes* (cookies covered in powdered white sugar), *baklava* (honey walnut dessert in layers of filo, basted with butter and honey), and Titika's *kalitsounia,* a delicacy made exclusively in Crete.

The couple had little time together before Mike returned to active duty. Mike and Noula didn't see each other in person again until 1959, almost a year and a half later, since he needed to complete the final time required of his Marine Corp enlistment. They kept in contact with each other through love letters, in which Mike enclosed poetry dedicated to her, their love, and their life together to come. Not long after his honorable discharge from the Marines, Mike and Noula married on July 5, 1959.

The next chapter in Mike's life had began.

───────────

After the wedding, it came as no surprise to anyone, knowing the closeness the twins shared, that Pete was determined to find his own nice Greek girl and future bride.

Fate intervened on his behalf.

John and Titika had not visited family and friends in Price, Utah, since the family moved to Modesto. Among the people they wanted to see was Pete's godfather, who was one of their closest friends. The opportunity arose to return to Price when the family was invited to a wedding there.

Price hosted a large Greek population and there were almost constant baptisms, weddings, and parties where Pete could socialize and maybe find the girl of his dreams. His parents thought the trip might be good for him.

Pete and Mike's younger sister Mary's graduation photo from Ceres High School, 1959.

He quickly volunteered to drive his folks to Price. His sister, Mary, now eighteen, offered to share driving duties with him and make the trip, as well.

The journey was long but uneventful, and the family arrived in Price and drove to Pete's godfather's home. Since Pete's godfather had been both *koubaro*, best man to John and Titika and according to Greek Orthodox tradition had also baptized Pete, the two families considered themselves related. Unlike the typical best man or best woman in any other wedding, the role of the *koubari* in the Greek Orthodox Church's Sacrament of Marriage is honored and cherished, as they are the ones who place ribbon-attached crowns, *stefana*, upon the heads of the bride and groom, crossing them three times (for the Trin-

The twins' sister, Mary, with their mother, Katherine, in the family's vineyard, Modesto, California, circa 1959.

ity) over the couple before placing the crowns upon their heads. The couple then take their first steps together as husband and wife, circling the table holding the Holy Bible three times, before ending their short walk as a fully married couple in the eyes of the church and finally taking their first communion as husband and wife.

The Pappas family and their *koubari* attended the wedding in Price to which they had all been invited. It proved to be a memorable event for the bride and groom but also served to introduce two young couples to each other. At the wedding, Pete met the sweet young woman who later became his bride—Bessie Katsavrias, who lived in town. That evening, Pete's sister, Mary, also met her future husband, Mike Alfieris, a practicing pharmacist who had graduated from the University of Utah School of Pharmacy. Titika, known for her successful matchmaking that resulted in numerous weddings in Modesto, couldn't take credit for the two couples meeting and falling in love that night, but she was thrilled, nonetheless.

When Pete, Mary, Titika, and John left Price and made the long trip back to California, all Pete could think about was Bessie Katsavrias, and all Mary could think about was Mike Alfieris.

Pete was certain that Bessie would make a perfect wife for him. Now, he just had to get to know her a little more. The couple wrote letters to one another for a month or so until Pete began calling her almost daily.

He could no longer take the separation from Bessie and popped the question.

Titika and John adored Bessie and excitedly congratulated their son. Soon thereafter, their daughter, Mary, became engaged to Mike Alfieris. They had met him previously (and even knew his father from their days in Utah) and had felt impressed with him, even hoping that he would one day notice their sweet daughter. In June of 1961, Pete and Bessie celebrated their engagement with Mary and her fiancé, Mike, at the Pappas home on College Avenue in Modesto, the same location as Mike and Noula's engagement party, just a few years before. Feasting on Greek specialties commenced, along with the requisite Greek dancing and gift opening. The night sparkled with the love of four young people.

The families of both couples rejoiced and toasted each other and their children with John's homemade red wine. The pending nuptials promised the creation of two new Greek homes, future grandchildren, and the joining together of three Greek families into one. John and Titika had seen the first of their twins marry a few years earlier, and now two of their remaining three children were engaged to marry young Greek people who were good, decent, kind, and from honorable families. John and Titika's eyes met across the yard as they both watched the young couples on the dance floor, dancing round and round, arms about each other with friends and family, and Titika thought, *God has smiled upon us. We have been through much, but life is finally good. Our children are happy and healthy, and they are marrying well. Our family is blessed!*

Titika's eyes glistened. Their hard times were finally over.

CHAPTER 14

1961–1962:
Broadcasting Beckons

FINISHED WITH THEIR MILITARY SERVICE, the twins felt ready to conquer the world. After Mike's marriage to Noula in July 1959 and Pete's marriage to Bessie in December 1961, they eagerly launched their professional broadcasting careers. Mike's first job was working as a newsman at KWG-AM. The station was the "big dog" in the Stockton radio market, and Mike was eager to make money and achieve his first success in the radio business. Typically, if someone wanted to climb the ranks and become a manager in the radio biz, advertising sales was the career road to take. Nevertheless, he enjoyed being a radio newsman and was determined to work his way into management, so he sold the station's owner on an idea: he'd save him money by doing two jobs—news *and* sales. A combination newsman's/salesman's position in the radio business didn't exist in the radio stations of the 1960s, and still doesn't today. Doing two jobs permitted Mike to make more money than doing just one job, and still put him in the running for a future management position.

He loved being on-the-air and enjoyed the programming side of radio, especially news. His idol was Edward R. Murrow, America's most prominent newscaster, and he reported the news holding high the standards of journalism that Murrow practiced. He believed that

Pete and Bessie's wedding in Price, Utah, in December 1961.

reporters must put aside their own views and look for the truth in every story, learn to sift through the spin, and differentiate between the pitch and the truth. As a news director, he prided himself on always presenting both sides of a story. For Mike, this was a journalist's primary task. Biased editorials belonged on the opinion page. If he had an opinion, he labeled it as such. When his audience heard Mike Pappas editorials, it knew what was being broadcast—commentary, not editorials disguised as news.

Just because working two jobs at one radio station wasn't done by others didn't mean it couldn't be done by him. He never believed he couldn't do it, which is why he *could* do it. He knew that to make money and get ahead in the radio business he had to work harder and smarter and had to plan every career move like strategizing for battle. Neither he nor Pete accepted what the public or business world believed to be their career paths.

They practiced positive affirmations before doing so was popularized by self-help gurus years later. They told themselves there was nothing that could stop them from reaching their goals. In later years, they discovered the book *Think and Grow Rich,* by Napoleon Hill, and the audiotapes summarizing the book's contents narrated by Earl Nightingale, which became their business "bible" and the basis for training their sales teams. The brothers purchased the entire series of the groundbreaking, positive-thinking audiotapes and listened to them religiously.

It only took six months for Mike to become the station's top salesman, and he was promoted to the position of local sales manager. A short time later the station was sold, and he took a job at KSTN-AM as the regional sales manager, a higher position than he had at KWG-AM.

While browsing through the classifieds in *Broadcasting Magazine* several months later, Mike saw an ad that the Golden Pacific Group, a highly respected broadcast company, was looking for a sales manager for one of their two stations in Stockton, KCVR-AM. He didn't feel he had much of a chance at the job, though. While successful, his recent full-time experience still classified him as a rookie, but he knew that one of the three owners, a well-known successful broadcaster, was the San Francisco restaurant owner and author George Mardikian. Since Mike was Greek-American and Mardikian was Armenian-American, and because the Greeks and Armenians traditionally had close cultural ties, he felt this might be his best chance to get in with a successful broadcast group rather than work for a locally owned single station. He sent his résumé to the address listed and hoped for the best.

Two of the partners who read his submission noticed that young Mike really didn't have a lot of experience. Still, Mardikian was inclined to give the young man an interview. He saw Mike's Greek surname and assured his partners that Mike was likely a nice Greek boy. And, knowing many fine Greeks through the years, he told his partners that hiring Mike would be a good decision. After interviewing Mike (and being impressed with his previous radio success and his evident enthusiasm), Mardikian and his partners hired him. Mardikian also met with Noula since it was their policy to interview the wives of potential employees. The purpose of doing so was to evaluate whether their new hire's home life was stable and if the employee's wife supported her husband's career. When Mardikian met Noula, her intelligence, beauty, charm, and love for her husband impressed him. Mike's wife helped seal the deal.

So Mike was hired as sales manager of KCVR-AM at the age of 24, one of the youngest sales managers in the radio business. Mike drove himself ceaselessly to meet every sales goal set for his department.

It was a momentous year for another reason. Noula delivered their first child, a girl. They named her after Mike's mother, Katherine, as was the Greek tradition. Their new daughter was called Kathy in English and *Ekaterini*, in Greek.

———

After Pete married Bessie, he too needed to find a radio job. He looked at help-wanted ads in *Broadcasting Magazine* and found a sales position available at KFIV-AM in his home town of Modesto.

After seeing Pete's record sales figures from the Juneau, Alaska, station, KFIV hired him.

In just a few months, he became the station's top salesman. It was while selling advertising for KFIV-AM that Pete was memorably turned down for one advertising sale he was trying to make for the station.

All business involves sales—someone has to sell something to someone else to make money—so salesmen like Pete or Mike do everything possible to make a sale, but even then, sometimes the answer is still "no." Most of the time for Pete and Mike, a "no" meant "not now," because they would make repeated attempts in the future to make that sale, and most of the time, they were successful.

However, one potential customer in Modesto repeatedly refused the station's previous reps' attempts to sell him advertising.

The account was assigned to Pete. He knew its history at KFIV-AM but was nevertheless determined to make the sale.

He paid a visit to the Sears & Roebuck store in downtown Modesto, hoping to sell them radio advertising. As he walked into the store mentally rehearsing his sales pitch, he finally came face to face with the store's manager. As Pete introduced himself and the two men shook hands, the manager paused and pulled his hand away.

"Pete Pappas? Did you say *Pappas?* Are you related to Titika Pappas?"

When Pete affirmed she was his mother, the store's manager shook his head.

"I don't know if I want to do business with you. She cost me a lot of money. All she said the whole time was, *no sir, yes sir, too high mister, too much money.*"

Pete didn't understand how that was possible, since Titika never learned to speak English well. It was broken English at best. Pete and Mike always suspected, though, that she knew more English than she represented. According to the manager, she spoke enough English to negotiate the price on the drapes she wanted, way below the retail price.

After enduring Titika's wheeling and dealing and agreeing on a final price, the manager had the drapes delivered to her home and installed. Titika took one look and decided she wasn't happy with them and insisted they were taken down and returned.

"If you're as shrewd as she is, I don't know if I want to buy advertising from you," the store's manager now said to Pete.

Pete couldn't help but laugh. His Greek immigrant mom from the village in Crete did this? Incredulous, he couldn't wait to get home and tell his family the story. They all laughed and had fun asking their mom about it, who didn't understand what all the fuss was about. She tried to get a good deal for the family, the man at the store was not cooperating, and, in the end, he delivered a low-quality product. Right was right and wrong was wrong, and she was right and he was wrong. Period! Her children were proud of their immigrant mother's innate business sense. Pete, Mike, and their two siblings always thought if Titika had been born in the United States and had the opportunity for an education and a career, she would have been a formidable businesswoman.

———

Mike introduced Pete to the Golden Pacific Group and after hearing of his accomplishments in Juneau and at KFIV-AM in Modesto, they hired him as well. The group presented the twins with their first opportunity for radio ownership. The Golden Pacific Group had launched a new AM station in Las Vegas. The group's partners wanted Pete and Mike to move to Vegas to make it profitable quickly. If they could do that, the partners would reward them with a discounted price to purchase a 5 percent ownership stake.

Here was Pete and Mike's chance to show what they could do and to earn what they wanted the most: an ownership interest in a radio station! That small percentage of ownership would hopefully lead to the fulfillment of their ultimate dream—to be the sole owners of their own radio station.

Pete and Mike accepted the opportunity and, with their wives, took the long, dusty drive to Las Vegas.

CHAPTER 15

1961–1964:
Twin Tempests Take Vegas

TWIN WHIRLWINDS OF DETERMINATION, energy, and fervor, Pete and Mike soon blew the top off the Las Vegas radio broadcasting market. Managing KVEG-AM, they were both tough competitors and creative promoters. They needed to raise $5,000 to buy 5 percent of the station, so the twins and their families lived frugally to raise the money. Bessie's office and bookkeeping skills and her pleasant, professional demeanor helped her find a nearby job. Mike negotiated a trade barter of a hotel room for the two families to live in rent free in exchange for advertising, which enabled them to save the money they would have paid for rent.

Initially, the two brothers and their families stayed in one room at the American Motor Motel on Las Vegas Boulevard South, which was on the Las Vegas strip. In that room, Noula cooked on a hot plate for the two families while pregnant.

Several months after their arrival in Las Vegas, Mike and Noula's second child, a boy, was born. In keeping with Greek tradition (as they had done with their firstborn, Kathy), he was named John, after Mike's father. He was *Yanni* in Greek. Mike found an inexpensive apartment for his growing family. At the same time, Pete and Bessie found an apartment of their own.

Pete and Mike raised $5,000 in less than six months and bought 5 percent of KVEG-AM. The station was profitable 120 days after they assumed its management.

———

The first of many business battles for Pete and Mike happened at KVEG-AM.

The twins worked long hours for months. They programmed the station's new format, hired and trained staff, established operational rules and procedures, and made a name for themselves as maverick broadcasters in Las Vegas. One afternoon, though, when the triple-digit heat made everyone feel like melting popsicles, the station's announcers and sales staff quit to form their own advertising agency. Presumably, they would then make sure that any station the Pappas twins were operating wouldn't get any advertising buys from their local clients.

The twins wondered why previously loyal employees would do something they knew had the potential of scuttling their ship, taking KVEG-AM off the air and perhaps causing it to fail permanently.

As always, Pete and Mike were energetic and ambitious, with a take-no-prisoners approach to achieving their business objectives. They were captains of the ship, and their crew (supervisors and staff) were required to take orders without question. They were both young with little management experience in the civilian world. Their management training came from the military, and that's how they ran their station.

Pete and Mike believed that employees who failed to give their best effort, which included working long hours, wouldn't be tolerated. If the twins worked 18-hour days, why shouldn't everyone else be willing to do the same to achieve success? They were on the same team. The radio stations' success ensured that everyone kept their jobs and eventually received raises.

In Las Vegas, a KVEG-AM 970 sign publicizes the station at a local car lot. The sign was bartered with the dealer's ownership in exchange for advertising on the station, as was the case with the company car featuring the station's logo, shown below.

Pete and Mike quickly turned the tables on their former staff. The twins' enemies list (which was previously composed of other radio stations in town) now had the new advertising agency at the top. Pete and Mike worked hard to discredit that agency, especially since the staff had only given them one hour's notice before leaving. (Pete and Mike went on the air, covering for the disc jockeys who left, until they could hire new ones.) It took months to fill all the positions left vacant by the mass exodus.

Pete at his desk after he was promoted by the Golden Pacific Group to the position of general manager of KVEG-AM 970, circa 1962.

For Pete and Mike, it was just more of the same, dating back to their high school days.

They were bold personalities, fierce competitors, and strong-willed, and they could be intimidating. The twins focused on a business target, took aim, and fired, never missing a shot. Resentment of Pete and Mike was the norm for those who couldn't keep up with them or deal with the dominating nature of their personalities.

Pete and Mike, a pair of cyclones blazing through Las Vegas, left their unsuspecting competitors, and some ex-employees, behind in a blinding desert sandstorm.

After giving KVEG-AM a Pappas twins' success makeover, the Golden Pacific Group wanted more of the same from Pete and Mike. In the intervening two years since arriving from California, the twins' younger brother, Harry, had come to town to attend the University of

Nevada at Las Vegas, while he worked part-time for his brothers. On the air, he was known as Harry Holiday. While at KVEG, Harry's remarkable intellect served him well as he learned everything possible about radio broadcasting.

Pete was entrenched in station operations but Mike was bored. They had taken over a station without billing and made it profitable, but Mike was ready to do the same elsewhere. He enjoyed planning and executing the twins' battle plans for the takeover and makeover of a money-losing radio property. Pete, on the other hand, enjoyed the daily challenges that came with keeping a radio station on top and in the black, and he was a master at reducing overhead while increasing sales, thereby generating profits.

Mike after he was promoted by the Golden Pacific Group to the position of general manager of KCVR-AM 1570 in Stockton, California, circa 1962.

Pete's talent was in operations, while Mike was the turnaround man. As always, the twins were a good balance for one another.

The Golden Pacific Group promoted Pete to general manager of KVEG-AM and transferred Mike back to the San Joaquin Valley, promoting him to general manager of the group's flagship station, KCVR-AM in Stockton. He improved the station's format and used trade deals, bartering advertising for promotional opportunities for KCVR, to increase ratings and sales. The group also assigned him the task of finding radio stations in other cities, such as Honolulu and Reno, so the group could expand. Mike and Noula, along with their toddler daughter and now a baby son, moved to an old house in Galt, just north of town, that was owned by his boss. The rent was free (a perk for being the station's general manager), so living there was advantageous. The old, white, wooden clapboard farmhouse out in the country had a gravel circular driveway in front. Mike drove a white station wagon painted with the KCVR logo and slogan on all sides, a rolling billboard paid for with bartered advertising. He traded out bus benches, the sides and backs of buses, and billboards painted on the walls of buildings that featured the KCVR logo. He gave building owners free advertising for use of their building's exterior walls.

The farmhouse's backyard had weeds and scrub brush two feet high. Mike regularly went out back and practiced shooting his pistol at targets and the occasional sparrow. The piercing echo of the firing gun would send his daughter dashing into the kitchen from the back of the house, just in time to watch her mother running across the wood floor, chasing a field mouse with a fly swatter (and usually killing it with one quick, powerful smack).

The Golden Pacific Group made an offer to purchase a radio station in Honolulu, and Mike was asked to move to Hawaii to manage its turnaround after the transfer of ownership was approved by

Mike's talent for "trading out" services in exchange for advertising helped establish the new branding for each station the Pappas brothers owned and managed. Each of the brothers "traded-out" what they needed to launch the station(s) they managed and, later, owned. Mike bartered both the vehicles from a local car dealer and the paint job for the signage on each vehicle. He also bartered advertising for a searchlight to use at evening remote broadcasts.

Typical radio control room of the late 1950s and early 1960s.

the Federal Communications Commission, the FCC (a requirement for the transfer of ownership of all radio and television stations in the United States). Yet the sale collapsed, and Mike continued with his job as general manager of KCVR.

Over time, the twins became unhappy with their arrangement with the Golden Pacific Group. They only had a 5 percent ownership of KVEG-AM and, therefore, no real control or decision-making authority. Pete and Mike decided to sell their ownership back to the group so they could go out on their own and buy a radio station, along with their brother Harry's additional capital investment. Mike began earnestly looking for a radio station the brothers could purchase without partners. Why should their hard work benefit the bank accounts of their bosses and not them? That was knowledge gained watching the partners of the Golden Pacific Group.

Mike did the reconnaissance and strategized. He relished the challenge. His job was to identify a radio station for sale, making it the flagship station of a radio chain that the twins and their brother, Harry, would build together. The brothers drew up plans for the turnaround of an unprofitable radio station that could be purchased inexpensively.

With the twins' savings, the profit from the sale of their KVEG stock, and Harry's investment of cash, they began their search for a radio station. Their experience with the Golden Pacific Group taught them what to look for in a radio station purchase, and they already knew how to turn a loser into a winner. Through research, they discovered a bankrupt, daytime-only radio station (signing on the air with each day's sunrise and going off the air with each day's sunset) in the small, San Joaquin Valley town of Tulare, California: KGEN-AM 1370.

The next chapter in their life's story was about to begin.

CHAPTER 16

1964–1971:
A Flagship Radio Station
when AM Was King

WITH THE MICROPHONE HOT, she sat next to her daddy trying to copy his words exactly, imitating his articulation and inflection.

"Now, Kathy, say exactly what I say, okay, honey?"

"Okay, Daddy."

She sat up as straight as she could, pushing back the brown ringlets cascading down her face. Little Kathy leaned forward toward the mic, ready to say her lines, careful not to get too close so the sound of her breathing didn't end up in the recording, forcing them to do another "take." She didn't like doing lots of takes, not because she got tired or bored, but because she liked getting it right the first time. Like any child, she loved the adoration and affection she received from her father for doing so, even though she was experienced radio talent.

At three years old, she was KGEN's Kathy.

"KGEN's Kathy" was her dad Mike's idea for a radio advertising package he could sell to merchants for a premium. Buying it gave them the talents of KGEN's Kathy to personally record their commercials, and she also made personal appearances at their remote broadcasts (broadcasts that originated from their businesses' location). Her mom, Noula, dressed her up in the cutest dress she had with a big bow in her hair when she went with her dad to visit the merchants who bought the package.

"Kathy, this is Mr. Smith. This is his store. Remember when you recorded the KGEN's Kathy commercial for him?"

Mike lifted her up onto the store's front counter.

"Yes, Daddy, I remember. We talked about selling clothes." The commercial was recorded just a few weeks earlier, so it was still fresh in her mind.

Kathy shifted further back onto the counter. It looked like a long way down and she was afraid that she might fall. Her father held

An early photo of KGEN's Kathy with her grandparents, John and Katherine, in Stockton, circa 1962.

onto her tightly so there was no real danger. She always felt safe with her daddy.

"Oh, well, lookee how cute she is!" said Mr. Smith. "Hey, everybody, come on out here quick-like and see little KGEN's Kathy!" Mrs. Smith put her bookkeeping aside and ran from the back of the store. Middle-aged and plump, she smiled sweetly at Kathy in her bright pink dress, a local radio star, sitting on the front counter of their store.

"I'm comin', Frank! I got a little treat for her, too."

"Well, Gladdy, hurry up now. She's got other stores to visit today."

Gladys scurried over to the front counter and pulled a lollipop out of her pocket.

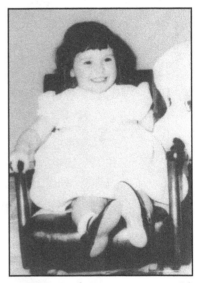

"Here ya' go, sweetie, you are just so precious!" She handed the orange lollipop to Kathy and gazed at her adoringly. "You are just about the cutest thing I've ever seen!"

By this time, Tommy (a local high school boy who helped in the storeroom) and the store's clerk,

KGEN's Kathy, age 3, circa 1964, in Tulare, California.

Lois, encircled them and told Mike how cute she was and how the customers talked about hearing the KGEN'S Kathy commercial for Smith's Clothing Store on the radio.

This scene replayed at every client's location they visited in Tulare.

The following Monday morning, Mike called Smith's and asked his client if he'd like to renew his advertising package.

Smith signed a six-month advertising contract to have KGEN's Kathy record all his commercials.

The Pappas brothers bought KGEN-AM 1370 out of bankruptcy. A daytime-only station, it had failed under two previous owners. Under-capitalized, the twins had just $5,000 left from the purchase for operating capital. Their unity of purpose, spirit, and hard work made the brothers a powerful force. Mike's family drove into Tulare, California, population around 12,000, with their possessions packed into the back of a station wagon and a trailer they towed. Pete, Bessie, and Harry drove from Las Vegas and met Mike and his family there. The Pappas brothers were taking their first step together toward achieving the American dream—the ownership of their own business, a radio station.

Radio was a means to achieve the financial success they craved. For KGEN's Kathy, radio was an escape and a place full of friendly people and great music. As they built their broadcasting business empire, she was raised on radio. Other kids went to parks as children. KGEN's Kathy went to the radio station. All her friends thought radio stations were very cool, very Hollywood, as though she and her family personally knew all the singers whose songs were played on the radio.

Exterior of the KGEN-AM offices in Tulare, California, circa 1964, before KBOS-FM 95 was put on-the-air by Pete, Mike, and Harry. After the construction permit was granted to the Pappas brothers and the station went live, the station's call letters were added to the office's exterior sign.

Kathy, her siblings, and her cousins all knew the truth.

The only connection they had to country crooners and pop idols were the black (and sometimes red) vinyl LP's and 45's the disc jockeys (they preferred the term "jocks") played on-air. Sometimes, they were the same discs the children in the family used as Frisbees in the acreage behind the radio station, after finding boxes of unused 45's (usually from unknown but hopeful singers who never made it big) trashed without fanfare in the dumpster.

As a youngster, Kathy could hear her favorite singers as she walked through the door of the family's radio stations—KGEN-AM and, later, its sister station, KBOS-FM 95—which were right down and across the street from her family's home and just down the street from her grandparents' house. She was infinitely blessed to have her *yiayia*, grandmother Titika, and her *papou*, grandfather John, just a block away, where she could go and watch reruns of *I Love Lucy* with Titika (who laughed until she cried) and could glimpse John working in his garden and afterward pour himself a lunch-time glass of his homemade Greek red wine from the barrel he kept in his garage. Kathy, her siblings, and their cousins loved spending time with their grandparents, listening to them speak a bit of Greek to each of their grandchildren but mostly to one another, as the aroma of

John and Katherine on their way to a Greek event at the Annunciation Greek Orthodox Church, circa 1964, Modesto, California.

Harry at his desk at the KGEN-KBOS offices in Tulare, 1966. Harry was Secretary-Treasurer of Pappas Electronics Inc., the first corporation formed by Pete, Mike, and Harry to purchase KGEN-AM 1370, in Tulare, California, in 1964. Harry was the driving force for the brothers' later foray into the independent television business. Photo Courtesy: Harry J. and Stella A. Pappas family archives.

Greek food, prepared lovingly with garlic, oregano, and lemon, wafted through the house.

Like most youngsters in the 1960s, she knew the lyrics to popular songs playing on KBOS-FM and, unlike her classmates, she got to read *Billboard Magazine*, delivered weekly to the stations and brought home to her by her dad. She knew all the disc jockeys at both stations by their real names and their radio pseudonyms and even helped organize the prizes for the radio contests (at the direction of her Aunt Bessie, who managed the office).

When she walked through the doors of those two stations, the childhood melodramas of her friends and school, along with the tumultuous world of the 1960s, faded away with every song playing on the radio. There were no Internet, iPods, or cell phones; local television only had three channels (until Pete, Mike, and Harry put the fourth station, KMPH-TV 26, on-the-air in 1971). In the little town of Tulare where she grew up, radio was her refuge, entertainment, and escape, as it was for most youth.

She could check in and out of reality with the flip of the radio dial.

Pete and Mike's story began before KGEN's Kathy's birth in 1961, but their later years in the radio and television business of the 1960s and 1970s became part of her life's story. She grew up listening to the radio stations Pete, Mike, and Harry owned that had been purchased as distressed properties, bought out of bankruptcy or in estate sales, or put on the air for the first time by them. One of her friends in their working-class Tulare neighborhood might hear her dad come home from work and talk for five or ten minutes about his day delivering milk for the local dairy, or his run-ins with his boss at the garage where he fixed cars, or how hot it was in the fields that day supervising the farmworkers picking beans. He might sit down, crack open a beer, and watch one of his favorite shows on TV. With only three stations to choose from initially, it didn't take too long to make a choice, kick his feet up on the recliner or coffee table, and relax for the night.

When Mike came home from work every day, life was different. It seemed that Mike always worked, and when he wasn't working, he was thinking about working.

Usually, he was still thinking—really, obsessing—about what he needed to do that night and what he needed to do the next day at the radio station. He came home, he changed out of his suit (if he didn't have to go out to meet a client somewhere), then he had a quick dinner with his wife and four children. The family's two youngest children were born in nearby Visalia—daughter Dena in 1965 and youngest son Jimmy in 1967, after the purchase of KGEN. He would give each child a hug and a kiss. They would sit together on bar stools around the semicircular counter that doubled as the kitchen table and talk with their father in 30- or 60-second bursts, during commercials on the evening news, in between Walter Cronkite telling everyone the nation's news of the day.

The children went to bed, always promptly at 8:00 p.m., since Noula's Spartan philosophy dictated that families, especially children, did better if they were on a strict schedule. Then Mike would spend much of the evening reviewing, repeatedly, the triumphs and losses of his day as well as his plans for the next day…and the next week…and the next month with his wife, who listened, listened, listened, without complaint, offering opinions when asked, as she went about cleaning the kitchen, folding clothes, or just sitting on the couch. Without the children present, he eventually relaxed enough to sit and watch a television show, though he talked about the business during commercial breaks. It was during this quiet evening time Noula told Mike what had happened with each of their four kids that day.

Pete and Bessie's ritual of reviewing business goals and plans happened daily as well, but first thing in the morning rather than at night. Pete, always the more happy-go-lucky twin, spent his evenings at "happy hour" with clients and then at home with his wife and twin sons. Unlike his twin, Mike, Pete left his worries at the office. Mike took his home with him each night and worried about the business right up until bedtime. Harry, as in most of his professional career, arrived early each day and worked at his desk until late into the night.

———

In Kathy's extended family, building the family business was at the forefront of their lives. There was no time for frivolity, except for the large parties thrown for advertisers of the stations, which really was

KGEN-AM and KBOS-FM's office manager was Pete's wife, Bessie, circa 1964.

work but which Pete, Mike, and Harry made into play. Life, she and her siblings learned, should be as it was for the fabled hero Odysseus: a journey they should pursue with faith and gusto, never losing sight of the destination, relentless in their quest. They were to brave the tempests of life with the same strength as Achilles, the wisdom of Athena, the courage of Leonidas and the 300. They were to live life fearlessly and adventurously. They must be daring, ambitious, and willing to take risks, unlike most people, who were safe and coddled.

By hearkening back to tales of old mixed with family tragedies and triumphs, her father, Mike, taught his children the high levels of achievement, honor, and performance that were expected of them. Her family's initial story, of simple villagers coming from the old country, their travails in America, and the subsequent story and success of the Pappas twins, had become the stuff of local myth and legend. The lives of Pete and Mike in many ways mirrored those of the ancient Greek heroes, albeit in the broadcast business.

CHAPTER 17

1964–1971:
An FM Radio Station Is Born

WHILE THE TWINS MANAGED different departments at the station, their brother, Harry, managed accounting, including all bank accounts, finance, and future business development, while also serving as an announcer in KGEN's early days. The twins and Harry discussed strategy and made major business decisions after consulting with one another. Pete's wife, Bessie, ran the office at no salary while Mike's wife Noula took care of the children, cooking and cleaning and caring for everyone in the rental house they all shared to keep their living expenses to a minimum. With everyone working together, KGEN-AM was in the black within 90 days.

Each day brought new obstacles and opportunities for financial success. Long hours of work and stress come with building any business, especially a new one without receivables, which was the only type the Pappas brothers ever had a chance to build.

Pete, Mike, and Harry didn't inherit money or have the education for careers in the professions. When aspiring entrepreneurs have no money, clawing their way up in the business world is their only option. They are faced with two choices: buy a business that is bankrupt (so it's worth little money and holds little interest for buyers), or start a business from scratch. The brothers knew they would have to do *both*.

While KGEN-AM was in bankruptcy when they bought it in 1964, KBOS-FM 95 had been built from the bottom up, a radio station born of a construction permit (CP) granted by the FCC.

Getting local merchants to consider buying advertising on either KGEN-AM or KBOS-FM wasn't easy, but the twins never ran from a challenge. Being creative thinkers, they knew they needed to spark interest and get the town talking. Doing that required more than playing great music and having a fun listening experience, at least at the beginning. No one would hear the great programming they put on the air if no one ever tuned in. They needed a hook—promotions turned into special events. This was Mike's forte.

One of their tactics was taking the radio stations out of the broadcast studio and to the public. If doing so and creating on-air sales promotions meant making money they couldn't get any other way, then they did it, Saturday, Sunday, and during weekdays if necessary. If it was too much trouble for the other local stations, Pete and Mike made sure it wasn't too much trouble for KGEN-AM or KBOS-FM to do it. They established mobile broadcast studios at a time when most small-town radio stations simply took their equipment (which was a unit the announcer used to broadcast through the client's telephone landline), sat at a table with a banner hanging down the front of it, and did their remote broadcast.

This sedate and somewhat boring setup, though, was not good enough for Pete and Mike's radio stations.

Mike was gifted at turning remotes into promotional events. So both he and his brothers agreed they needed a mobile studio.

Consequently, Mike went shopping and bought a peanut trailer.

The trailer had been used to sell peanuts at county fairs, so he discussed with his brothers the changes he was going to make to turn it into a mobile broadcast studio. The exterior would be rebranded with the stations' logos. All the construction and materials used for the remodel came from Mike's gift for making trade deals. The brothers were building a business with next to no money, so they used what they had: the many minutes of unused airtime that could be bartered for whatever they needed to grow their stations, including converting a peanut trailer into a mobile broadcast studio.

Mike was a marketing genius and created promotions that often took a whole Saturday—a Western day, for instance, that they once sold to a business. He brought in a live band, bales of hay, decorations, a live remote broadcast from the location all day, and employees wearing Western clothes, which helped create a carnival atmosphere. Some remotes occurred at shopping centers, while others were sponsored by downtown associations. Some towns even blocked off streets in their downtown for one or two days to host the remotes.

The custom-designed promotions were Mike's passion.

Promotional events built around remote broadcasts attracted people, created talk, and brought new customers into clients' stores. It was a lot of work putting promotions together, but no one else was doing it, so the brothers made them their specialty.

Nighttime was not the usual time for radio station promotions, but Mike found a way to make money during evenings, too: he bartered for searchlights mounted on trucks to light up the night sky at whatever advertiser's location they were broadcasting from that night.

Business was war, and they did everything they could to outflank the competition.

During those early years in business, the twins, their link as large as the trunk of a sequoia, worked feverishly. Mike awakened at 5:00 every morning, went to the gym, and was at the stations by 7:00 a.m. He led the sales meetings, which doubled as training and motivational sessions. Pete tackled the first operational issues of the day. Often, Mike left the office and spent the day double-pitching advertisers with his salespeople and took clients to lunch. They both worked late as necessary, many times on weekends, managing the stations. Each took potential and new customers, like advertising agencies, retailers, and car dealers, out to dinner. Every single day, Pete and Mike thought and talked about building, creating, modernizing, and ultimately succeeding in the radio business. Mike spent many Saturdays behind the typewriter, making attack plans for increasing sales through promotions for the stations, while Pete met potential clients at local watering holes. Harry worked late into the night, every night, learning everything he could about the broadcast business so the brothers could build a chain of stations.

Pete and Mike, always the underdogs, attacked the local radio market with every weapon they could muster.

Mike's creative juices flowed like a rushing river throughout each day: at work, while he was at home with his family, and even while dreaming in his sleep. His first thoughts in the morning were always solutions to problems on his mind from the night before.

———————

As a child, Kathy watched her dad and Uncle Pete steal a little time away from a house full of noisy children and family on weekends or holidays so they could "take a drive," as they called it. They always came back laughing, smiling, and relaxed. When any of the kids asked to go along, they were firmly and politely told that the drive was reserved for the dads, so they went back outside to play.

One year when she was about 6 or 7, Kathy pleaded with her dad and uncle to let her go on their drive. They looked at one another doubtfully and then back at her.

"My little intellectual will stay quiet, won't you, Kathy?" said Mike.

"I will! I promise! Please let me go with you, Daddy!" she begged.

With keys in hand, her Uncle Pete smiled at her. Mike took her hand and they all climbed into the car. She sat in the middle of the back seat, with her knees on the hump over the floorboard, leaning forward, balancing herself with her elbows, the air conditioning blasting her face with arctic-cold air, and they drove. And drove. *And drove.* It seemed like hours, going in out of neighborhoods, her dad and uncle waving at strangers.

"Why are you waving at those people?" she asked. "We don't know them, do we?"

"People get suspicious seeing strange cars driving through their neighborhoods," her father explained. "If you make eye contact and wave with a smile, they'll wave back, and think you must be a neighbor they haven't met yet, or someone who is nice and no trouble. Besides that, if you wave and smile, even if they don't know you, you won't look stuck up."

Pete steered the car through the downtown, made a big circle, and then drove through more neighborhoods. The whole time they drove, Pete and Mike talked and talked. They talked about the business: how to get ratings up, how to get more business in, how to out-maneuver competitors. They brainstormed new ideas and wondered how they might get local business owners to try out their radio stations. The car's movement seemed to stir up their creative pot of ideas, and they usually came up with a solution to at least one business problem.

Kathy was enthralled.

Several times during the drive, her dad looked back over his shoulder at her. She sat so quietly and attentively, he didn't hear her stir and thought she fell asleep.

Pete and Mike's ritual of driving around happened almost weekly, sometimes more often, throughout their lives.

As time marched on, AM radio formats moved with it. Johnny Cash, Loretta Lynn, George Jones, and Tammy Wynette dominated the country music charts on AM radio. In the early 1960s, Elvis Presley ruled the pop airwaves as the king of rock 'n' roll. Later in the decade, the Beatles dominated the music business, along with the Rolling Stones, the Doors, and the Motown sound. Recording artists' new music became the foundation for innovative formats on radio's newest frequency, FM.

Pete and Mike relied on industry publications like *Broadcasting Magazine* for radio broadcasting industry news and *Billboard Magazine* for programming their stations. In a time before the Internet and social media, broadcasters scrutinized those publications and attended their annual *California Broadcasters Association* and *National Association of Broadcasters* trade organizations' annual conventions, to stay abreast of the latest advancements in the industry.

As their children grew into "tweens" and as the popularity of pop and rock music on FM radio dominated the airwaves, the twins would ask them, "Is this what the kids are listening to?" or "Is this a hit with the kids?"

CHAPTER 18

1964–1971:
Local Broadcasters
and the Coffee Shop Scene

COFFEE SHOPS IN RURAL CENTRAL VALLEY TOWNS served as informal community town halls. Pete and Mike decided during their early days in Tulare that they needed to connect with local merchants daily at what Mike called "the coffee shop scene." He himself visited local coffee shops in rotation. Sitting at a coffee shop counter at 5 a.m., he might find a farmer to his left and the mayor to his right. Across the aisle, local merchants talked conservative politics and agricultural business. This setting was fertile ground for the Pappas twins, natural communicators, being every bit at ease talking with local judges as they were with farmers wearing dusty overalls from working in fields and orchards.

In a rural area like the San Joaquin Valley, knowing the small talk of the town was crucial in building a business strategy. Understanding the enemy (in this case, their competitors) and what the local business community (their potential advertising customers) were doing and thinking was a key tactic of the brothers, one that Mike had learned well in Marine Corps intelligence and that he put to good use as a local broadcaster.

Mike established his own personal spy network in the local towns of Tulare and Visalia via the contacts he made in the area's coffee shops.

Local business or advertising agency owners whom Mike befriended would report to him what was said by competitors, his own employees, or even the management of other radio stations. He anticipated that keeping informed of what was happening with their staff or competitors gave the Pappas brothers an advantage: they could adjust their stations' programming if needed, introduce a new advertising package to sell to local merchants, or counterattack a competitor's plans before they were implemented. Was a radio station planning a format change? Did an advertising agency owner personally dislike one of the twins so that advertising would never be purchased from them? The possibilities were endless.

Neither Pete nor Mike ever wiretapped or committed illegal acts, but they did routinely communicate with local folks who might have information that could be helpful to their business. Pete and Mike jokingly referred to their network of informants as their Greek intelligence service.

The twins always took the approach of establishing personal relationships with the businesspeople they met. This extended to time-buyers at national advertising agencies who rarely purchased airtime in markets the size of Tulare or Visalia. Mike was particularly adept at establishing rapport with these buyers, typically young women who were beginning their careers in advertising. He knew that building camaraderie was critical because even in those days, having good ratings (being in the top three stations in a market for a particular demographic—for example, women 18–49) was the main reason an advertising agency placed its national buys for commercials on radio or television stations. Since the Pappas brothers always bought bankrupt stations or put new stations on the air, at the beginning, there were no

151

ratings, and they still needed the business, so how did they do it? By doing what they did best—they got to know the decision makers and worked constantly on establishing personal relationships. When most small-market stations spent little or no time pursuing national advertising money (maybe taking a quick two-day trip to Los Angeles or San Francisco, or no trip at all), Mike spent as much as a week at a time in each city, visiting advertising agencies with a very well-rehearsed pitch, lots of promotional materials, and photographs of community promotions he was particularly talented at creating.

———————

Beginning with KGEN-AM, to build morale and stir up the community, the brothers also remodeled or moved facilities to attractive, modern sites sporting the best, newest equipment. In radio's early days, there was very little emphasis on interior furnishings and image. In the 1950s and 1960s, radio was like most local businesses—mom and pop operations. Pete, Mike, and Harry looked at other industries like banking and finance, and determined that by expecting their own employees to dress professionally, act professionally, and work professionally, they needed to give them a professional environment in which to do these things. This facility and image enhancement helped communicate their message to the local community that their broadcast stations were serious businesses and thereby cemented their stations' reputation as first-class operations.

Businesslike behavior and decorum prevailed at non-broadcast companies and was in fact the norm, so why not broadcasting too—and especially, why not radio? Many radio stations in those days had makeshift offices and studios located inside cheap trailers at the base of their tower and transmitter sites. Gray or green, beat-up metal desks bought from military surplus stores generally made up the office furnishings.

Portable, loud, window-mounted air conditioning units blew cold air into smoke-filled spaces, while staff and disc jockeys attired in T-shirts, faded jeans, and casual clothes crammed behind their desks and into studios to get work done. At that time, some small-town radio stations could be found in industrial, low-rent areas.

The Pappas brothers' stations, located in professional offices they owned, were so unusually clean and professional-looking that advertisers were given tours of their contemporary facilities, which acted as a selling tool for the stations. By doing so, Pete, Mike, and Harry ignited a positive buzz among the local merchants, accomplishing their goal of distinguishing themselves from the other media in town. They built a reputation for having very modern broadcast facilities, beautifully designed and equipped with state-of-the-art-technology. The emphasis on a professional working environment also gave their employees a morale boost by making them feel that working in the radio business was just as respectable as any other business.

The Pappas brothers also established relationships with local bankers by first becoming the bankers' customers, establishing personal checking and savings accounts with a few different banks in town to cultivate personal relationships with local bankers. In the 1960s, local banks were operated by local managers who had full authority to grant loans. When Pete, Mike, and Harry needed loans to build their broadcast business, it was local bank managers who first saw their potential and early success and granted the brothers their initial commercial loans. These local relationships helped finance the building of their second radio station, KBOS-FM 95, including legal fees, for an application to the Federal Communications Commission for the construction permit (CP) and also to purchase equipment for the station.

The mammoth banks of the twenty-first century, with multiple strata of management, loan committees, and such, didn't exist in those days. Local banks and local managers, even larger regional banks like Bank of America, had vested interests in their local communities and were granted full power to make loans, and they did so. This method of bank operations was a great advantage to local businesses, unlike current mega-banking practices that make it incredibly difficult for small businesses to obtain loans from corporate banking giants. Businesses sprang up with regularity in communities across the United States and stayed open for generations, unlike many of today's locally owned businesses that are undercapitalized, face insurmountable competition from chain and big box retailers, and are often doomed to an overwhelming and quick failure. The decades of the 1960s and 1970s were dominated by small business. In that climate, the Pappas brothers worked together, bound by their love and devotion to one another, ambition, enthusiasm, and an unmatched work ethic, all to make sure their stations would be profitable and, when necessary, be able to borrow money from local banks to help fuel their stations' future growth.

CHAPTER 19

1967–1971:
Self-Made Men as Mentors

As PETE, MIKE, AND HARRY PAPPAS established a protocol of profession-alism and excellence at their first stations (to be followed by others in later years), they entrenched themselves in their city of license, Tulare, California. Mike joined the local Kiwanis Club while Pete joined the Rotary Club. It was at local community service clubs and their morning coffee shop haunts that Pete and Mike met men who inspired them. One such man was Manuel Cardoza, a Portuguese immigrant who came from a poor family that had migrated from the Azores, the lush, emerald-green islands off the coast of Portugal.

Cardoza escaped from poverty by the sweat of his brow, hard work, honesty, and integrity—the kind of man one could shake hands with, make a deal with, and know that his handshake and word held more power than any written contract.

When Cardoza met Pete and Mike, he immediately liked them, recognizing the same ambition in them that had burned within him as a young man. Cardoza had started working on other contractors' construction projects, learned the business, saved money, and started his own business that successfully developed homes in single-family neighborhoods. He also owned a neighborhood grocery store with his brother. If Cardoza could become a successful businessman, the Pappas brothers could do it, too. Although a few decades older than the twins, he mentored and helped them in any way possible.

Cash flow is always an issue for businesses in their early days, and it was no different when the brothers built both KGEN-AM and KBOS-FM. As Mike got to know Cardoza, he asked for a few favors to help the twins when money was tight.

"Manuel, could you rent us a house and, instead of cash, we'll give you advertising?" Mike asked one day as they sat together in one of Mike's favorite downtown coffee shops.

Cardoza looked at him, smiled, and took a sip of coffee. "To help you boys out, I'll do that for you."

A few months later, Mike asked for Cardoza's help again.

"Manuel, we can't afford groceries right now. Would you give us groceries in exchange for advertising for your market?" Cardoza was fond of the brothers and their families, so helping the family with a barter arrangement for his groceries was a quick and easy decision.

Cardoza's neighborhood market was a regular stop for Mike's daughter, Kathy, who was routinely sent to pick up bread, milk, cheese, and staples for her mother. She was always greeted with hospitality and a warm smile by Cardoza's brother, the instant she walked through the double stainless-steel swinging doors of the store. The place smelled of cleaning solution (the floors were always being mopped), fresh green vegetables and fruit from local farms, and freshly cut meat and cheese at the butcher counter. Little Kathy was greeted again by the butcher, who knew her well and who waited patiently for her to read her mother's meat and cheese order to him. When she went to check out, Cardoza's brother stopped whatever work he was doing elsewhere in the store to personally wait on Kathy. He watched her sign the charge slip to buy that day's groceries, as she regaled him with her latest school adventures.

Cardoza didn't need to advertise either his store or his construction company on the Pappas radio stations, but he did it because he saw these young Greek scrappers, Pete, Mike, and Harry, working hard like he did. He wanted to help them succeed.

Pete and Mike surrounded themselves with entrepreneurial men like Cardoza who were not from the enclaves of old money, but were fresh upstarts, aggressive and ambitious entrepreneurs with a pioneering spirit. Ray Farmer, who became a lifelong friend of the Pappas brothers, was one of these men. Mike met Farmer when he sold him advertising on KCVR-AM, and Mike immediately clicked with this self-made man 20 years his senior. Farmer started a used car business and eventually opened his own dealership, Payless Motors, which later evolved into the dealership called Toyota of Stockton.

Pete and Mike learned much from older, successful men like Cardoza and Farmer, and they put that experience to work. The twins quickly realized that knowing their community and all the potential customers in it helped them understand each merchant's needs. If one understood their needs, one could help fulfill those needs by selling them advertising that brought more customers into their stores, thereby increasing their sales and profits. Helping *them* achieve success in their businesses led to the radio stations also succeeding. Thus, Pete and Mike wanted to know everything that was happening in their communities.

The twins were forever thankful to people who inspired them with their kindness and generosity, because they knew that a person never becomes successful on their own without the help and support of friends and family. They related to individuals who were predicted never to succeed as entrepreneurs simply because they didn't graduate from college or have advanced degrees. Those were always the people the brothers could relate to the best.

Using their positions both as broadcasters and as great believers in the freedom of the press and its obligation to hold government accountable to the people, both Pete and Mike often wrote and voiced editorials on local, state, and national topics. The twins' willingness to take a conservative political stand and be controversial was mostly unheard of in much of 1960s and 1970s radio and helped foster their goal of creating talk. Whether or not people agreed with them was not the issue or the objective. They wanted to generate publicity for their stations, and it worked. Additionally, Pete and Mike always believed that radio stations were more than jukeboxes and boom boxes. They were in fact businesses and servants of the communities to which they were licensed.

As predictions by naysayers often are wrong, especially from fellow broadcasters in each community in which the Pappas brothers owned stations, they were astonishingly wrong in the case of the brothers. The predictability of their competitors' underestimation of Pete, Mike, and Harry's drive, gusto, and tenacity made it impossible for them *not* to succeed. When the enemy expects the opposition to fail and does nothing to defend itself or its borders, the invading army has an automatic advantage. For the Pappas brothers, this was an axiom. Business was *war,* and the element of surprise that came with their invasion of a new radio market resulted in the pummeling of their competitors, with many local radio listeners turning to Pappas stations first for both news and entertainment.

———————

Because the three brothers now owned their own nicely furnished homes, the entertainment of clients became home-based as they hosted lavish parties for advertisers and, later, for investors in their stations. Most of them happened at Pete and Bessie's house, where they had built a large party room at their rear of their home that featured a full bar (like the sort usually found at restaurants), a new spacious pool in the backyard, and a custom barbecue unit designed by Pete to cook a special Greek entrée: a whole lamb barbecued on a spit. His father-in-law, Nick Katsavrias, taught him the intricacies of cooking lamb on a spit during one of Pete and Bessie's trips back to her hometown of Price, Utah.

A whole lamb cooking on a spit was something not seen in the little valley towns of Tulare and Visalia, likely because there were few Greeks in the area, either American born or immigrants from the old country. In addition to lamb, the wives Noula and Bessie; the twins' sister, Mary; Harry's wife, Stella (they were married in 1969 after a whirlwind courtship when Harry used an "assumptive close" to confirm she would marry him—saying *"when you marry me, Stella..."*); and her mom, Mary Vouros (John and Titika knew Stella's late father many years earlier before he was married to her mother, Mary), cooked all the accompanying Greek entrées and desserts: *moussaka, spanakopita, tiropites, pasticho, karydopita, kourambyethes,* and the requisite *baklava.*

Clients and potential customers at their parties devoured the Greek delicacies, amazed at the foreign but delicious variety of entrées and desserts prepared by the Pappas family wives and relatives. Leftovers were nonexistent. All the food was wolfed down by guests and hosts before the end of the night.

───────────

When Mike left the house each morning, briefcase in hand, as he walked out the front door, he would wave to his children, all gathered around the breakfast counter with their mother, and say, "Goodbye, my beautiful kids, I'm off to fight the world!" And he was. They were a family, and they were all in it together.

Regardless of how hard or how many hours they worked, Pete and Mike always made time to spend with their children and families.

Weekends for Mike's four kids were time with Daddy. Saturday morning breakfast was spent at Nielsen's coffee shop in downtown Tulare, eating all the pancakes they could eat, or a midmorning snack of a single plate of french fries, shared by all four kids with their father, and each was allowed only one soda (no free refills in those days, and they probably wouldn't have been permitted to have one if there were). Their father was in their lives, in good times and bad, in good moods and bad—not merely a weekend parent entertaining them if it fit into a datebook. Pete spent most weekends at home with Bessie and their twin boys at poolside barbecues with friends and family.

The children, like others of their generation, were lucky and didn't know it.

They had their mom and dad living with them in the same house sharing their lives each day. Times were truly different in the small towns of the 1960s.

Having a mom and a dad living in the same house together with the children was commonplace. Mom could stay at home, not worry about having an outside job if she didn't want one, and could volunteer at her kids' school and in the community. The kids could walk to the neighborhood school without fear of kidnappings and molestations or shootings, and Dad could work hard all day to pay the mortgage on a nice, three-bedroom, two-bath, middle-class house that cost about $16,000. A family could own a few cars and maybe even a boat or trailer for weekend outings with the family. They could travel now and then to the local lakes in the Sierra mountains and to beaches on the Central Coast. The country was at war, there were student protests on the college campus at Berkeley and hippies in San Francisco's Haight Ashbury, but in the little town of Tulare, in a small neighborhood, where the kids of radio station owners played and grew up with the children of dairymen, deliverymen, farm workers, mechanics, and truck drivers, life was peace, and joy, and fun. The Pappas children's biggest worry was who the teacher liked best, who got to take the homemade ice cream they made in class to the principal that day, and who got to sit next to whom on the bus coming home from school. They didn't worry about someone grabbing them off the street, or seeing anyone's bare breast from a wardrobe malfunction on TV, or hearing language they weren't supposed to—they were living secure in their childhood, with each new day an adventure filled with the minutiae of their little school, in their friendly little neighborhood, in their quiet little town, with their family's radio stations down the street from their house, playing a part in the daily drama of their lives.

CHAPTER 20

1967–1971:
Taking Care of the Folks

WHEN KGEN-AM BECAME MORE SUCCESSFUL and then they were able to put KBOS-FM on the air, the brothers purchased a home for their parents. Harry managed the purchase of the home and all its furnishings. The three brothers decided that their parents, who had worked hard all their lives and never owned anything that wasn't used or second-hand, should have a newly built, "never-lived-in-by-anybody-else" home, plus a brand-new car. Pete, Mike, and Harry insisted that their parents move to Tulare, three doors down from the radio stations and about five doors down from Mike's house. They bought their father a new four-door Buick Electra (their mom didn't drive). However, their always humble dad, John, though impressed with the beauty of the new car but also worried about the expense ("too much money, boys, too much!"), refused to drive it, since he hadn't paid for it himself.

He still had his old car, he insisted, and it ran fine.

Understanding their father's practicality but still wanting him to drive a new car, they put an announcement on KGEN-AM and sold his old 1950 Ford for $50. Since he no longer had his old car, he was forced to drive the new car.

It still took about 20 days for John to summon the nerve to drive the new Buick.

Pete, Mike, and Harry climbed into the car with him when he finally took the wheel. After going two or three blocks, he looked back at them with a big smile and said, "Hey, if I take this to Greece, they gonna' think I'm the King of Greece!"

Seeing the smiles and wonderment on the faces of their father in his new car, and of their mother, blissful in her new home with her all-new furniture, made every sleepless night, every moment of worry, and every hour of work well worth it to the three sons. As ambitious as they were, their goal wasn't about accumulating money for money's sake.

Achieving financial success was how their families' lives, including those of their parents, became easier.

The new little subdivision house purchased for John and Titika suited them perfectly and fulfilled a promise the brothers had made to each other: as soon as they were successful enough to do so, they would buy their parents a new home and get new furniture. When the brothers showed their parents the newly furnished home for the first time, the tears in Titika's eyes, her radiant smile, and their father shaking his head with amazement, they knew they had accomplished their goal of providing the very best for their parents in the golden years of their lives.

John and Titika spent their entire lives loving, caring, and providing for their children, doing everything necessary to raise them, without any help from the outside world. They worked six days a week, spent the seventh day taking their children to the Greek Orthodox Church, and welcomed friends and family into their home each Sunday afternoon. They taught them compassion, ethics, kindness, honesty, integrity, moral values, responsibility, and self-reliance. Titika had filled their hearts with love and their heads with positivity before such a concept even existed, inspiring her children to achieve great personal and financial success. Both John and Titika taught them that success meant *nothing* without the love of family, and that faith and family must be the foundation of their lives.

Pete, Mike, Harry, and Mary, all married with families of their own, made their parents' senior years as happy and stress-free as possible. John and Titika deserved every good thing in life that their children could provide. It was their children's turn to take care of them.

After settling into their new house, John immediately went to work establishing a little orchard with a variety of fruit trees—peaches, plums, and nectarines—along with a vegetable garden and a few rows of grapes in the backyard. When the grapes were ripe and ready for harvest, he made his traditional homemade Greek red wine. With the help of his sons, he found some used wine barrels and aged the grape juice in his suburban two-car garage until it was ready to drink. Every day, he had a four-ounce glass of red wine at lunch and one at dinner. He had done so all his life. Growing a garden, fruit trees, and grapes, then later harvesting the crops and making wine, was a lot of work for anyone, especially a man in his late 70s. But for a Greek immigrant like John, *not* working was not being productive, and that was something a Greek never wanted to be—since life was about contributing and producing, not slothfulness.

The same was true for Titika. While her husband kept busy with his garden and orchard, she cooked and baked all the Greek delicacies she had always prepared, flavored with affection and love for her family. Now, she was cooking not only for her husband and children, but also for their growing families, including all her delightful grandchildren. The Greeks have an old saying: *ta agonasou ene san theeo ta pethya sou*—your grandchildren are twice your children. This is every Greek *yiayia's* and *papou's* creed. Titika's earlier life had been lived for her children, and she would live her later years for her grandchildren. Every morsel of Greek food and pastry she cooked and baked as a grandmother were bites of love with which she nourished the family's littlest members, filling them up with a grandma's eternal affection.

The holiday most cherished by those practicing the Greek Orthodox faith, like the Pappas family, was *Pascha*, known by the rest of the Western world as Easter. *Pascha*, in the Orthodox Christian faith, celebrates the Resurrection of Jesus Christ. Orthodox Christians observe *Pascha* based on the ancient Julian calendar and not on the Gregorian calendar that is used by the Western world. Thus, Western Christian churches and the Orthodox Christian Church only celebrate the holiday on the same day peridocally. During all other years, the dates can be over a month apart.

John sharing a peach grown in the backyard orchard of his home in Tulare, California. John was a man of the land, happiest working in his farm or garden, circa 1970. Photo Courtesy: Harry J. and Stella A. Pappas family archives.

When the family moved John and Titika into their new house down the street from the radio stations in Tulare, their home continued to be the center of the family's celebrations, including *Pascha*. Titika's health began to fail after many years of Type 2 diabetes (due to a negligent primary care doctor in Modesto who had misdiagnosed her illness as being "all in her head" when she was younger). Despite being on insulin and fatigued, with the help of her daughter, Mary, and daughters-in-law Noula, Bessie, and Stella, she still reigned over the festivities, forever the queen of the kitchen and in the hearts of her family.

As always, Pete, Mike, Harry, and Mary cherished the times, like *Pascha*, Thanksgiving, and Christmas that they, their spouses, and their children came together with John and Titika to revel in their closeness, private jokes, memories, joy, and laughter. Their loving ties now included their grandchildren, building their own memories and bonds of love with their siblings and cousins. John and Titika were growing old, so their children, acutely aware of their parents aging, didn't let life's obligations prevent them from getting together as much as possible, especially for the celebration of *Pascha*.

On *Pascha* morning, the aroma of garlic, lemon, olive oil, and oregano that came from the marinated legs of lamb in the oven wrapped the Pappas home in a warm and cozy embrace, while the sweet smell of baked goods, including *baklava, diples, karythopeta,* and *kourambyethes,* enveloped the house in the days and nights leading up to *Pascha*. Titika made sure everything was perfect for her family on this most revered of Orthodox Christian holidays.

In the week leading up to *Pascha*, Titika's daughter, Mary, and her daughters-in-law also cooked main dishes like *pasticho, moussaka,* and *keftethes* in their own homes, while enlisting the children to bake the favorite American cookie of the three brothers, Snickerdoodles. Noula also brought her special *dolmathes,* prepared with a frothy *avgolemono* (egg lemon) sauce, a recipe common to Sparta but not to Crete. She also cooked her husband Mike's favorite Cretan appetizer—Titika's unique version of *kalitsounia,* a mixture of cheeses wrapped in a light, flaky dough and quick-fried on the stove. The delicacy is eaten hot, immediately after cooking.

As everyone arrived, aprons were donned by all the women in the family, who immediately worked to help Titika. The adults' table was set with the china Mike had bought for Titika when he was in the Marines and stationed in Japan, along with crystal that was a gift from her children. Hydrangeas and roses from John's garden graced the table as a centerpiece.

When the food was finally ready and placed in bowls and platters on the dining room table, the family gathered around, and the chatter stopped. All eyes focused on John.

John first led the family in the *Lord's Prayer*, in both Greek and English, and then spoke to his clan in Greek.

"Emaste olly etho, we are all here together, by the grace of our Lord Jesus Christ." John paused to look at his family—his sons and daughter, his son-in-law and daughters-in-law, his grandchildren, and his wife, Titika. Tears welled in his eyes as he said, "May God always bless us; may he allow us to be together as a family always; may he keep our family strong and our honor clean." His voice broke with emotion. "May he protect our grandchildren and keep them in good health; may he protect our *Ellatha*, Greece, and may he watch over and protect our blessed America, the land of our present and future." John's tears flowed freely, something that as a young man he would have never shown. But now, in his later years, it was difficult to rein in his feelings. Tears filled the eyes of all four of John and Titika's children.

Mike put his arm around his father's shoulders. "It's all right, Baba."

Titika's eyes also filled with tears as she watched this big, tough man who had worked so hard all his life providing for their family, always stoic, now showing his emotions to all. Mary wrapped her arms around her mother. *"Emaste olly kala meetera,* we are all fine, Mother." Titika nodded as she held the hand of her little granddaughter.

The family finally sat down, but before serving the children and eating themselves, one Greek Orthodox ritual remained.

In the center of the table, a large bowl held many boiled eggs, dyed a deep, dark red. Each family member took one boiled egg and tried cracking another's egg. The person offering an egg said, *"Chistos Anesti,*

Christ has risen!" while the person on the receiving end said, *"Alithos anesti*, truly He has risen!"

Then the two eggs are smashed together, and the one that does not crack is the winner. The person with the winning egg moves to the next person with an egg to crack, and so on. At some point, when all the eggs are cracked, one egg is the lone winner, having survived all the challenges at the *Pascha* table. Tradition holds that the eggs are dyed red, symbolizing Christ's blood shed at the crucifixion, and the cracked eggs represent Christ's emergence from the tomb upon His resurrection.

While the family practiced Greek Orthodox *Pascha* customs and though the mood was always fun and celebratory, the Pappas and Alfieris children, just like their parents, had been born in America, so American Easter holiday traditions were added to the mix. (Even though Greek-born, Noula never could understand the relevance of the Easter bunny, Easter chicks, Easter baskets, or Easter egg hunts to the resurrection of Jesus Christ.) While clean-up was happening after the meal, the family's Easter bunny of the day, Bessie, led the charge to hide all the chocolate and candy eggs in the front yard while the children were kept busy inside opening Easter baskets. Once the yard was ready, the children gleefully raced outside, checking under every azalea and begonia bush, each shrub and tree branch, for the desired candy eggs. Their parents laughed and rejoiced in the enthusiasm of their brood (Mike made Kathy promise she would share her candy with him), while John and Titika laughed heartily at the spectacle of their grandchildren running about the yard.

After the eggs were found (with Bessie pointing them out to the smallest children so every child would get a fair chance at a basket full of Easter candy), the family moved back indoors to enjoy all the Greek pastries their bellies could hold.

Pascha celebrated the resurrection of Jesus Christ, but for the Pappas and Alfieris clan, it was also a celebration of family—the bounty of each family member's unconditional love for one another, and the knowledge that no matter what challenges life brought them, they would face them united, bound by love, loyalty, and a shared history.

Time now showed in the wrinkles on Titika's once-porcelain complexion and in John's weathered hands and face. Pete, Mike, Mary, and Harry's parents were now aged, and the time that once seemed to stretch into infinity now seemed limited. How long would they all be around to celebrate life's happy moments and successes together? How many more years would their parents be with them? To be all together as they had always been now had an urgency to it. The twins, Mary, and Harry each vowed that they would continue gathering as a family to celebrate every holiday, but also to celebrate life itself—something they discovered later could be taken away in a few terrible moments, shattering a bliss they thought would last forever.

CHAPTER 21

1970–1972:
The Independent Giant
of the San Joaquin Valley

KATHY'S PARENTS AWAKENED HER in the middle of the night, which was something they never did. On any other night, she would immediately think that something catastrophic happened. She did have two elderly grandparents living five doors down, and her *yiayia* Titika had not been doing well lately.

That night she knew why they did it. Kathy had asked them to do so.

This was a big night for the family: the first time a picture was broadcast on the family empire's new television station, KMPH-TV UHF channel 26, based in Visalia.

She ran into the family room and sat on the floor, as close as she could to her family's Zenith console television set. Kathy's siblings were asleep, but there was a lot of quiet excitement in the family's den with herself, her mom and dad all staring at a snowy, static picture on the television, its channel control set to 26. Then—voilà! There it was, the first picture broadcast from the Pappas family's new television station: color bars, shown when television stations went on-and-off-the-air, in the early morning and at midnight. They let out a collective cheer, and while Kathy smiled, her parents' faces beamed like bright lights on a black, moonless night. The last time Kathy had seen her parents with those radiant smiles and happiness on their faces was when they brought her baby sister, Dena, and later her baby brother, Jimmy, home from the hospital as newborns. In her mind, this was a parallel situation. A new television station was born, letting out its "first cry" that night. Its call letters—KMPH—stood for Mike, Pete, and Harry (the name suggested by their sister, Mary, as they all had sat around a family dinner one evening brainstorming ideas for the new station's call

Harry J. Pappas with one of the first cameras used at the KMPH-TV channel 26 studios after its launch in 1971. Harry's knowledge, research, enthusiasm and inspiration convinced his brothers Pete and Mike to launch KMPH-TV 26. As President of Pappas Telecasting Inc., he led the station to stratospheric success in later decades as the flagship station for the largest privately-owned television station group in the United States. Photo Courtesy: Harry J. and Stella A. Pappas family archives.

letters). They were three brothers and sons of Greek immigrants, whose collective dreams and hard work had culminated in the creation of a brand-new independent television station—a dream that came to fruition and went on the air that very night.

Pete and Mike had always been very happy to continue building their radio station empire. On the other hand, their brother, Harry, felt motivated to research another avenue of broadcasting. He saw opportunity for the Pappas brothers in a place Pete and Mike would have never thought to look: independent television (meaning a station not affiliated with the big three networks: ABC, CBS, and NBC). So KMPH-TV 26 was born of Harry's vision: television's allure had captivated him, and he was determined that his dream—the three brothers all succeeding in the television business—would become a reality.

But first, he must convince Pete and Mike.

They loved and respected Harry and admired his brilliant intellect. However, the twins had no experience in the independent television business and felt unsure that putting an independent television station on the air should be their next broadcast project. Using his research and knowledge, Harry knew that he had to educate them about the enormous opportunity that independent television presented and how that prospect would make them a great deal of money.

Pete, John, Harry and Mike at a KMPH-TV 26 launch party, circa 1971.

KMPH was his idea, his baby, and it was born and had grown from Harry's long days and nights of research and planning. He had contacted business executives of established and successful independent televisions stations across the country. He met with many of them personally and asked pages of questions, often returning home with multiple yellow pads full of notes. He asked them how they got started, how they programmed their stations, what obstacles they faced, how long it took to make money, and what, if they were to do it all over again, they would do differently.

Harry became the self-educated expert on independent television, carving out his own niche in the Pappas broadcasting legacy. Indeed, in later years, he surpassed his brothers in his achievements, building a television station empire and making his company, the Pappas Telecasting Company's group of affiliated stations, the largest privately held commercial television broadcast group in the United States, in terms of household coverage, as was defined by Nielsen Media Research. Just as with Pete and Mike, driven by the need for success and freedom from the poverty and hardship their immigrant parents endured, Harry's motivation also came from his determination to succeed after being relentlessly bullied in elementary school.

Pete and Mike always marveled at Harry's genius and as they grew older, the twins proudly talked up his immense success in the television broadcasting industry to everyone they met.

As Harry worked from early morning until late into the night, every night, learning and researching the television station business, by day he worked with Pete and Mike to continue the success of their two flagship radio stations, KGEN-AM 1370 and KBOS-FM 95. There were seven previous television stations that went on the air, then later off, in the Tulare-Visalia-Fresno, California, television market. Pete and Mike weren't as enthusiastic about entering the independent television field since those seven stations had failed. There was a lot of risk, and they didn't want to lose the stations they had already built. Harry studied the previous television stations' failures and was determined that the Pappas brothers would succeed, not fail. None of the three local network affiliated stations was for sale, nor could the brothers afford to purchase one, even if it were for sale. Their only option: do what they did with KBOS-FM, and build a station from the ground up.

The twins and Harry needed investors and first had the idea to approach wealthy businessmen. They sent letters of introduction and presented the opportunity of investing in KMPH to men like the movie star Gene Autry, who already owned television stations, and the Skouras brothers, Greek movie moguls who had built a theater chain and were instrumental in the management of both Warner Brothers and 20th Century Fox.

With much anticipation, they waited for a response.

They never received a reply from either Autry or the Skouras brothers.

Discouraged, Mike went to a local watering hole, bellied up to the bar, and ordered a bourbon on the rocks. He sat next to one of the most successful local farmers he knew and told him what happened.

"It seems to me," said his friend, downing a shot of whiskey, "that if you can't find one fella with $100, you can always find 100 fellas with $1 each. In the end, you'll still have your $100."

It wasn't just the proverbial light bulb that went off in his head, but 100 flashing spotlights. He and his brothers then created a plan to find smaller investors to get the capital they needed to launch KMPH. Their first group of investors were extended family and many of the self-made men the brothers had befriended, including local businessmen and farmers. The stress of building KMPH with the investment of other people's money put a huge strain on the brothers. Sleepless nights fueled by anxiety were commonplace, because the brothers were conscientious and responsible. They didn't want to lose one dollar of the investors' money, and they were committed to producing a profitable return for each.

Pete, Mike, and Harry were accustomed to, and proficient at, doing battle for radio and television construction permits (CPs) against competitors for licenses. They were tough negotiators and diligent in forming comprehensive contracts in the purchase and sale of properties. When people said it couldn't be done—whether it was selling stock to put together a television station, building new radio stations, or buying them out of bankruptcy, like they did with KGEN—that's when the Pappas brothers set out to prove they could do it.

Because of his training in Marine Corps intelligence and his three years in the Marines, Mike approached a business problem, or the building of a new radio or television station in a new market, as a commanding officer originating an attack on an enemy position in time of war. Radio stations were launched in new markets because each marketing assault was strategized and organized with the best possible equipment, programming, and army—meaning its carefully selected employees—to achieve success quickly. The Pappas brothers didn't believe in slow roll-outs of new stations.

So the brothers sold stock to local investors to put KMPH-TV on the air. These were local people—merchants, owners of family farms and businesses from Central Valley towns like Tulare and Visalia—who saw the three brothers roll into town with a few vehicles and a U-Haul trailer between them, work hard, and achieve success with KGEN-AM 1370 and KBOS-FM 95.

With KMPH, the twins and Harry utilized the same strategy and tactics as they had at KGEN and KBOS. Ever the underdogs, they initiated the station with creativity and promotions.

For the launch of "all-color KMPH-TV 26," the brothers planned three celebratory grand opening parties. Advertisers, shareholders, politicians, and prominent members of the community received beautifully engraved invitations to attend the festivities. Mike spearheaded the design of promotional materials and bartered advertising on other media outlets, which were distributed in a five-county area and featured KMPH's new logo:

- 20 billboards advertising the station's launch
- 11 branded company vehicles
- 10,000 notepads distributed to every business
- Advertising placed on 10 theater screens
- 500 special KMPH pens
- Commercials aired on local radio stations in Fresno and Bakersfield, including KGEN and KBOS
- 100 KMPH branded wall clocks placed in restaurants, night clubs, and barbershops
- 100 KMPH ties, jackets, and pocket patches provided to employees, management, and shareholders

Mike traded out the promotional advertising and materials. In a speech to shareholders before KMPH went on the air, he outlined the Pappas brothers' plans. The goal was to get as many cash contracts as possible presigned, so cash billing was established for the station. One incentive used at the start was to offer one free commercial for every five commercials purchased by clients. In his speech, Mike emphasized the importance of the shareholders' participation in the promotion of the new station, including buying commercials on KMPH for their own businesses.

With gusto and enormous optimism, the brothers launched KMPH-TV, UHF channel 26, on October 11, 1971.

Later, when the brothers needed more operating capital for new equipment and programming upgrades, they couldn't simply go to a bank and borrow the money, because Pete, Mike, and Harry each had already personally borrowed as much money as possible and bankers wouldn't extend any more credit to them. They decided to sell more ownership in KMPH-TV in the form of stock to folks that weren't already investors. They needed to widen their circle.

Mike researched and checked the Yellow Pages. He looked in the listings labeled "accountants," "attorneys," and "doctors." The brothers hosted Tuesday night VIP receptions. Mike made a presentation to the gathered group. Appetizers and soft drinks contributed to a cordial, low-pressure atmosphere. While the brothers could be hard-sell when necessary, on this night, Mike used charm and congeniality to convince their potential customers to buy. In this case, Mike sold KMPH as a money-making investment.

The invitation sent to each guest was mailed from Mike, as president of KMPH. At the VIP reception, Mike personally introduced himself to the accountants, doctors, and lawyers present.

"You've been selected by a special committee to become investors in Pappas Television Inc.," Mike began. "You were invited to tonight's meeting because we select our investors very carefully—VIP's only— and you're here tonight because you were selected by a special committee of our board of directors."

In fact, Mike was the single member of the committee.

Eager to raise money, he presented the opportunity: invest with KMPH, and the Pappas brothers will ensure you a profitable return.

With the second group of investors' money, the Pappas brothers accessed the additional capital they needed to continue building the station.

Pete and Mike also used their passion for travel by creating advertising packages they sold to local business owners. Clients were sold radio and television airtime in one-year packages (which gave the stations base billing—meaning that they started every month with business already on the books). The brothers' customers were rewarded with a group trip to the Caribbean, England, Italy, Mexico, Spain, or similar destinations. The cost of the trip was figured into the pricing of the advertising but was negotiated at such a good group-travel rate by the twins' local travel agency that their rate per spot—the cost paid per commercial—worked out to be the same as those of competitor's stations, or very close to those rates, so advertisers loved buying airtime from a Pappas station. The merchants received creative, effective television commercials that brought more customers into their businesses,

Stella A. and Harry J. Pappas, circa late 1970's, at a KMPH-TV 26 event. Stella managed the KMPH-TV 26 front office after the station went on-the-air in 1971. Photo Courtesy: Harry J. and Stella A. Pappas family archives.

and each received a free trip for two to whatever place the Pappas brothers chose that year as their destination. It was a win–win proposition before the term existed. The advertisers received more for their money than the other stations offered, and the brothers could also indulge their love of travel, seeing places they only dreamed about as poor young boys from Crows Landing Road.

The station faced many roadblocks. As the new, independent station in town, at the beginning, there were no ratings and KMPH faced programming competition from the three major network affiliates broadcasting from Fresno. Additionally, in October 1970, a cable television operator received approval from the FCC to provide television coverage to the Tulare County area by importing signals from five Los Angeles area television stations, two stations from San Francisco, one from San Jose, and one from Bakersfield.

Pete, Mike, and Harry knew foreign television signals cabled into the local television market would doom their infant KMPH. It was like an NFL team playing against a Pop Warner team from the local elementary school.

That level of competition from out of town would effectively kill KMPH before it had an opportunity to grow and succeed. The brothers, on behalf of Pappas Television Incorporated, filed a complaint against this proposed action, listing all the reasons why bringing the cable system into Tulare County would crush KMPH, its only local station, owned by local people.

In the end, the FCC ruled on behalf of KMPH and against the cable system, prohibiting the import of television stations' signals from outside the Tulare-Visalia-Fresno television market. With this victory, Pete, Mike, and Harry marched onward and upward, working 16-hour days to build KMPH. Their slogan was: *KMPH—the Independent*

Giant of the San Joaquin Valley. It wasn't just a tag line for their promotional spots on the station or for merchandise. It was their mission.

———————

Even with long hours and enormous stress building KMPH, Pete and Mike still loved spending as much time together as possible. Certainly, time together was harder to come by. In addition to their business responsibilities, they had wives and children who needed their attention. Still, the twins made time for each other. It was commonplace for Mike to think about Pete, pick up the telephone receiver, and find Pete already on the line. And the same thing happened in reverse—Pete picked up the phone to call Mike, and he was already on the line. The twins' psychic connection was a regular occurrence, with Pete and Mike coming up with the same ideas or walking to the other's office to speak with his twin and finding the other one already in the hall walking toward him.

Just as in their youth, both Pete and Mike found that their best ideas and solutions to problems always happened when the two shared their thoughts, ideas, and feelings with one another. There was Pete and there was Mike, and there was also a hybrid born from the two of them. Their best, most creative selves existed when they worked together. They were older, their lives changed over time, but the attachment between them intensified with each passing year. When they had an idea or thought, Mike called Pete and Pete called Mike, and it would always be so, they thought.

The fates still wove their tapestry and had not yet finished with Pete and Mike's destiny.

CHAPTER 22

1972:
Saying Goodbye

THE TEACHER ANSWERED THE CALL on the wall-mounted telephone in Kathy's classroom. Even with her back to the students, they could hear their teacher's conversation.

"Yes, she's here. I see. Right now? Is someone here to pick her up? We're right in the middle of a spelling test. Oh, I understand. I'll send her to the office right away."

The teacher told Kathy to get her lunch box and jacket and go to the office. Her mother was there waiting for her.

Kathy packed quickly. She knew something was terribly wrong. Her mother never picked her up from school.

Never.

If she or her siblings missed the bus either in the morning or after school, they had to walk to or from school. Their mother, Noula, told them the exercise, sunshine, and fresh air were good for them. She wasn't going to indulge their lack of discipline and give them a ride to school or home when they knew full well they should take the bus.

When Kathy arrived at the school's office, her mother's face was pale and strained.

She took Kathy by the hand, and they walked outside to stand under the shade trees that lined the school driveway where she had parked the family car.

Noula knew her twelve-year-old would be the most upset of their four children. The other three children were waiting inside the principal's office and were yet to hear the news. Kathy was the oldest and had the closest relationship with Titika and the most memories of her. She put her arm around her daughter.

"Kathy, your *yiayia* is gone."

"She's gone? She's not at *Thea* Mary's anymore?"

Noula sighed as she stroked her daughter's long, brown hair.

Titika had survived a stroke a few years earlier that left her bedridden. She needed round-the-clock care.

Pete, Mike, Mary, and Harry and their respective spouses had gotten together after Titika's health deteriorated and decided the best care she could receive was with her daughter, Mary. Mary had three little ones at home; Mary's husband, Mike, worked full time as a pharmacist, and she herself had recently enrolled in nursing school. She quit nursing school to take care of their dearest mother, whose every breath and moment in life was dedicated to her husband, their home, and raising their four children. The brothers pledged to help financially and to visit as much as possible.

Placing her hands now on Kathy's shoulders, Noula looked into her daughter's eyes.

"Kathy, your *yiayia* has passed away. She is in heaven now with God and the blessed *Theotokos*, our ever-Virgin Mary. She is not at Thea Mary's anymore. Only her body remains but her spirit still lives. She is in heaven now. She isn't sick or suffering anymore."

Kathy, stunned and silent, stood quietly. Her heart ached for her *yiayia* whom she would see no more on this Earth and for her father, Mike, who she knew was devastated. Her father, uncles, and aunt adored and revered their mother, Titika, and their father, John. As their mother, Titika was the core and soul of the family. Everything they knew, everything they were, everything they believed, was rooted in the teachings and love they received unconditionally from their parents Titika and John.

And now she was gone.

"How is Daddy doing? How is *papou?* How is everyone? Does Johnny know? Do the kids know?" ("The kids" were what Kathy called her younger siblings, Dena and Jimmy.)

Noula embraced her daughter.

"My little mother, always worrying about everybody else. Your daddy is sad, but he will be okay. We are all sad, but we will be okay. *Yiayia* is young, happy, and healthy in heaven now, just like she was when she was a young girl like you. She is not suffering anymore. Daddy knows this but he hurts. He will miss her. We all hurt. We all miss her. I want you to wait here. I am going to get the other children so we can all go home together, and I will tell them about *yiayia* there. The little ones are too young to understand but I will try to tell them."

———————

The funeral was held in Los Angeles. In the year prior to her death, John had selected two burial plots at Forest Lawn Cemetery.

"A man must choose his final home for himself and his wife," he said at the time.

John and Titika had grown old, and it was wise to prepare for their final journey to the Lord. A practical man, he didn't want to burden their children with those details, so he took care of it with his daughter, Mary, and son-in-law Mike while he was visiting them to see Titika. It was hard to see the vibrant young girl he married now ill. He was older than Titika but healthier, so he took care of the particulars. They had a hard life together, but it was a good one. The Lord blessed them with four wonderful children. No man or woman were more blessed than he and Titika, but their time was near. It would be hard to say goodbye to the woman who shared his life and bore his children. She was the perfect wife to him and a devoted, dutiful, and loving mother to their children. When he looked at icons of the blessed *Theotokos* and ever-Virgin Mary, John thought of his wife, Titika. The love the *Theotokos* had for her son, Jesus Christ, paralleled the love Titika bore for Pete, Mike, Mary, and Harry. And soon, it would be time for him to say goodbye to his children and grandchildren—for now. He knew he would see Titika again when he went, by God's grace, to heaven. He was certain she would be there waiting for him.

Kathy had never seen her family so overcome with grief, the grown men and women of the family crying as they remembered and mourned Titika, and especially when they all traveled to the funeral home and saw her in the casket for the first time. She had never before seen her father break down and she never wanted to see it again.

Most of Titika's grandchildren were too young to go to the funeral, so Mary and Mike arranged for a family friend to watch the children at their home in Alhambra during the sacramental funeral service at St. Anthony's Greek Orthodox Church in Pasadena.

The previous evening, they asked Kathy and Johnny if they wanted to attend the funeral. Kathy said "no" and Johnny said "yes." Kathy didn't want to see her *yiayia* in the casket again. She wanted to remember all the times her *yiayia* laughed as they watched *I Love Lucy* together; all the times Titika laughed until she cried watching her grandchildren's antics; all the times she hugged and kissed Kathy all over her face and called her *"matakya mou"* (my eyes) and squeezed her so hard she thought she might stop breathing; all the times she taught her songs in Greek, like the *fegaraki* (little moon) song or the *papakia* (the little duck) song; how she taught her the Greek alphabet and showered her with love, love, love, because that was Titika's greatest gift: she loved with every cell in her body, down to the essence of her soul.

Kathy knew Titika was in a better place, but she missed her terribly and didn't want to show weakness by crying at the funeral. She wanted her father to mourn his mother without worrying about his daughter, and her *papou* to mourn his wife without worrying about his grand-daughter, so she stayed home with the younger kids. She told her parents she would help take care of her siblings and cousins. They didn't doubt her because she always helped her mother. That day would be no different as far as they knew. But she knew the real reason.

Kathy wanted to hold on to her *yiayia*'s love that lived inside of her, and she didn't want to think about death or that she wouldn't see her anymore.

It was too much.

Kathy wanted to remember Titika's love and nothing else.

CHAPTER 23

1972:
A Work Ethic and Self-Made

As TIME PASSED, Pete and Mike never forgot their humble beginnings, regardless of their financial success. With their mother's passing and their father aging, their credo to never forget where they came from became more poignant and urgent. Whether dealing with Ivy League–educated attorneys in negotiations for buying or selling stations or with local farmers and merchants, inside Pete and Mike lived two poor boys from the immigrant neighborhoods of Crows Landing Road who never forgot their beginnings. Their extroverted personalities were unchanged by their business accomplishments and, at times, caused misunderstandings with some who found them too outgoing and dogmatic and judged them wrongly for it. Most folks appreciated them for their forthrightness and perseverance. They were determined not to be hypocrites, but rather to live life by their own rules and to always forge ahead, whether people appreciated and approved of them or not. Pete and Mike detested snobs and they treated all people with the same respect, whether they earned their money themselves, inherited it, or were working class.

They didn't tolerate those with inherited wealth looking down on them or other hard-working folks pursuing their version of the American Dream.

Neither of the three brothers sought to take on vocal minority groups but were forced to do so when the license renewal for KMPH-TV was challenged. One radical group that gained steam in the 1970s targeted broadcasters like the Pappas brothers, attempting to persuade the FCC to take the licenses of stations away from current license holders and to instead give those broadcast licenses to their group. Their leaders asserted they should receive entitlements, like television station licenses, that would provide them with opportunities they hadn't received before, due to past mistreatment of their ethnic group or race. These opportunities and preferences, they believed, should include preferential consideration for construction permits for radio and television stations, even though they had zero broadcasting or television station operations experience. Additionally, it was thought more advantageous for them to exert control over or seize stations that were already operational and successful. Consequently, they filed complaints at the FCC against current, licensed owners of broadcast outlets, when the renewal process for those radio or television licenses came due. The group that targeted KMPH-TV also filed complaints against other stations in California.

Pete, Mike, and Harry felt livid.

They fought back with every legal weapon available to keep the license for KMPH-TV, the station they metaphorically gave birth to, and had fought so hard to make successful.

They didn't believe this group deserved preferential treatment over other immigrant groups. Why should their struggle be any different from that of any other immigrants? When European immigrants, including Greeks, struggled and worked hard to achieve success, why should the government grant other ethnic groups special treatment?

In their legal documents, the group that filed a complaint against KMPH argued that licenses should not be renewed to current owners, even if there was no reason not to do so, and that radio and/or television station licenses should be taken away from owners like Pete, Mike, and Harry and their shareholders, and instead given to *their* group. The purpose of seizing the licenses and stations was to right the wrongs of the past which, in their view, favored Caucasian owners who didn't provide enough programming to serve non-Caucasian viewers, particularly Latino and African-American audience members. Their complaints also alleged that targeted stations, including KMPH, didn't employ enough minorities in staff and management positions, even though, in the case of KMPH, the station did attempt to recruit from local minority groups by advertising open positions in publications that were popular with those specific populations.

KMPH, still a new station, only had a staff of 25 people. In one of its responses filed with the FCC, KMPH listed the ethnicity of the station's non-Caucasian staff and management as five Mexican-Americans (a film editor, a camera operator, an on-air personality who doubled as a producer, and two office administrative assistants), plus two Japanese-Americans. It also stated that there were no African-Americans on the staff because none had applied for any of the advertised positions, and that the station had retained all applications and resumes of applicants for the time required by law and the Equal Employment Opportunity Commission. (The station's EEO (Equal Employment Opportunity) plan was submitted to the FCC on October 28, 1971.)

KMPH shareholders had invested in the station because they thought the area was long overdue for a local television station, so they placed their faith, and their dollars, with Pete, Mike, and Harry, to launch the station and guide it to financial success. They wanted a profitable return on their investment. Predictably, they supported the brothers' fight against the special interest group filing against the station at the FCC. They knew the Pappas brothers would never capitulate to any group attempting to wrest control, and ownership, from the share-holders and the Pappas brothers.

Harry reigned over KMPH as general manager and directed the station's response to the complaint both at the FCC and locally. KMPH's Washington, D.C., based FCC attorneys countered the group's assertions by showing that the station aired Spanish language programming four hours a day, had recently hired a husband-and-wife team to produce and star in a Japanese language talk show originating from KMPH, and was executing EEO plans to recruit employees of *all* ethnicities and races.

Harry also met personally with representatives from the local group who wouldn't back down from their minimum demand—that KMPH, the Pappas brothers, and KMPH's local shareholders would all agree to a "statement of policy" granting the group permission to exert control over the station's hiring and daily programming.

Harry assured them that the Pappas brothers and KMPH's share-holders would *never* surrender to their demands.

The group held an inflammatory protest at the local community college. At one point, another protest even occupied the station's parking lot. One of KMPH's Spanish-speaking administrative assistants found group members gathered in the parking lot and, feeling fearful of their presence, asked Harry to escort her out to her car. When they entered the parking lot, they found a dozen or so younger protestors taking pictures of Pete's car (a Mercedes), leaning against it, and potentially damaging it.

Harry asked them to move away from the car because it wasn't their property and told them they were also trespassing by protesting in KMPH's parking lot, which was not public property.

He remained calm and polite.

Nevertheless, the group belligerently continued its protest against KMPH while sitting on, and leaning against, Pete's car.

Harry asked his assistant to mediate since she spoke Spanish, but the group wouldn't leave the premises, so he asked her to go into the station and call the police. He waited outside for their arrival. The group quickly dispersed when Visalia Police Department squad cars pulled into KMPH's parking lot. Harry requested that the police department increase patrols around the station indefinitely, and it agreed to do so.

Both sides continued presenting their cases to the FCC. One letter, submitted on behalf of the Pappas brothers, was especially powerful, as it was written by a local Mexican-American owner of a Mexican food-manufacturing company who had hired Pete to serve as vice president of the company:

"...It has come to my attention that a complaint was filed against KMPH-TV 26, Visalia, California.... It is my understanding that this organization implies that Pappas Television Inc., permittee of Channel 26 TV, discriminates against Mexican-Americans, has no concern for the poor, and uses underworld tactics. Mr. Pete Pappas let me read the demands this group presented to the T.V. station, and I feel they are utterly ridiculous."

The letter continued: "I have been running my business for approximately 21 years, and of all of the people I have known and been associated with, I could think of no one better qualified than either of the three Pappas brothers, to bring into my organization. Since the company is mainly made up of Mexican descent employees, I definitely could not hire someone to fill this high position [Vice President–General Manager] who would be prejudiced and discriminatory against Mexican-Americans or other ethnic groups.

"I have known the three Pappas brothers—Pete, Mike, and Harry— for several years. They are of Greek ancestry—their parents being foreigners. I know the Pappas brothers do not believe in discrimination of any sort, period. This statement being substantiated by the fact that the two radio stations, owned by the Pappas brothers, employ Mexican-Americans, Portuguese, and [people of] other ethnic backgrounds...."

The letter concluded: "When the discriminatory accusation was brought to my attention, I became very upset and felt a letter stating the facts as they are might help to clear up this matter. Anyone making remarks of this nature, simply is not aware of the facts. Someone with a prejudiced attitude certainly would not or could not be associated with these firms." (Letter of April 7, 1972)

After reviewing all the presented documents and letters in support of the Pappas brothers, the FCC dismissed the complaints against KMPH's license.

KMPH-TV Channel 26 was the sole station that didn't sign hiring and management agreements with the group that challenged KMPH's license, or with any other groups.

Just like their childhood fracases, as broadcasters and businessmen, Pete, Mike, and Harry didn't like being pushed around or threatened. In this particular business battle, they fought hard—and won.

Pete, Mike, and Harry's views toward minority preference in ownership and hiring were well known—they opposed it. While this was perceived as racism by some, the brothers simply didn't see any difference between the prejudice directed at them throughout their childhood and teen years and that aimed at vocal minorities of the 1960s and 1970s. If the Pappas brothers could overcome the same disadvantages of poverty and prejudice, they believed, then it was possible for anyone to do so.

The brothers tenaciously worked hard to achieve success despite nasty names like *dirty Greeks* being hurled at them daily as youngsters and teens. They grew up in mixed racial neighborhoods in south Modesto, not in the middle-class or affluent parts of town. Although raised in a poor family, they were taught the importance of hard work, dignity, duty, honor, moral standards, and ethics rooted in their culture and their Orthodox Christian faith. They never believed they could fail at *anything* they pursued, because they were gifted with a mother and father who believed in them. If they could pull themselves up and out of the poor side of town working in America's free enterprise system, then others could do it, too. Prejudice was no excuse. Just because people might underestimate someone because of the color of their skin, nationality, or religion, those were not reasons for failure.

If someone used those excuses to fail, the failure was theirs and theirs alone.

Pete, Mike, and Harry truly believed that the most important power any immigrant or ethnic group could possess was "green power"—the power of earned money or wealth. When all Americans, regardless of national origin, race, or ethnic heritage, earned economic success, they would be like all other immigrant Americans who came before them, and their color or ethnicity wouldn't matter. Their friends Toby and Stella Castillo, who had built a chain of Mexican restaurants from the ground up in the Central Valley (Toby's immigrant father had done the same), were proof that with hard work, dedication, and fulfillment of a need, anyone could be successful. In the case of this Mexican-American family, their authentic and delicious Mexican food, served in clean, welcoming restaurants to customers treated hospitably, resulted in immense success for them.

Mike and Harry later encouraged Pete to participate in a forum at an upcoming California Broadcasters convention. At the convention, Pete debated a representative of a militant group challenging broadcasters both at the FCC and in court to take their radio and television licenses away.

He was the only broadcaster willing to do so.

Mike enjoyed watching his twin brother speak on behalf of the broadcasters gathered in the room.

During the forum, Pete told the group's representative and the audience that anyone can be successful if they work hard enough.

"Look, I'm a Greek-American," he said, "and in addition to co-owning and operating our radio and television stations, I'm vice president of a tortilla factory that makes tortillas in over 50 brands for Mexican-American people. Why was I hired by this local, hard-working Mexican-American family? Because the owners saw how hard my brothers and I work (just like their family) and [noted] that every business we've started, including KMPH-TV 26, is financially successful, and that's what they wanted for their business."

The group's representative at the forum said that a Greek making tortillas shouldn't be permissible.

"It should be a Mexican-American making Mexican tortillas for their people, and not a Greek."

Pete smiled, then responded: "If you are smart enough and work hard enough to make tortillas for your own people and make money, you should do it, but until then if a Greek sees an opportunity, he'll take it, even if it is making tortillas for your people."

While Pete's opponent was visibly upset with that remark, the debate was civil and ended with the two shaking hands at the center of the stage. Later that night, Pete elbowed up to the bar where his debate opponent sat with a friend, and Pete's conviviality eventually won them over, the three of them spending much of the night telling each other jokes and laughing the night away.

In the end, the Pappas brothers persevered.

CHAPTER 24

1972–1973:
Love, Support, and Fear of Failure

JUST AS STEEL BEAMS SUPPORT the structural integrity of the tallest and grandest skyscrapers, the support of their wives to Mike, Pete, and Harry was no less critical. All three worked long hours and took great financial risk because they were determined to succeed for both their investors and themselves. One Saturday night after a particularly harrowing week, Mike and Noula drove to a big Armenian-American dinner dance. Mike was feeling a bit melancholy. KMPH had been on the air just a short time, business was arduous, and he feared failure.

He couldn't let the 113 small investors who had placed their faith, trust, and money with the Pappas brothers, lose their money. That loss would be the brothers' loss too, because they had borrowed against KGEN and KBOS. Thus, a bankruptcy of KMPH meant they would lose KGEN and KBOS as well. Everything they dreamed of, worked for, and achieved would be lost if Mike and his brothers couldn't get better ratings for KMPH and take in more advertising dollars as a result.

On the way to the dinner dance, he told Noula how bad the work week had been, and how he feared for their future. He hoped their hard work would pay off, but he wasn't sure it would.

Mike was, as always, worried and anxious.

His palms felt cold and clammy as he held the steering wheel tightly.

"Be prepared, because we may lose everything—everything we worked for, everything we sweat for," he told Noula.

She moved closer to Mike, held his arm tight, and looked over at him as he drove.

"When I married you, you had nothing—we only had each other," Noula said. "Now we have four children, we have your brothers, and if we were to lose everything today, knowing you and your brothers, in five years, you'll have started again, and you'll be successes in the future. But whatever happens, honey, I'll always be by your side."

Mike had always respected his wife's strength, love, and support, but at that moment, he particularly admired her, and felt that he could conquer the world if his dear Noula was at his side.

During the early years of KMPH, Mike, as all the brothers, worked late into the night and came home exhausted and stressed. He only slept five or six hours and went back to work. When he labored to find investors for KMPH, he stopped his early-morning routine of going to the gym. Introduced to smoking by his brother Pete in high school (who began smoking when a girlfriend shared her cigarette with him at Modesto High School), Mike chain-smoked two packs a day (as did Pete), and they both ate for comfort and stress relief. They knew smoking, even though advertised in the 1950s as "cool" and healthy, was bad for their health. They couldn't focus on living a healthier lifestyle when their job was to build KMPH into a profitable television station.

The twins both gained weight and smoked constantly at work and at home. Pete beat Mike to the 300-pound mark, but Mike wasn't far behind.

Bessie and Noula feared the outcome of Pete and Mike's excessive weight gain and smoking. But while each might say something privately to their husbands, sharing their worries about the twins' health, they were told all would be fine and the twins would work on quitting smoking and losing weight when KMPH was "in the black."

On weekends, Mike, unlike Pete, spent much of the time sleeping, exhausted from the work week. His body was also rebounding from diet pills—amphetamines—that he stopped taking on weekends. Amphetamines were often prescribed by physicians in the 1960s and 1970s to help patients lose weight. The brothers' advertising parties gave the twins ample opportunity to enjoy rich, fatty, buttery foods and hard liquor as they drank at Pete's commercial-style bar in his home's game room. They concentrated on enjoying life with each other. Counting calories and physical fitness weren't even considerations. Pete and Mike, who had been thin and in good physical condition all their younger lives, watched the numbers on their bathroom scales creep upward as they entered their thirties.

Pete often warned Mike about taking diet pills. He thought they were dangerous and tried to talk his brother out of taking them. At one point, Noula was so worried she called his doctor and told him how the pills exhausted Mike on the weekends when he took a break from them. Mike's doctor assured her that the pills were safe and she shouldn't be concerned. While Mike was losing weight from taking the amphetamines prescribed to him, Noula innately knew the pills were harming her husband. Deep down, Mike feared the pills' long-term effects, so he didn't take them on the weekends. His body eventually crashed from being on a metabolic high five days a week. At a follow-up appointment, his doctor once again reassured him the pills were safe and would help him lose weight.

He lost weight in the short term but paid a price for it in years to come.

CHAPTER 25

1973-1974:
Hollywood Comes to the Valley

ALONG WITH KMPH ITSELF, the Pappas children were growing. KGEN's Kathy was only 10 years old when KMPH launched in 1971. The station became her small-town link to Hollywood, and she found it thrilling that television programming sales reps came to the family's independent TV station in Visalia to sell programming. Reps from Warner Brothers, 20th Century Fox, and others paid the station a visit before every new television season. The various studios owned programming, usually old films and television shows, that they packaged up and sold to independent television stations. Some were also sold to network affiliate stations that didn't have as much time to fill as independents. While viewers now have access to thousands of both old and new television programs and films through cable television and streaming services, it's hard to imagine that during the early 1970s, there were only local television stations to air programs. In Tulare and Fresno counties, there were four television stations, including independent station KMPH-TV 26. There was no cable TV, no satellite TV, no streaming services, and no VCRs, DVRs, or Blu-ray players.

If viewers missed a show, they missed a show, and they had to wait until it came back as a rerun. With such a limited choice of channels, it was both a privilege and exciting for rural cities like those in the San Joaquin Valley to have an independent television station offering programming, in addition to the big three national network stations. Locally, before KMPH launched in Visalia, all television stations in the middle of California's Central Valley were located in Fresno, an hour's drive north.

After KMPH got into the black and was making money, Harry later created a new company called Pappas Teleproductions (PTP), born out of KMPH and originally created to produce commercials and promotional announcements (called "promos") for KMPH exclusively. After a short time, he saw the potential profit the company could make selling PTP's commercial production services to businesses requiring television production, not just for use on KMPH, but also on the ABC, CBS, and NBC affiliate stations in Fresno and even statewide. With PTP's location in a Central Valley town (but only three hours north of Los Angeles and four hours south of San Francisco), PTP's production costs were low, but its production values high, so PTP attracted the attention of independent productions and advertising agencies in both Los Angeles and San Francisco.

PTP's low production costs and high quality were why Chuck Connors, an actor best known for the television series *The Rifleman,* came to Visalia for a few days to shoot a pilot for a new television series.

The children stayed home with a babysitter while Noula and Mike met the actor at their favorite hangout in Visalia, a bar/restaurant on the "good" side of town. The requisite list of regular barflies and party girls (although most were too old to be called *girls*) were at the bar, all there either by coincidence or tipped off by someone at the restaurant that the actor was there, and all were very willing to share their affections with a TV star. There was an abundance of hanging on, cleavage spilling out of tops, kisses, and perhaps invitations for private rendezvous.

Mike always got along with everyone, the gift of a great salesman, and he talked with each person he met sincerely, asking the right questions (all people enjoy talking about themselves, one of the first rules a salesperson learns in training). He also had an easygoing, affable personality. Connors had met Mike earlier in the day at KMPH and warmed up to him quickly. Not knowing anyone in town (an actor's life on sets and in hotel rooms can be a lonely one), he eagerly accepted his invitation for a night out on the town. When he saw Mike and Noula arrive and walk over to the bar, he strolled over to them and shook Mike's hand. After chatting for a few minutes, the actor was respectfully enchanted by Noula, knowing she was Mike's wife. Noula was dazzling. Beautiful, sexy, and demure, Noula was the only woman in the bar not fawning and falling all over him. Being used to an overabundance of willing and friendly attention from all types and ages of women, he really didn't understand this woman who didn't act like any other woman he met in social situations. Noula's unique Grecian beauty and charm captivated most men, just as it had Mike the first time he saw her, and Mike, unlike most men who would be jealous of others staring at their wives, always considered it a great compliment to him that men found her alluring. After all, he had won her and she would go home with him that night—and every night—so what did it matter if other men stared at and desired her?

When Mike's back was turned, Connors coyly flirted with Noula and asked for a kiss.

She charmingly smiled and said, "No."

He smiled and said, "Why not? Do you know who I am?"

She turned her head to the side, smiled, and said very sweetly, "I know who you are, but I won't kiss you because I'm married, and I only kiss my husband." She gave him a quick kiss on the cheek. The actor threw his head back, laughed, and raised his glass, toasting Noula.

Mike looked over his shoulder, saw the look Noula gave him, and when she said, *"Epeetah,"* meaning "later," to him in Greek with a wink, he knew the usual flirtation had taken place, and his wife had yet again sweetly rebuffed another suitor, a television star notwithstanding.

CHAPTER 26

1974–1976:
Going Home to Where
the Dream Was Born

AFTER MAKING KMPH A TOP-RATED and profitable operation and with
Harry at the helm to continue building upon its success, the brothers
wanted to buy another AM-FM radio station combination: two stations, consisting of one AM and one FM radio station. Because they
already owned the combination of KGEN-AM and KBOS-FM serving
the Tulare–Visalia radio market, FCC rules dictated they couldn't own
other radio stations in the area. Thus, the brothers started searching for
a radio station combo elsewhere in the San Joaquin Valley. As general
manager of KMPH-TV, Harry was primarily responsible for the successful operation and continued growth of the station. Pete managed
moneymakers KGEN and KBOS. Mike was ready for a new challenge,
and the brothers wanted their broadcasting business to grow.

From their longtime friend, the broadcast engineer Cecil Lynch
(who earlier helped them with the construction permit for KMPH),
Pete, Mike, and Harry learned that two stations were being sold by the
estate of the late Bill Bates (who had put the station on the air in
the 1930s)—KTRB-AM and KTRB-FM in Modesto, the same station the twins toured as youngsters that fueled their boyhood dreams

of radio broadcasting careers. Pete, Mike, and Harry, with investment from local partners, formed Big Valley Broadcasting and bought KTRB AM-FM in 1974. Of the three brothers, Mike was the turnaround man. Consequently, he moved his family to Modesto to work the Pappas brothers' magic on KTRB AM-FM.

In 1973, when the movie *American Graffiti* (rumored to be based on writer/director George Lucas's teen experiences in his hometown of Modesto) was released, it rebooted the 1950s in American culture. The hit television show *Happy Days,* debuting in 1974, also helped bring the 1950s to life again in popular culture. Many kids and teens of the 1970s fell in love with the 1950s and lived there in their fantasy lives, listening to the era's singers on greatest-hits LPs and on the radio. At dances patterned after sock hops of the 1950s, girls dressed in poodle skirts and boys were attired in dungarees, T-shirts, and black leather jackets. Their parents, who grew up in that era, were thrilled the 1950s were back again. Every song brought back a special memory of their youth. Many parents didn't like the music of the 1960s and 1970s, so they got a kick watching their kids listen to the favorite songs of their teen years.

The country itself was nostalgic for the 1950s—the clothes, the cars, the music. It was a time of innocence for America's youth, when the worst trouble a teen got into might involve taking a drag on a cigarette, drinking beer on the sly, and cruising the main boulevard in cities like Modesto, which could double for any rural town in America.

Mike noticed the phenomenon and soon figured out how to make money from it.

He changed KTRB's format from the country music it played since its inception, to an oldies format playing hits from the 1950s and early 1960s. The format was simulcast (aired simultaneously) on both the AM and FM frequencies.

Mike and his daughter Kathy were much like the other parents and teens in Modesto. He loved the music of the 1950s and so did she, introduced to it by the movie *American Graffiti* and the TV sitcom *Happy Days*.

Kathy liked her generation's music. The 1970s had great musicians and songs, but she also loved the fun music of the 1950s. Teens from the later decade grew up during the turmoil of the 1960s. The assassinations of President John F. Kennedy, the Reverend Martin Luther King Jr., and Senator Robert Kennedy as well as protests against the Vietnam War dominated the headlines and changed the country's zeitgeist. It was a much more serious decade than the postwar 1950s of *Pete and Mike's Dance Time*.

Finding music for KTRB's new oldies format wasn't difficult to do since the popularity of *American Graffiti* and *Happy Days* spawned a wide selection of 1950s compilation albums advertised on television. Each album contained 20, 30, or even 40 songs, all hits from the 1950s.

Allegedly.

If they weren't hits that Mike remembered playing as a teenage DJ with his brother Pete, they didn't make it on the air. He remembered those songs and the original singers well, so after he had ordered and received the albums, Mike asked Kathy to help him pick out the best songs. They sat together near her turntable and Kathy acted as DJ, playing the songs Mike selected on each album. He asked her to take notes (as she always did for him throughout her childhood, with what he called her "beautiful penmanship") and make a list of the top songs he selected from all those albums. Only the hit songs he had played as a teen DJ aired on KTRB.

Mike took the albums with the chosen songs to the radio stations the next day. His program director followed his instructions, since Mike knew the oldies format better than the PD did, and they proceeded to transfer the oldies onto eight-track cartridges that played music on the station using the latest high-tech track machines. Mike knew Kathy loved the music of that era, so he later brought the albums home and gave them to her.

When the 1950s fad passed, Mike's task was to choose a new format for KTRB to replace the oldies format that was initially so successful. By this time in radio history, FM radio was well on its way to becoming king of the airwaves, so the brothers stopped simulcasting KTRB-AM on the 104.1 FM frequency and cleverly changed the call letters to KHOP-FM (with FCC approval); the "HOP" was intentional. They programmed it to play current pop and rock hits. Consequently, it didn't make good business sense to program KTRB with music. Mike did his market research and talked about it with Pete and Harry. His recommendation was to program KTRB-AM 860 with a talk radio format, although not your typical one of the times, which featured interview programs and shows focused on the personality of the host.

Mike was a fan of controversial talk radio and enjoyed listening to it when he visited Los Angeles and San Francisco during business trips. After presenting the case for a controversial talk radio format to Pete and Harry, they all decided quickly and decisively that a provocative talk format would take KTRB into the ratings stratosphere.

Mike arranged for local talent because, unlike many radio stations in small to midsized radio markets, he didn't want to use what broadcasters called "canned," syndicated shows of the day. He only used them during non-peak radio listening dayparts: from 6:00 p.m. to 7:00 a.m. on weekdays and on weekends. His goal was to have a slate of local, talented people whom he could mentor.

More importantly, he wanted them to have polar-opposite opinions and philosophies.

Controversy created talk in the community, and when people talked about what they heard on a radio station, other folks subsequently tuned in who weren't previous listeners. The result? Ratings, and thus profits, went up. After making calls and interviewing folks who he thought were good communicators and possessed the potential for building a following on a local radio talk show, he settled on two important local people—the president of the local chapter of the John Birch Society, a politically right-wing group, and the president of the local chapter of the National Organization for Women (NOW), a politically left-wing group. All the station's talent, from early morning to early evening, Monday through Friday, was locally sourced.

Mike strategized the best way to launch KTRB's new talk format. Following the Pappas brothers' modus operandi of publicizing a new radio station or format from its very first day, he initiated an extensive advertising and promotional campaign. Soon, KTRB's new slogan, *Talk Radio 860 KTRB*, could be found all over town on bus benches, the sides and backs of buses, and even on billboards and murals on buildings. He bartered advertising for the ads. Every company vehicle was painted to match, with logos prominently displayed on the sides and back of each vehicle. (All was paid for by trading the station's airtime for the graphics and paint jobs.) KTRB's format change was done with the customary Pappas brothers hoopla, including grand opening parties for local VIPs and public officials.

The new format debuted with the station's local hosts, and Mike sat in as a guest on each show for the first day. He privately had coached the hosts to be controversial, to challenge their listeners to think, and to present their views forcefully and with conviction. And, just as he thought, it worked. Phone lines lit up, and he grinned as he listened to the shows. Talk was his favorite radio format, and he thoroughly enjoyed the give-and-take between his hosts and the audience.

As his new radio personalities grew more comfortable on the air, Mike became a local celebrity himself when he went on air as a guest playing the role of devil's advocate, taking the opposite though equally extreme point-of-view, challenging both the host and the audience. On the John Birch Society's show, Mike acted as the libertarian. On the show hosted by the feminist and NOW local chapter president, he acted as the resident "male chauvinist pig," the king of all misogynists.

Mike loved it. He relished every moment of his time on the air and the controversy it created.

Pete and Mike both ran editorials at KGEN-KBOS and continued that tradition at KTRB-KHOP. Firm believers in conservative

Mike moved his family from Tulare to Modesto to launch KTRB-AM 860 as the newest Pappas brothers' station. As was the case with every station owned by the brothers, he used bartered advertising to re-brand the station. He "traded-out" the vehicles, the trailer that functioned as the mobile broadcast studio, bus benches, billboards, and KTRB's new logo. Photos circa 1976.

economic and political ideals, they felt compelled to editorialize on the airwaves of their radio stations because they were convinced that political and social movements of the times were eroding the fabric of American ideals, individual rights, and constitutional liberties. Both men became popular with listeners and local businesspeople in the mostly rural, agricultural area, which was predominantly conservative, regardless of Democrat or Republican Party affiliation. The twins, outspoken in their private lives, even wrote editorials reflecting their opinions. They were forceful yet not argumentative. Mike's editorials were also printed in a local, Stanislaus County weekly newspaper. The column, called "Open Mike by Pappas," was labeled as an editorial opinion. Their editorial commentaries were meant to elicit thought and emotion from their listeners, but not to incite anger or altercations.

One day a man showed up at the KTRB-KHOP studios clearly angry and actually packing heat, but it wasn't in response to their commentaries. The fellow was furious that he lost his job when Mike and his brothers bought the stations and terminated the employment of staff not meeting the brothers' high standards. Fortunately, Mike kept his cool and calmed the man down, escorting him out of the stations' building on Norwegian Avenue, while keeping an eye on the man's hand and the gun holstered at his hip.

Following what could have been a disastrous confrontation with an angry and unbalanced ex-employee, Mike got his own concealed weapons permit and began carrying a pistol with him at all times. Pete and Harry did the same. Trained in the Marines, Mike knew how to shoot calmly and with precision. He also practiced shooting at targets regularly.

He'd never use the pistol unless he, his family, or his staff were in danger, but Mike wasn't afraid to aim and pull the trigger if necessary.

The Pappas brothers weren't concerned with negative reactions to their commentaries. They believed it was their duty to challenge inequities or injustices, whether political or social in nature. Pete and Mike welcomed controversy and dissenting opinion. They always practiced freedom of speech and freedom of the press. These were freedoms that had helped make America the greatest country in the world. Their neighbors might disagree with Pete and Mike's editorial opinions, but they could still get together with them for an enjoyable Saturday barbecue.

America wasn't a place where a person might disappear in the middle of the night or get savagely beaten or shot because they had a differing opinion.

The twins didn't expect every listener to agree with them, and they weren't intimidated by those who disagreed or who insisted that controversial shows be taken off the air. Pete and Mike had fought hard as youngsters to be accepted as sons of Greek immigrants who were proud Americans. They were no more intimidated by those who might oppose their views than their forebears were when fighting for freedom from the Ottoman Empire.

They knew that it was part of a Greek's DNA to never surrender.

Pete and Mike didn't hesitate to use the power of their own local press—meaning their radio stations—to air editorials, because they hoped to inspire positive change at the local, state, or even national level. They felt it was their duty, as local licensees of the public airwaves, to do so. One of Mike's earliest campaigns on KTRB-AM was to put pressure on the City of Modesto to remove its parking meters from downtown, which is something downtown merchants felt was essential to the redevelopment of the city's center as a vibrant shopping area. Because the city's residential development was moving north, shopping centers and the local mall emerged there, luring merchants to move north along with their customers.

At each new shopping venue in northern Modesto, parking was free.

Mike spent many of his early mornings in downtown Modesto coffee shops connecting with local business owners (just as he and Pete did when putting KGEN and KBOS on the air in Tulare County). He listened to their concerns and, being a business owner himself, often adopted their causes. He made a trade deal to produce buttons with a "no-parking meters" graphic (an image of a hand with a thumbs-down, along with an image of a parking meter and the KTRB logo) and distributed them, with matching posters, at the KTRB-KHOP studios, at remotes, and at every downtown merchant's location. The merchants also teamed up to buy a special advertising package of commercials on KTRB, promoting the cause along with their businesses.

In his anti-parking meters editorials, Mike said that every home should have a parking meter in its backyard as an antique relic, because parking meters were an old, passé way for cities to make money.

Predictably, Mike was *not* a favorite at City Hall.

In the end, the campaign to eliminate parking meters from downtown Modesto was successful, giving the downtown merchants a more-equal opportunity to compete with stores in North Modesto that had free parking.

The anti-parking meters campaign was an example of the brothers getting involved with and leading local efforts in their communities to make them better places for everyone to live and work. At one point in their earlier days, Pete even ran for mayor of Tulare to help usher in changes he believed were needed to improve the city for all its residents. Pete and Mike could have gone to work each day and just focused on making money, which of course they did, but they were not the kind of broadcasters who got out of bed every morning, went to work, and got home without having accomplished something beyond making money. Creating talk or interest in a community cause, like opposing parking meters, was good for the city they served as licensees and for business overall.

Pete, Mike, and Harry believed broadcasters were essential servants of the public interest and functioned as the fourth estate—watchdogs of the government. Radio and televsion stations functioned as an outlet for local freedom of speech, they firmly believed. So they provided an opportunity for the little guy to have a voice. The Pappas brothers took that responsibility, and mission, very seriously.

———————

The twins, no longer living in the same town, still spoke by phone multiple times daily. Mike picked up the phone to call Pete, and he would already be on the line, having called just seconds ahead of his twin. There was an intuitive connection between the two of them, one not readily quantifiable, but which their families saw repeatedly. Whether across town or across the state, Pete and Mike's thoughts were an invisible, telepathic line of communication not heard by anyone but them. Only other identical twins understood that connection.

CHAPTER 27

1975–1977:
Together but Separate

ANOTHER PROBLEM SOON EMERGED.

Pete and Mike, both married with young children, began thinking about the future, and their heirs. The San Joaquin Valley was composed almost entirely of family businesses. The twins saw many sold or closed when families didn't have succession plans. Families and businesses were often torn apart when second-generation heirs fought with one another over control of the inherited assets and money. Businesses were lost due to family "civil wars."

Pete, Mike, and Harry (at this point Harry had no children but planned to have some in the future) consulted various tax attorneys and made their plans.

Contractually and legally, they decided to go their separate ways as owners, swapping stock and selling each other shares so that each brother had sole ownership of specific stations (some with partners they would eventually buy out). Pete became the owner of the Pappas shares in Big Valley Broadcasting, owner of KTRB-AM and KHOP-FM in Modesto. Mike became the single owner of KGEN-AM and KBOS-FM in Tulare. Harry became the sole Pappas owner of KMPH-TV. With each brother owning his own individual station or stations, they preserved their close family relationship as brothers, always relying on one another's support and talents, yet hoping to prevent future family conflict when they were no longer alive. (Pete and Mike, though still young men, always thought ahead to their deaths, having been convinced since youth that they wouldn't live long lives.)

Lack of financial and succession planning by the brothers wouldn't be the reason the second generation might implode and lose their inheritance. Hopefully, as good parents, Pete, Mike, and later Harry would teach their children how to responsibly manage the businesses and money. In the end, if the family businesses were lost after the deaths of the first generation, it would be due to the second generation's failings, not the lack of planning by Pete, Mike, or Harry.

After the ownership change, Pete and Bessie, excited to return to the Greek church and community that John and Titika had helped establish, moved to Modesto with their twin sons. Harry and Stella continued living in Visalia, since Harry was now the president and general manager of KMPH. Mike and Noula moved their family from Modesto to Visalia, a move of some 137 miles that was met with tears and hostility from their children, since all four loved living in Modesto and didn't want to leave their friends behind. Nonetheless, the family moved to Visalia, and Mike assumed daily operational management of both KGEN-AM and KBOS-FM in Tulare.

CHAPTER 28

1978:
Another Indie Station Needs Help

AFTER THE SALES MANAGER HE HIRED had proven himself competent, Mike promoted him to station manager of both KGEN and KBOS in Tulare. Always looking for another opportunity and missing the process of turning money-losing stations into winners, Mike then began a broadcast consulting business. He placed ads in *Broadcasting Magazine* promoting himself as a management consultant to radio and television broadcast groups. The first call came from an investor who represented his fellow partners, a group of senior citizens who owned independent television station KMUV-TV channel 31 in Sacramento. The fellow originally called a friend of his who had been a neighbor of Mike's and a radio broadcaster in Modesto. Mike's former neighbor gave the investor Mike's contact information, since he thought Mike might be able to help.

KMUV's investor told Mike the station was on the precipice of failure and all the investors stood to lose everything they owned, since they had personally guaranteed loans taken out by the station's management. The banks were preparing to demand payment in full, and the station's debts were a mile high. Could Mike help them?

After discussing this opportunity with Noula and Harry and negotiating his fee with the Sacramento station's owners (in a volley of phone calls), Mike started commuting to Sacramento weekly to consult with his new clients.

Noula, Pete, and Mike all supported Mike's foray into broadcast consulting, because Mike was known as a phenomenal turnaround artist in the radio broadcast business. He could take any station losing money and turn it into a moneymaker. Mike's certain success at KMUV-TV would also be a success for Pete and Harry, because when one brother succeeded, they all emotionally shared that win and were each other's biggest supporters. When Harry later dominated the independent television station industry, there were no two prouder men than Pete and Mike.

Enthused, Mike plunged headfirst into the daily management of the station.

Working eighteen-hour days, he saw the enormity of the what the investors faced. KMUV-TV Sacramento was buried in a pit of debt and required a radical change in its operations. He terminated the station's general manager and superfluous staff. He evaluated the station's programming and any contracts in force, while keeping the investors who hired him informed. With Harry's connections in the television industry, Mike reprogrammed the station using ethnic programming, mostly Spanish language, with other shows in Japanese, Korean, and additional languages. At the time, there were more than 200,000 Spanish-speaking people in the greater Sacramento–Stockton–Modesto metro area, so the bulk of the programming was tailored to that audience.

Additionally, the station aired religious programming, which paid for time on the station, providing KMUV with an influx of revenue. Since the station had terrible ratings, the stream of revenue from religious programming helped keep the station afloat. With the new programming and Pappas-proven sales training of his handpicked sales team, advertising sales revenue grew from $2,000 to $50,000 per month, which, while not enough to make it profitable, was sufficient to keep it on the air with a skeleton staff.

When Mike executed his battle plan to take the station out of debt, he would achieve his goal: make KMUV successful enough so it sold for the greatest amount of money possible. Selling the station for a decent profit would save its investors from financial ruin. The first step was to purge the station of its debts. The only way to do this was to hire attorneys and have the entity that owned KMUV-TV declare Chapter 11 bankruptcy. Doing so would pay back creditors about ten cents on the dollar, based on a payment plan established by the court. Chapter 11 bankruptcy would be the tugboat towing the ailing KMUV-TV ship, giving it a chance to reach shore, get repaired, and go to sea again with another captain at the helm. With Mike as the current captain of a financially recovering KMUV, he charted a new course for the station and steered it toward a successful horizon.

———

In a Sacramento courtroom in late 1978, during one of the bankruptcy proceedings involving KMUV, Mike felt his chest tightening.

He just shook it off.

It had been a long day and he had slept little the night before, anxiously reviewing his plans for the next day. Feeling tired and a little lightheaded was probably the result of little sleep and excessive worry.

When court was adjourned for the day, Mike walked to his car parked in the underground lot. Then he broke into a cold sweat while his chest pain worsened.

"What the hell is going on?!" he thought. He felt nauseated and "saw stars" swirling inside a black hole as he dropped to his knees. It felt like a brick wall was bearing down upon him.

He clutched his chest and grabbed the car door to pull himself back up to his feet.

He instantaneously knew something was terribly wrong and he was going to die alone in the parking garage. Was the angel of death going to succeed this time and take him to the next world?

He couldn't die alone.

Hunched over and grabbing his chest, he slowly walked back toward the stairs that brought him down into the garage. He clutched the stair rail as he pulled himself back up the stairs, step by step. He was short of breath, unable to breathe. He looked up and, though bleary-eyed, saw his assistant Sue and his friend George, one of the investors, coming down the stairs.

He again fell to his knees as he reached out to them. His vision was failing as he was losing consciousness.

"Help me, please!" he said, "I don't want to die alone."

———————

When that metaphoric wall came down on Mike, his world shattered beneath it. He was only 41 years old and had suffered a massive heart attack, putting him in the cardiac intensive care unit for two weeks and changing the course of his life forever.

Death's dark angel failed again to take Mike from this world.

KMUV-TV was a pressure cooker, and he was in the pot. Mike had been working day and night, seven days a week, at full speed, not realizing that at 41, he had the damaged heart of a man twice his age. The days of his life, like the sands in an hourglass, were close to running out.

Mike's weekly commute to Sacramento while also supervising the manager operating both KGEN and KBOS hadn't been worrisome to Noula or his brothers because he was young and energetic. But he was overweight and had since quit smoking (a result of chest pains that struck Pete the year before, frightening Mike so much that he quit smoking immediately and begged his brother to do the same—though Pete did not do so). Still, the stress of operating KMUV was taking its toll on his health. Mike was exhausted and had become short-tempered.

Mike and Noula were raising four teenagers, ages 13 to 17, so when he returned home on the weekends the house shook with doors slamming, music blaring, and the usual arguments over curfews and grades, not to mention the typical bickering between siblings over bathroom use ("Can you turn the AD/DC down, and hurry up! There's other people waiting out here!"). There were weekends when he stayed in Sacramento and Noula drove up to see him, sparing him the weekly drive to Visalia and the household commotion.

At the time, Mike thought he was managing his life and responsibilities well and weight gain was the short-term price he paid, so he could continue making a substantial amount of money for himself and his family, with the added accomplishment of turning yet another money-losing station into a winner. When that happened, KMUV's senior citizen stockholders, whom he wanted to help and with some of whom he had become friends, would recoup their initial investments. He vowed to lose weight and get into good physical condition (close to his Marine Corps fitness—which was always his goal, accounting for middle age and so forth). When he sold KMUV-TV, he would come home to build a chain of radio stations. That was his dream. After all, he had experienced this level of stress before, as when he and his brothers launched KMPH. This would end just as successfully, he was sure of it.

What could possibly go wrong? He was young and had plenty of time.

Or so he thought.

After Noula received a call from Mike's assistant that he was in the cardiac intensive care unit at Sutter Hospital in Sacramento, she sat down and cried, stunned that this had happened to her resilient husband who always seemed to carry the weight of the world on his shoulders—her very own Atlas. Then she composed herself and called their children to come into the kitchen.

At her direction, they all sat around the kitchen table, leaving the chair at the head of the table empty. That was Mike's chair. Holding back tears, she stoically told their four children the terrible news.

"Your father is all right for now but…"

She held it together for them. She had survived so much in her life as a young girl in Greece—trials like the Nazi occupation, a Communist civil war, and a long famine. As a family, they now faced a frightening reality: her husband and their father was close to death and might not survive. She asked them to band together and for the two eldest children to take care of the two younger ones and to keep the household going. They were to be good to each other, care for their pets, go to school as usual, and carry on, just as their father expected them to do. All four sat silently, with Kathy and Dena openly crying and Jimmy and John blinking back tears.

Noula called Pete, Mary, and Harry to let them know of Mike's condition. Both brothers were speechless and choked up. Mary immediately broke down crying. How could this happen to Mike? Noula told Harry she was leaving to drive to Sacramento. Since they lived in Visalia, Harry told her he and Stella would help and would check in with the children often.

After hanging up, Pete blinked back tears and quietly told Bessie, who stared at him, shocked at the news. Mike was his other half, his identical twin. For Pete, there was no living without Mike. His twin brother *must* survive, or both of their lives would be over.

Noula quickly packed and drove to Sacramento. The four children knew their father was alive, for the moment. They didn't know if he would live or die. Their powerful dad, ever the resilient Marine, ready to take on the world every day, lay in an intensive care hospital bed, connected to an IV and monitors. As the days passed, they went about their routines as normally as possible, not knowing if they would get a call to come and see him or get a call that they would never see him alive again.

While Harry and Stella were a short drive away and called to offer support, Mike and Noula's four children never accepted help during his recovery in the hospital. They followed their usual routine as much as possible, with Kathy and John going to high school every day, while making sure their younger siblings, Dena and Jimmy, got to school on time. They all worked together to keep the house clean, prepare meals, get laundry done, feed the dogs, and complete their homework as their parents expected of them. They took good care of themselves and each other.

It was two weeks before they drove up to Sacramento and saw their dad. Noula came out of her husband's room to prepare their children for what they would see.

After greeting her four children, she smiled kindly but spoke firmly.

"It is a shock to see him like this. Don't get emotional, don't cry. We have to keep him calm."

The four children looked at one another and agreed to do so.

She was right, it was alarming to see their seemingly indestructible father connected to a plethora of monitors. He looked pale and weak.

Nevertheless, they held it together.

They slowly walked into the room to the right of his bedside. Their mom went to the left and held his hand. He became emotional seeing them, choking back tears.

"My kids…."

Tears poured down his cheeks and his pulse went up but Noula reminded him, "Relax, keep calm, remember what the doctor said."

Mike took a deep breath, bringing his pulse back down. Each of his kids took turns taking his hand and leaned in for a kiss on his cheek.

"We love you, Daddy," said Kathy, speaking for herself and her siblings. "Everything will be okay, don't worry."

―――――――――

Mike had always liked to move from project to project, town to town, and he was about to do it again. This time, the project wasn't a bankrupt radio or television station, or a newborn station that must be built from the ground up. As he was driven home by Noula from the hospital where he nearly died, he thought about his new project and realized it held more value for him than any other goal he ever worked toward.

This time, his goal was to never have another heart attack.

He never wanted anything more. No goal he ever aimed at or achieved was more important than attaining just one more success. More than anything else, he wanted to live a long life and not look death in the eye again until he was a very old grandfather, a *papou*, playing games and chasing his grandchildren around the backyard, taking them to Disneyland, showing them this country he loved so much as he steered his motor home through it, and watching the children of his children grow into the next generation of the Pappas family.

Upon their return to Visalia, Noula and Mike visited his cardiologist and learned all the new rules of life for a heart attack survivor— what medicines he would take, what his new diet and exercise regime would need to be, and all the other changes he needed to make in his life, if he wanted to live. Reducing stress was a priority. While he still dreamed of building a chain of 14 radio stations, he set that goal aside to concentrate on transforming his health.

His dream, for his new post–heart attack life, was becoming healthy enough to live it.

―――――

After his recovery and with a modified work schedule, he still had to get KMUV sold for its investors.

As Mike led the station out of the red and into the black, he started contacting television broadcasters, primarily through Harry's contacts, to gauge the interest of potential buyers. The station was making money and he sought to sell the station for as much money as possible, as soon as possible. During a trip to Southern California with a KMUV-TV investor who was also an attorney, Mike met a true Hollywood character—a shrewd and very wealthy producer who entertained them at his home in Malibu, as they began talks to sell the station.

While in the middle of negotiations, the KMUV investor took out his guitar, which he had brought on the trip. Mike had seen him load the guitar into the trunk of the car and assumed it was brought along for relaxation, to be played by the investor in his hotel room or perhaps at the beach.

He discovered, embarrassingly, that wasn't the fellow's plan.

On the deck of the producer's home, the investor began playing his guitar and singing.

The Hollywood producer smiled, accommodatingly.

Mike took a deep breath and tried not to act surprised, even though he was certainly not planning on the impromptu performance.

Having been in the radio business for so many years, the three brothers were used to people wanting to be stars, either on the radio as singers and announcers or as spokesmodels and announcers in television commercials produced by their stations. Mike never expected that a successful lawyer in his sixties, participating in negotiations to earn millions of dollars for himself and his fellow investors, would stage a spontaneous audition, singing and playing his guitar. Mike later recalled that while he was negotiating for the best deal possible to make the most money for KMUV's investors from a sale of the station, his traveling companion was busy being "entertainer of the year." It became a running joke among KMUV's investors—how could they use his talents in future negotiations?

After he accomplished his goal of selling KMUV for the shareholders and extricating himself from his final responsibilities, he decided to sell KGEN-AM, the brothers' flagship station, as well as its sister station, KBOS-FM. Having already lost a literal chunk of his heart to the irreversible damage of his heart attack, the time had come to retire. He didn't know how much time he had left, so he wanted to spend it with his beloved wife Noula, traveling to all the places he wanted to see in his lifetime, both in the United States and abroad. He wanted to help his children transition from the safety of life with Mom and Dad to independent, adult lives, and, with some urgency, to also share those experiences with his twin brother, Pete.

Pete and Mike always had a psychic and emotional bond with one another, knowing how the other twin thought and felt. As youths, they shared everything—their frustrations, hopes, desires, and dreams, both conscious and unconscious. Frequently, they awakened from a night's sleep and found that each of them experienced the same dream on the same night.

Now that Mike had narrowly escaped death himself, he obsessively worried about his brother Pete. He spent much time talking, at times pleading with Pete, to have medical tests to check his own heart. Pete still smoked and was also overweight. They both had long practiced the same bad lifestyle habits and disregarded the negative effects on their health.

Mike knew it was by the grace of God, or perhaps sheer dumb luck, that he survived his heart attack. It was a frightening warning to change how he was living his life. He wouldn't have another chance.

Would Pete have such a warning?

Pete fainted once at the wheel of his car a few years prior to Mike's heart attack. Pete regained consciousness and thought nothing of it. While this episode worried his wife, Bessie, as well as Mike, Mary, and Harry, it didn't concern Pete. Mike repeatedly begged his twin brother to exercise, to lose weight, and to change his lifestyle completely. They talked on the phone daily, sometimes more than once.

Pete's response was always the same.

"I'm not the sick one, brother," said Pete. "*You* had the heart attack. Don't make yourself sick worrying about me. Just take care of yourself. I'm fine! You never have to worry, brother. I'll always be here."

Nevertheless, Mike felt uneasy and anxious. He experienced repeated nightmares of Pete going to the mountains, "someplace high" Mike said, and dropping dead of a heart attack. In his nightmare, Pete didn't get a warning heart attack like he did.

Mike frequently awakened in the middle of the night terrified, sweating, tears pouring down his cheeks, watching his brother die over and over again, in a terrible nightmare that repeated night after night, would disappear for a while, then begin again. He felt a sense of foreboding about losing his twin, as the dark angel of death stole Pete away from this life, from *him*. He prayed this wouldn't happen, that these were only nightmares, for he couldn't face life without his brother Pete, ever. He remembered what it was like when that metaphoric avalanche came down upon him as his heart attack struck, and how he fought with every breath to live.

He now feared an avalanche would not only come down on Pete but would bury him.

CHAPTER 29

1979:
The Old Warrior Fades

SINCE TITIKA BECAME ILL AND PASSED AWAY, John lived alone. He was a loner by nature, so this didn't distress him, but it did worry his children. Mary called him every morning and evening from her home in Alhambra. Noula checked in on him a few times a day by phone, and his other two daughters-in-law, Bessie and Stella, also called John. His sons Pete, Mike, and Harry talked with him every day after work. John was in his eighties and the family, having already lost Titika (who was over a decade younger than John), couldn't take for granted they would have endless time with him.

When John later suffered a stroke, he knew what it was and hoped it meant he would soon be taken by God to his new heavenly life where he would see Titika, his mother, father, sister, and brother again.

But he was not yet meant to leave this Earth.

When he awakened in the hospital, he couldn't feel the body he knew as a boy: the body whose skin was burned and browned in the hot sun; the body whose muscles cramped and ached from days and even decades of hard labor in the mines and the fields; the body whose arms embraced his wife, children, and grandchildren. This body didn't seem to be his anymore. This body didn't move as he needed. He lay paralyzed from the waist down in his bed.

How could this be happening to him? He had made mistakes, but tried to redeem himself all his life. Perhaps paralysis was his retribution, and he still must atone for lives lost at his hand in the Balkan War or at home in Crete protecting his family?

He accepted this illness if it was God's will.

———————

Pete, Mike, Mary, and Harry spent a few hours by phone debating the pros and cons of how they could best care for their ailing father. John couldn't return to his home, now that he needed round-the-clock nursing care. Harry and Stella arranged for John to move into a guest wing of their home so he still had privacy but could also be cared for by nursing assistants who worked alternating eight-hour shifts. They waited a few more days to bring up the subject with their father because they wanted to make sure he understood the severity of his condition. They also didn't want to break his spirit. Their honorable father had come to love his home in Tulare. After Harry spoke with John, his father agreed he would move in with Harry and Stella.

Over time, John's furniture, garden, fruit trees, and row of grape-vines were sold, along with the house. Pete, Mike, Mary, and Harry knew their resilient father was heartbroken by losing his home and independence. John convalesced quietly and engaged with his grand-children who were brought over to visit with him. Even when John was surrounded by family, he was contemplative. He wasn't accustomed to being inactive and unproductive. The stroke changed his life in a way he never imagined. He always thought that when it was time to die, God would take him quickly, but he knew now that wouldn't happen to him.

He didn't fear death.

He feared the act of dying.

The arrangement at Harry and Stella's home became a short-term one when the local nursing agencies couldn't provide nurses strong enough to move John frequently. Although ill, he was still a large man and was too heavy for a female nurse to physically lift and move him as required to care for him properly. Pete, Mike, Mary, and Harry faced a decision they vowed as a family to never make. They would have to choose a long-term nursing facility to care for John as his health declined.

Tears flowed.

As their parents had aged, the children pledged they would never admit them to skilled-nursing facilities. That's why Titika was sent to stay with Mike and Mary when afflicted with her stroke. With heads bowed and after much emotion shared with each other, they agreed to search for a reputable facility for John's care. They promised one another they would visit him daily and call multiple times a day. Harry and Stella would bring him home on Saturdays frequently for lunch with his family.

In the next few weeks, John solemnly accepted his fate as he was transported to a nursing home just a few miles away.

On many Saturdays, Harry arranged for medical transport to have John brought to his home for a family lunch, seating him at the head of the table. Everyone at the table—Harry, Stella, Mike, Noula, various grandchildren, and some family friends—carried on a plethora of conversations. They included John by asking him questions, taking his hand, patting his shoulder, giving him a kiss on the cheek—whatever they could do to try to engage him. In most cases, he gave a slight smile or didn't respond at all, keeping his hands folded in front of him.

One Saturday, however, was different.

The family had gathered around the table, passing bowls of Greek food to one another, cooked by Harry's wife, Stella, and her

Harry J. and Stella A. Pappas in their home in Visalia, California, prior to attending a family wedding. Photo Courtesy: Harry J. and Stella A. Pappas family archives.

mother, Mary Vouros, who was visiting from Sacramento. The next generation of the family began asking questions about the origin of the family's surname—*Pappadojiannis*. They knew it was the result of a *Papa Yanni*, the name of an ancestor of theirs who in fact was a priest called "Father John," and the family had been so honored to have a Greek Orthodox priest in the family that they took the surname of *Pappayannis*, which, over time, became *Pappadojiannis*. The question they asked their *papou* now was: what was the family's original surname? Harry remembered his father told him the original family surname at one time, but he couldn't recall what it was.

"Daddy, what was our family's original name before *Pappadojiannis?*" Harry repeated the question in Greek. *"Baba, tee etaneh to onoma tis ekoyyenias protou Pappadojiannis?"*

John didn't answer, so Harry repeated the question.

"Baba, tee etaneh to onoma tis ekoyyenias protou *Pappadojiannis?*" There was still no response from John.

Everyone began speaking at once (which happens frequently at large Greek family meals) while passing around plates of lamb, Greek salad, and *pilafi.*

"Tsafaris!" John said.

"Wait, shhh, everyone, *baba* just said something! What is it, *baba?* What did you say? We didn't hear you. Will you say it again? *Baba,* will you say it again, please?"

Everyone abruptly stopped what they were doing and saying and looked at John.

"Tsafaris! Tee onoma tis ekoyyenias protou Pappadojiannis etahneh Tsafaris!" The family's name before Pappadojiannis had been Tsafaris!

"Quick" said Harry. "Get a paper and pen—someone, write that down."

———————

The family's original name, suddenly recalled by John at one of his last family lunches, became one of the memories the children and grandchildren laughed and cried over in the days, months, and years after John's passing.

The old, proud soldier who battled in the Balkan War; worked on the railroad; dug coal in the bowels of Utah; fought to protect his crops and livestock against the bitter cold of Utah's winters; picked peaches, grapes, and every crop grown in the crushing heat of the San Joaquin Valley; and raised his children alongside his sweet Titika, with humility, dignity, and honor, left this world peacefully, in late September of 1979.

He died surrounded by his children and their spouses, all the love and tears for this gentle giant pouring out in an abundance of hugs and sobs over the loss of a truly noble man.

John was gone.

Titika was gone.

With their passing, Pete, Mike, Mary, and Harry—once the children in the family—transformed into the family's leaders. As such, they were tasked with molding the next generation, both born and unborn.

Time swept away their youth along with John and Titika.

After laying their father to rest next to their mother, through torrents of tears the family shared all they learned from their humble and noble parents—to live their lives truthfully; to treat others with respect, especially those who worked hard to rise from the purgatory of poverty; to work hard every day, because working and productivity are intrinsically dignified pursuits (God does not want his flock to be lazy); to be moral and raise their children to live their lives honorably, as their Pappadojiannis ancestors had done; and to be, as John always told his children, "an A-number-one person."

The three brothers and their sister, Mary, lived their lives with the hope that they had made their parents proud and would continue to do so. The challenge, now, was to learn to live without their father, as they had done with their mother, while carrying on the family's credo and traditions, as they continued to raise their families and build their businesses and careers.

Collectively, they agreed to share all they learned from John and Titika with their children—to emphasize their Orthodox Christian faith as the foundation of their lives and to tell them the stories and history of their family and Greek culture itself.

For Mary and her husband, Mike Alfieris, teaching their children the blessings of faith, honor, and duty came naturally, since both already lived their lives as John and Titika, and Mike's Cretan-born immigrant parents, had taught them as youths. That they would pass along those same lessons to their children was a given.

For Pete, Mike, and Harry, following their parents' footsteps in their homes happened without question. At work, they vowed to conduct their business with an ethical foundation while dealing with competitors and others that didn't have the same beliefs or values.

As they achieved their goals of greater success, they often wondered if that would change them. Would they forget all they were taught by their mother and father? The challenge was to achieve success and still be "an A-number-one person," as their father reminded them throughout their youth.

Titika had been their coach and mentor, and John their moral compass. Now that they were gone, the Pappas brothers and sister must absorb and live those roles as they raised their own children and continued building their broadcasting careers.

Would they succeed at this profound task?

They were always dreamers, planners, and doers, but fate was fickle. Would their lives to come and future generations be as successful and morally centered as John and Titika?

The future was not in their hands. Perhaps destiny would decide.

CHAPTER 30

1979–1983:
Unexpected Challenges of Retirement

WHILE MIKE WORRIED ENDLESSLY ABOUT PETE and made radical changes to his own daily routine, life changed in other ways for himself and his family after his return home and retirement. He was now home all day, every day, and this was a new world. Previously, he worked all week long, coming home only in the evenings. Now, watching the comings and goings and ups and downs of a home with four lively teenagers, he realized how much more open they were with Noula than with him, and he grew envious. Retirement was everything he hoped for, but while being home and not working proved to be a great thing for his health, at least at the beginning, it was stressful in ways he didn't anticipate. His wife and children weren't used to having him at home all the time, and he certainly wasn't used to being there. A simple disagreement between siblings would become a major conflict when Mike drew conclusions and made judgment calls too quickly and often with biting criticism. He learned that dealing with four teenagers wasn't anything like running a business and eventually realized that he didn't need to be a peacemaker.

His wife had been home with the kids for years, and let squabbles between siblings (which she wisely knew were inevitable, especially with teens) solve themselves. He was amazed to watch his children argue over the bathroom, the noise, music, what show to watch, and the family phone in one minute—and then find them all sitting together, laughing, in the next. His first two years home were difficult for the family, because his need to be more involved in his teenagers' lives clashed with their need for more independence. He forgot how he and his brother Pete had usually been on their own as teenagers, since his immigrant parents didn't fully understand the ways of American teenage life. However, he vividly remembered their teenage antics and was afraid his own children would replicate behavior that, as a parent, he didn't want to see repeated. He was a strict and unrelenting disciplinarian, resorting to Marine Corps drill instructor behavior when dealing with his kids. His own parents had given Pete and Mike freedom and independence as teens without fearing that either would do anything to bring shame upon the family.

But these were the 1970s and early 1980s, and times were different from the more-innocent 1950s when he was a teen. Mike felt afraid of what might happen to his children if they made bad choices that could perhaps lead to addiction, jail, or even death. He worried constantly about their safety and teenage rebelliousness. As the head of the family, it was his job to make sure nothing happened to any of them, even if it meant they got angry with him for his rules and restrictions. They were the next generation of the Pappas family, and in his view they should *not* act like typical teenagers. His job, as he saw it, was to be their father and not their friend. Hopefully, friendship would come later when they were adults.

However, his assumption that they should not act as typical teens led to a lot of conflict and even more rebellion. He got frustrated and angry, and so raised voices, fueled by hormones and hurt feelings, became the norm around the house.

"If you worked for me, I'd fire you!" Mike said to his children when they rebelled and resisted his control.

"If I was out in the world working, I would never work for you!" his children would counter, with that same response each time they argued with him.

After slammed bedroom doors and Mike retiring to his recliner in front of the television set, everything cooled down when Noula, acting as the family peacemaker, went from the family room to the unruly teen's bedroom for a few words and back again until there was peace in the household.

Eventually, Mike adjusted to life at home as a retiree, learning to understand everyone's teenage drama and to not react emotionally. His children also learned how to better communicate with their father.

In the five years after his heart attack, Mike was diligent about losing weight, keeping it off, and maintaining what health he had left. By quitting smoking two years before his heart attack, he had given his body more ammunition to fight the constriction of his arteries and preserve what was left of his heart muscle. He took up regular walking, stationary cycling, and swimming, significantly altering his overall lifestyle, with Noula's help, and even losing 60 pounds. He struggled to not eat what was forbidden to him, both in the type and amount of food he loved (calorie-dense, high-salt, fatty foods) and the foods he must eat to live longer (the type of food Noula always cooked—a Mediterranean diet, long before the term was popular).

Much of his discipline came from his wife's constant reminders, at his request, of what he could and couldn't eat. She admonished him by addressing him as *Manoli* (his name in Greek) whenever he disappeared into the kitchen between meals, prowling the refrigerator and cabinets, looking for a treat, but not finding any—because there were no foods remaining in the house to tempt him.

His burden to regain his good health was shared by his wife, just as every other goal or project had been since the day they married. During his most physically fit period, he was walking up to 10 miles a day. Having been in an executive management position with the resulting long hours, stress and lack of exercise through the years had greatly contributed to his health decline, and he was determined to not repeat those mistakes. He ate food for enjoyment and celebration but also at other times—to relieve stress or cope with anxiety or depression—that invariably resulted from business problems. Food was his pacifier.

During the early years of his retirement, he worked to learn, with Noula as his coach, that he needed to not live to eat, but to eat to live.

Noula was glad to see her husband lose weight, adopt an exercise program, and achieve the best health he had been in for years, all as a result of his commitment and her support of his efforts. Yet, she worried. The cardiologist warned the two of them at the start of Mike's recovery that the five-year anniversary of a heart attack was a pivotal marker for cardiac patients. Those who continued their new health regimes and remembered that no matter how great they might feel, they still had a damaged heart, usually did well in the long term. Those patients who felt great and forgot they had an injured heart and typically returned to a strenuous lifestyle of high stress and extraordinary pressure, went back to bad habits, and decided they no longer needed their medications, would inevitably and tragically suffer another heart attack. If they survived, they became long-term cardiac patients who lived chronically ill, until their damaged hearts beat no more.

CHAPTER 31

1984–1985:
Back to Work

MIKE ENJOYED HIS EARLY RETIREMENT. It allowed him to travel with Noula and to spend more time with his children, with Pete, and with the extended family. However, after the fifth anniversary of his heart attack, he began to think more seriously about money and the future.

His initial concern turned into extreme anxiety.

What if he lived to old age? He was certain his wife, Noula, would do so, as she was healthy, never smoked, and only drank a glass or two of Scotch or wine when they were out on the town socializing on weekends. Since he had retired at such a young age, he fretted he might run out of money before reaching his golden years.

He took the profits from the sale of KGEN-KBOS and invested them for the long term, but he had an expensive lifestyle—a large home in the countryside, luxury cars, and a new motor home and a boat to support his passion to travel. He was still supporting four children, with two in the middle of high school and two entering college one year apart.

Mike enjoyed the novelty of buying new clothes in smaller sizes, though he looked at his reflection in the mirror and saw himself as fat. After his weight loss, he was determined to buy himself new Levi's, the brand of jeans he and Pete always wanted as kids but could never afford, in a size that he had not been since his 30s. He was proud of losing so much weight and enjoyed modeling his Levi's for his two daughters when he got home from shopping.

"Do I look good now, Dena? Do I still look fat, Kathy?"

"Of course not, Dad. You look great!" said Dena.

"Keep up the good work, Dad," added Kathy. "We're proud of you. You don't look fat, because you're not fat anymore."

But every time he bought a new pair of pants, shorts, or a new suit, it was always the same question, "Do I look fat?" and his family repeatedly told him he wasn't fat anymore. Still, he was afraid of gaining weight back and fearful of running out of money in his senior years and being poor again. Even though he instinctually knew he should stay retired, Mike eventually decided he needed to go back to work. So he started shopping for a radio station.

In California, the cost of buying a broadcast station was prohibitive at the time. Higher prices for stations benefited him as a seller, but didn't as a buyer, so purchasing a radio station within the state was not possible. He enlisted a radio and television station broker to begin his search nationwide.

No one in the family was in favor of his return to the working world.

Noula was terrified that Mike would have another heart attack and tried to get him to reconsider his decision. She remembered what his cardiologist said about the danger of the fifth anniversary for cardiac patients, and she was afraid that this was now happening to her husband.

Petrified of losing Mike, Pete tried repeatedly to talk him out of it. He was certain that buying a radio station was a terrible decision that might kill Mike. How could Pete live without his twin brother? It was unthinkable. Harry also advised Mike against going back to work full-time, and his sister, Mary, agreed with her siblings and Noula that Mike should stay retired and focus on keeping his new, good health.

If he went back to work, Mike might be stricken with another heart attack and die this time.

He didn't understand why everyone was concerned.

He felt fine.

He would be just fine.

So he shopped for radio stations in Paducah, Kentucky; Tupelo, Mississippi; and even one in Savannah, Georgia. He loved those cities, especially Savannah. The stations didn't meet his criteria, though, so he kept looking until he found the perfect station: KZEL-FM 96 in Eugene, Oregon.

Against the advice of his wife, family, and children (who also pleaded with him to stay retired), Mike bought the station and took

At a family wedding in 1984, this is one of the last photos taken together of Harry, Pete, and Mike Pappas.

his eldest son, John, and daughter-in-law Litsa (they had married in early 1984) to help him turn the station around. As always, he knew he must take the station from the red into the black in short order.

Mike didn't feel like a man who lost part of his heart. Rather, he felt *great* and planned to build a chain of some 14 radio stations, finally fulfilling his dream. KZEL-FM was to be the flagship station of the Mike Pappas Superstations—his new broadcast group.

Mike's strategy for KZEL was the same as for any new station the brothers owned. Whether they put a station on the air for the first time or purchased a station already operational, they began a business reconnaissance.

Mike analyzed the demographics of the greater Eugene–Springfield area using information from the last U.S. Census, the local Chamber of Commerce, and the most recent ratings book. He evaluated the formats of other stations, their individual ratings, and promotions (if any). He planned one of his signature-blitz business attacks in the form of a new format (classic rock), along with promotions and fresh advertising. He bought an abundance of billboard, bus bench, newspaper, and television advertising all debuting the station's brand—a Mike Pappas Superstation—with a fresh logo, format, and new ownership. He evaluated the staff and management team, keeping the most talented and terminating the employment of those who he felt weren't the best fit. He hired the finest personnel available in programming, production, sales, and promotions. Even though KZEL was well known as a rock station, with the launch of the station's new branding and updated format, it was born again under Mike's leadership.

He imposed a professional dress code for his staff and managers even when he was advised not to, due to Eugene's laid-back atmosphere. KZEL-FM 96 had been the area's dominant rock station for over 20 years. He updated the format but wanted to obliterate its old

*Mike replicated the Pappas brothers' method of operations when he purchased
KZEL-FM 96 in Eugene, Oregon. Just as with their other stations, he bartered
advertising for various local services to publicize the station's new ownership
and format change. He used a local firm to design KZEL's new logo, traded out
company cars, and bartered furniture for the new office/broadcast studio, local
billboards, bus benches, and buses to advertise the launch of KZEL's new format
and Mike's purchase of the station. He also created buzz in the community by
placing his announcers and broadcast studio behind a window on the first floor
of the building, broadcasting live 24 hours a day. He borrowed the idea from
a station he competed against in Stockton during his KCVR days. Photos circa
1985.*

hippie reputation and launch it anew by putting a fresh, professional
face on the station. He bought a new building on a major Eugene thor-
oughfare to house the new KZEL, and he created a lot of immediate
buzz in the community when he put his announcers in a studio facing the street, doing their show live. Behind bulletproof glass, the disc
jockeys played Mike's new format of current rock hits with classic rock
interspersed, and the public could stop by and watch the announcers
while on the air.

Pete and Mike didn't believe in a slow roll-out of a radio or television station any more than a general attacking his enemy slowly and deliberately. To win a battle, one struck with force, surprising the enemy. With that strategy, Mike hosted an invitation-only grand opening event for KZEL. He invited city officials, prominent businesspeople, likely advertisers, advertising agencies, local attorneys, and the most prominent citizens of Eugene to a well-orchestrated grand opening event, held over three evenings. Each night featured catered appetizers, a harpist, and a barbershop quartet.

In a matter of months, KZEL-FM became the ratings leader in both the morning and afternoon drives in the Eugene–Springfield, Oregon, market. It was common for one of Mike's sales representatives to run into a listener or advertiser who said, "Right—KZEL, a *Mike Pappas Superstation*. Hasn't he always owned KZEL?" Mike found such comments both amusing and promising since he had only owned the station for about six months.

The station became profitable in a short time, but misfortune loomed.

Until Noula sold their home, Mike lived in Eugene while she stayed in Visalia, commuting up to Eugene when possible. Mike battled his health issue and made great progress losing weight before buying KZEL and moving to Eugene, but he and his family knew that much of his success was due to his wife's coaching and coaxing to keep him on track. With Noula not yet in Eugene full-time, Mike abandoned his previous good habits and returned to his negative habits of old. He also forgot what the cardiologist said about the dangerous five-year anniversary for cardiac patients who felt great but weren't.

He forgot he had a damaged heart.

He forgot he couldn't smoke.

He forgot he couldn't drink hard liquor.

He forgot to follow his healthy diet.

He forgot he needed to take all his medicines, every day.

As the months passed in Eugene and he worked some 18 hours a day to launch KZEL, one morning he looked at himself in the mirror and saw the physical manifestation of his self-imposed neglect, especially his dramatic weight gain. He was under a lot of stress building KZEL into a profitable business. By the time Noula, his daughters, and his youngest son moved to Eugene, the damage was done.

Mike gained back all his pre–heart attack weight, was chain smoking again, and determined there was no going back.

Looming over him when he looked in the mirror was something else—the memory of the angel of death whom he denied victory when he had survived his heart attack in Sacramento. If she came back, he knew she might succeed this time! She would do everything possible to succeed in taking him from this Earth, and he made it easy. He expected to have a second heart attack any day and not survive.

He contacted the same broker who helped him find the station initially, to sell KZEL. He needed to make his profit and go back to retirement.

If he could live long enough to do it.

Mike loved the natural beauty of Eugene and had big plans for KZEL. And his eldest son, daughter-in-law, and two daughters worked with him; his youngest son would join everyone later. His original plan had been that his children would help him build a broadcasting behemoth—a chain of 14 stations—and it would be his legacy. The Pappas brothers' broadcasting torch would pass onto the next generation. His children would fulfill his dream and continue building the broadcasting empire that would be his greatest gift to them. He was fully aware of the challenges that could face the second generation of a family business, so he was determined to give them the best possible training and support, especially since he might not live to see his dream come to fruition.

At a lunch one day with his Eugene-based attorney, Mike talked about his (and Pete's) philosophy for bringing his children into the radio business and how he handled employee conflicts that might arise. He knew his children had experienced more than their rightful share of jealousy from employees at every broadcast station the brothers owned.

"Employees thought *'here comes the kid of a rich and successful businessman who's going to show us how it's done.'* All four of my children had to prove themselves!" said Mike to his attorney. "They knew about the jealousy and resentment that employees could feel and that it would be directed at them."

The "Zel bell"—a promotional tool used at live remotes in Eugene, Oregon, circa 1985.

Mike took a drink of his red wine. The inn where they were having lunch, nestled on the banks of the Willamette River, had a great wine selection, along with delicious food. The decor was rustic, with a blazing fire in the oversized fireplace in the lobby. His attorney paused in between bites of his roast beef sandwich.

"Well, how did you direct them to handle that? Your kids are young, right? What did you tell them to do?"

"I taught them to be *more*—more professional, more hard-working, more friendly, to always work more hours and to show more commitment. I also told them to treat each employee as an individual, to get to know them and their personalities. One thing I always did was stick by them," said Mike. "And I always told my employees that I never raised my children to be spoiled. I've given them a good life, but I'm not building these radio stations for anyone else, so it's a waste of time for you to downgrade or denigrate them or play politics to try and turn me against them. I'm your employer, but first, I'm their father, and I won't allow it."

"Did it work?" the attorney inquired. "Did the kids follow your advice? How did the employees take it?" Mike's attorney had never owned a family business. He was curious how it worked when a business owner brought the next generation into the business.

Mike smiled and put his wine glass on the table.

"You know, from the time I introduced the kids to my station staff, they'd go on to work hard and not expect special treatment, they gained the respect of the employees, and we never had any trouble."

The Pappas brothers' stations were family-owned and operated. The feeling of family that Pete and Mike tried to instill in their radio station staff at each station is rarely found in a corporate-owned business. Pete's, Mike's, and Harry's names were all on the license of their broadcast outlets (whether "Pappas Electronics," or "Pappas Television

Inc.," or "Pappas Telecasting Inc.," and on both the "Pete Pappas Company" and the "Mike Pappas Superstations"), and their name and reputation *was* the business. Like many family business owners who helped to build America, they took personal pride in their business and their communities. That pride of ownership is disappearing in the United States, as large conglomerates and multinational corporations conquer America's backwoods and small towns.

As KZEL's ratings and revenues increased exponentially, Mike's health deteriorated at the same rate. His wife, Noula, his children, and his daughter-in-law Litsa, each talked with him privately about the dangerous road he took by returning to his bad habits. *But Dad,* they cajoled, *don't you want to live out the rest of your life with Mom, doing all the things you planned to do—travel, see the world, do everything you worked for all these years? Don't you want to see us get married? Don't you want to live to see your grandchildren, watch them grow up, graduate from college, get married—you and Mom married young, so you will be able to do that. Don't you want these things more than food, more than smoking, more than a social shot of bourbon? Come on, Dad!*

Mike told them the conversation was pointless. He would either survive another heart attack (it was coming, inevitably, he admitted to his wife and kids) and get another chance at life, or he wouldn't. He would also say they were right, he would go back to good habits when he sold KZEL and made his profit. He would begin anew when he returned to California with Noula. He said the same thing to his twin brother, Pete, to his sister, Mary, and to his brother Harry.

"Brother, come on," Pete told him by phone. "What about our plans? All the trips we're going to take together—you can't leave me behind. You can't leave me here without you, brother!"

Mike heard the fear in his twin's voice every time they talked.

"I'll be okay, brother, I just need to get the station sold for Noula and the kids, my retirement—just this one last deal and I'll come home, go back on my diet, start walking again. Don't worry, brother."

But Pete did worry about Mike. He nearly lost him to one heart attack and didn't want another one to strike him down. And while Mike disregarded his own deteriorating health, he worried desperately about Pete. They shared the same genes, they were identical twins, Pete probably already had arterial blockage he wasn't aware of, and he would likely be next. Mike's nightmares of Pete, killed by a sudden, massive coronary, had followed him to Eugene.

Mike couldn't lose Pete. He could never live without him. He was his identical twin, his other half; there was no living without Pete. So, while his brother Pete did everything he could to get him to change his ways, Mike worried he would lose Pete, that the angel of death wouldn't be satisfied with just one twin.

She wanted them both.

Mike, who had always been so disciplined, simply couldn't control this aspect of his life. He believed there was nothing he could do about it. He would either live or die. All his life, he had believed he was in control of his own life and fate.

But not anymore. Now, it was in destiny's hands.

Mike felt depressed and demoralized, but he would keep going forward and make sure the family didn't worry. For Mike, it was a foregone conclusion—he'd suffer another heart attack and he might not survive, therefore his job became to ensure that his station was sold in advance of his death. His conversations with his two eldest children often began with his saying, *I hope it doesn't happen, but when I have my next heart attack...* Not "if," but "when." He couldn't focus on anything but selling KZEL, and his health was already out of control (he thought), so he focused on what he could control, which was his business.

Fortunately for everyone, the broadcast broker he retained found a buyer for KZEL-FM in just a few months.

———————

As predicted, and not unexpectedly, Mike suffered a second major heart attack in 1985.

He once again found himself in cardiac intensive care, fighting for his life, praying he would get just one more chance to live.

Weeks later, when he was released from the hospital, he finished negotiating the sale of KZEL, setting the sale in motion for FCC approval. After the contract was signed, Noula arranged for movers.

His dream to build a chain of 14 radio stations with his children working alongside him faded, as he saw Eugene, Oregon, disappear in the rearview mirror a short time later.

The return to California was bittersweet. He would be happy to see his extended family again, especially Pete. Their home in Visalia was leased to tenants prior to the Eugene move, so now they moved to Stockton, where Mike could live near the water, the San Joaquin Delta, and still be in the valley close to family. Mike always loved boats and dreamed of living near the sea. Moving to Stockton gave him the chance to live near water, with access to the ocean via the delta's extensive waterways, and still be about 40 minutes from Pete's home.

He desperately needed a fresh start. He was ready to go home to the San Joaquin Valley for good.

CHAPTER 32

1986:
A Chapter Closes

IN THE SUMMER, Pete and Bessie traveled back to her hometown of Price, Utah, to visit her widowed mother, brother, and extended family. Bessie's mother was from a large family, so there were many loved family members to visit. And this was not the stereotyped, obligatory son-in-law visit to in-laws, ready to go home at any time, the sooner, the better. Pete was unlike those sorts of sons-in-law because he truly loved his in-laws. They were warm, hospitable, and kind people who considered him a son the day he married their lovely daughter Bessie. During this trip, the family enjoyed many nights out, sitting around tables full of Greek dishes like *moussaka, pasticho, dolmathes,* and *baklava.* Pete was just as excited to visit this great family of his that he acquired through his marriage to Bessie, as she was to go home and see her relatives. This trip back to Price was not going to be any different from any other they made in the past.

However, they were gravely mistaken.

This trip would be unlike any other they had ever taken.

And it would cost them dearly.

If only they hadn't taken this trip. This trip his doctor advised him not to take. This trip his twin brother Mike begged and pleaded with him, tearfully and with much anguish, not to take.

If only.

But Pete wouldn't listen to his brother's fears.

Mike was the sick one, not him. Mike was the twin Pete and the family nearly lost twice, the twin brother whose hand he held in the hospital a few months before, both trembling. The two of them had looked at each other then with love and fear, knowing that despite everything they went through—the worries, the work, the sacrifices, joy, and laughter—that their lives could come to a crashing end, two once-mighty oaks fallen by sickness and decay, crashing to the ground with fury, leaving each of them separated from the other, a tangled mess of loss and grief. In the split second it takes for a fertilized egg to divide, when the one of them became two, the force of life brought them into being. In the same split second, death could reach out and snuff the lives they were given, reducing them to twin brothers torn apart by an angry fate, with one twin left behind, shattered. Pete and Mike could be separated from one another—a destiny, a life, that neither could face without the other twin at his side.

CHAPTER 33

1986:
A Twin's Nightmare Comes True

"It's the end of an era."

Tearfully, his face twisted by grief, Pete's longtime best friend, side-kick, and general manager of KHOP-FM couldn't stop weeping.

Fiercely loyal and hard-working, Dave Jacob went to work at the KTRB-AM and KHOP-FM studios in Modesto, like any other work-day. He was waiting for Pete's niece and Mike's daughter, Kathy, who also arrived just before 8 a.m., the norm for her as KTRB-AM's station manager.

They embraced.

Kathy held onto their family's longtime friend as his chest heaved. A torrential downpour of tears struck them both.

How could this reality be the truth?

It was unimaginable that Mike's dearest twin brother, Pete, was dead.

───────────

How could Mike and their family accept the death of someone so full of life? While Mike could be dark and brooding, Pete was the light one, from the time they were children, always there to reassure Mike that their plans would work out and their dreams would come true.

Nonetheless, he was struck down by the explosion of an artery in his heart at only 48 years old, just weeks before his 49th birthday.

A month prior to Pete's death, Kathy was visiting her parents in Stockton. One morning, she saw her father, Mike, sitting at the kitchen table, ashen and drawn, with the troubled look of his she came to know through the years, as he battled in business each day, clawing his way from poverty to success. She asked him what was wrong. Was he feeling all right? He looked at her with tears in his eyes.

"I just got off the phone with your Uncle Pete. I had that night-mare again last night. I dreamed he died in Utah. I begged him not to go. The altitude is too high there for him. I couldn't convince him not to go. He said I'm the sick one, not him, *don't be such a yiayia, stop worrying, I'll be all right.* But how can I? I just have this terrible feeling I'm never going to see him again."

Mike and Pete's bond was prenatal and preternatural, as with all twins. But their lives were so intertwined, like the twisted branches of an old olive tree, that their life together seemed as if it would go on forever, together. When Mike was admitted to a Stockton hospital for congestive heart failure shortly before Pete left for Utah, Pete drove hurriedly with Kathy from Modesto to be at his side. As she watched the two of them, Pete, in his silk suit and diamond rings, stood over his pale, sickly twin with tears in his eyes. Choked up, Pete reassured Mike not to worry.

"Everything will be okay. You know I'll always take care of Noula and your kids, like we always promised each other—that if something happened to one of us, the other would take care of his brother's wife and kids, but *this won't happen because you have to get better.*" They held hands and Pete looked down at his ill other half with sadness and fear. The twins held hands tightly, tears streaming down both of their faces.

Neither ever imagined one would live without the other.

When he walked out of the hospital room that day, Pete blinked and wiped away his tears as he turned to Kathy, who was waiting just outside the door.

"Pray your dad gets better, Kathy, because if he dies, I won't live much longer. I can't live without him." When he walked away, she went back to her dad's room, took his hand, leaned over the rail, and kissed him on the cheek.

"Love you, Dad."

"Love you, honey."

"I'll see you tonight after work."

"Okay.... Kathy?"

"Yeah, Dad?"

"Talk to him. Maybe he'll listen to you. You see him at work every day. When you have time alone with him, try to get him to lose weight, take care of himself—you know? I keep having the same nightmare, over and over." He looked away, wiping his tears with the back of his hand.

"In my nightmare, he has a heart attack but he doesn't get a second chance like I did. He just dies. He drops to the ground and dies."

"I don't know what I can do, Dad. You're his twin brother. You two only listen to each other, no one else, not really. But I'll try, I'll try."

"If something happens to him, honey...." his voice trailed off and he looked down. "I love you kids and your mom, but I'm not long for this world if something happens to him. He's my twin brother. I can't live without him."

It turned out Mike's fears and nightmares were premonitions.

Thankfully, Bessie was not alone when her husband died. When Pete was hit in the middle of the night with sudden cardiac death in her family's home in Price, Bessie's screams resonated throughout. Her brother ran from down the hall and began administering CPR while her mother called 911. Paramedics soon arrived to render aid, but despite her brother's valiant efforts, Pete was gone.

After Pete's body was taken from the house, Bessie sat with her brother and mother for a few minutes, still overwhelmed with the suddenness of Pete's death. Her husband was gone. They had just had such a wonderful evening visiting with family and friends, eating delectable Greek food, and drinking homemade wine. It was a vacation like no other. They laughed and listened to Cretan *mandinathes*, Greek stories recited as poems.

It couldn't have been a more wonderful week.

With the support of her brother and mother, she must call the Pappas family in California. Her first thought was to contact Mike, but she knew, as everyone did in the family, that neither twin could survive the loss of the other. Mike had already been near death with two heart attacks. How would he survive this? Who would tell him? How? And she still had to somehow tell her twin sons that their father had passed away. Bessie also had to call his other siblings, Mary and Harry.

She felt so overwhelmed with her own shock, grief, and loss that she could only make one call before contacting her sons. She first called Pete's brother Harry, who at that time was living with his wife, Stella, in Omaha, Nebraska, where Harry had launched KPTM-TV. Soon thereafter, Mary and Mike's wife, Noula, were informed of Pete's passing.

Mike was the creative one, the storyteller and poet whose passion for life was expressed in the many poems he wrote while in the Marines, the broadcast promotions he designed, and the editorials he wrote and broadcast. Pete was the comedian, the one who gathered folks around to tell a good joke. He loved to make people laugh. He loved to laugh himself, and his greatest audience was Mike, who thought Pete was the family's Jackie Gleason. Pete loved to dance, to put on an apron and barbecue, to host people at his home every weekend since he and Bessie practiced the Greek tradition of *philoxenia*—hospitality.

Mike was the leader of the twins, but both Pete and Mike loved being the centers of attention. Since they began their careers as teen announcers on live radio, creativity and performing came naturally to them. Mike's adult children used to watch the two of them, at the center of a crowd at a party or bar, and noted how people gravitated toward them. Strangers quickly became friends as the twins jockeyed for the admiration and laughs of the group. Had they known the right people, they could have been nationally successful and famous—not as actors, since their personalities were too dominant for that, but perhaps as a twin set of talk show hosts, natural, gifted communicators blessed with good looks and charisma.

It was unthinkable that Mike's much-adored identical twin brother Pete was gone forever.

When Mike's daughter Kathy was in elementary school, she tried climbing to the top of the monkey bars for the first time. She was about six years old and felt a sense of achievement when she reached the top. She had tried so many times before, and failed. Kathy was overweight at the time, clumsy and embarrassed that everyone could climb to the top and she could not. Nevertheless, she was determined to reach the top, kept trying, and finally made it. Unfortunately, when she reached the top, Kathy lost her grip and dropped suddenly to the soft ground, landing on her belly. She was breathless, desperately gasping for air and crying because she couldn't seem to get her breath back.

A teacher in the schoolyard came over, picked her up, dusted off her legs and dress, and consoled her.

"It's all right, ya' just got the wind knocked outta' ya', that's all—you're okay." And, after a few minutes, she was fine.

When Mike found out Pete died, he felt just like that six-year-old in the schoolyard who got the wind knocked out of her. Suddenly and catastrophically, Mike no longer could say *I love you, brother* to Pete, or continue sharing his life as they always had, ever since the spark of life that created them in their mother's womb.

For Mike, losing his twin brother, Pete, was getting the breath knocked out of him in a nightmare he could never awake from for the rest of his life. He not only lost his brother, but he felt part of himself had died with Pete, because Mike never lived without Pete, and Pete never lived without Mike.

With Pete's death, the inseparable Pappas twins were torn apart—one left in this life, and one in the next.

CHAPTER 34

1986:
Saving Mike

PRECEDING PETE'S DEATH, Mike's daughter Kathy had bought a micro-cassette recorder, which was the latest technology of the time. She paid $98 for it and could only afford to buy one recorder per paycheck. She intended to write Pete and Mike's life story (as she promised her father when she was a child), so she wanted both brothers to always keep a recorder with them. When a memory or thought appeared, they could promptly record it. She bought the first one and took it to her Uncle Pete's office, to give him the recorder in advance of his trip to Utah. She knew the drive there and back was long and he might use some of the time to begin recording his memories.

He gave it back to her, unused.

"I don't need this. Your dad is the sick one. Give it to him first. I'll be around. Give me a recorder later when you buy another one."

He died in Utah a short time later.

The family decided that the best way to break the news to Mike was to get him to a medical facility first. Thus, if he had another heart attack when hearing of Pete's death, he would receive immediate medical attention. Shocked and emotionally overcome, Noula didn't believe Mike would survive hearing the news that Pete was dead. She prayed she wouldn't lose her beloved husband. She was tough as steel, but this day would take every bit of her Spartan fortitude and spirit to continue acting as if the day was normal and no different from any other. She could not shed a tear or show emotion to Mike. She would tell him nothing of the news he was about to receive.

Mike was told that he needed to be seen by his cardiologist at St. Joseph's Hospital that day to go over the results of tests taken when he was admitted a few weeks before for congestive heart failure. Only 24% of Mike's heart functioned at that time, so the story was plausible that there might be more issues with his heart. Noula decided that John, their eldest son, would be the one to break the news of Pete's death to Mike.

John called Mike's cardiologist and told him what was happening. The cardiologist would be on-call, Mike would be in a private room when told the terrible news, and a nurse would be nearby with oxygen, a code-blue crash cart, and any drugs that might be needed to resuscitate Mike, should the worst happen.

Mike saw John running toward the hospital as he and Noula drove into the parking lot. He suspected that if John was there, the results of his tests must be catastrophic. It was 107 degrees outside, a typically blistering August day in the San Joaquin Valley. When John saw them, he ran over and leaned into the car through the open passenger window. He assured Mike everything would be explained soon.

As planned, upon their arrival, Mike and Noula went directly into a hospital room where they met Mike's cardiologist, a nun from St. Joseph's, and their son John. He had the life-changing, horrific task of telling his father that his twin brother, Pete, was dead. Noula stayed strong but feared this trip to St. Joseph's would be the last for Mike and these would be their final moments together. She still didn't expect her dearest husband to survive the news.

Mike noticed the nurses and doctors were extra kind to him and seemed to be looking at him strangely. Perhaps, he thought, the news about his heart meant his life would soon be over.

John stood up and walked over to where his father and mother were sitting together. He needed to be strong and keep it together. There was a large lump in his throat. He swallowed hard and was determined to not break down as he told him the terrible news.

"Dad, there is no other way I can tell you, except to say to you that Uncle Pete is dead. Your twin brother is dead. He died this morning at 2:30 in Price, Utah."

Mike wailed and sobbed, his heart shattering, his mind flooded with a reality he couldn't bear.

"Pete is dead. Oh my God, how could this be true? This can't be true! Not my identical twin brother, Pete. Oh my God, how could you have let this happen?! Not to Pete! It was supposed to be me! God should have taken *me!* How can this be real! Not Pete!"

John's words echoed in Mike's brain, over and over again: *Your identical twin brother Pete is dead, your identical twin brother Pete is dead, your identical twin brother Pete is dead....*

Some time before, after Pete had declined using the microcassette recorder, Kathy gave it to her father. The day after Mike was told of Pete's death, he began recording his thoughts, saying aloud and recording what his family knew: his heart was irretrievably and infinitely broken.

I went into all kinds of crying and hysterics. There was no way I could believe it, and the nurses were trying to calm me down with the doctor. I just grabbed ahold of myself and I said to myself "I got to watch out here so I don't have a third heart attack."

It hit me also that could happen very, very easily but—how could it be?—that this happened to the brother that was waiting earlier when I was in the hospital, put his hand on my arm and said, "Don't worry, I'll take care of everything for you"? Not that brother, not the brother who's my identical twin brother, whose life has been like mine.

Tears came down my cheeks. I dreamed he would die of a quick heart attack, but one that lasted long enough, at least a minute or two, when he grabbed his heart and he had pains around his neck, and his right arm, and he knew he was suffering a massive heart attack. That brother? I'm sure he suffered, for a minute can seem like a lifetime. I know, I've had two heart attacks and I know the feeling. You're telling yourself, "now is the time that I might be going—please, God, don't let me go," and you pray to yourself, and it happens so quickly.

Mike couldn't understand, from the terrible few moments when he first heard of Pete's death, to the last days of his own life, why he had survived two heart attacks and repeated congestive heart failures but his twin brother didn't get a second chance.

Why did *he* survive? Why did Pete die? How could he live without Pete? Mike wept uncontrollably, his heart aching for the brother he would never see in this life again.

With Pete, there were so many memories. I can't sleep at night. It hit me like a bolt of lightning, like a bomb, like an explosion, like nothing I can describe the shock that I felt.

No one knows, except an identical twin brother, that when one twin brother dies, the one that is alive feels that half of him is dead also. It's just that the other half that is alive represents that Pete Pappas did not die 100%. My identical twin brother, who I loved and cherished so much and would do anything for me, and for my family and for my children, and who I in return would do anything for, lives a little bit in me. We were inseparable from the day that we were born, and now today, I'm separated from my brother.

Up until she heard by phone from her mother that her Uncle Pete had died, Kathy never spontaneously cried before. Her knees buckled and she dropped onto the bed in her hotel room in Miami Beach (she was on vacation), head bowed, crying a waterfall of tears, flowing from the bottommost part of her heart. She broke the news to her sister, Dena, who responded in the same way. When Kathy first heard the song *Cry Me a River*, she didn't understand that depth of sadness over a broken heart. As she cried her personal river of tears, Kathy instantly knew her father, Mike, would cry oceans of tears for the rest of his life. And both girls feared the worst—that their father wouldn't survive the news of his twin brother's death or the funeral to follow.

Culturally, the preparation for the funeral of a Greek Orthodox Christian begins for a Greek family, as it does for others, by letting everyone know a family member has passed. With Pete's death, word spread quickly, especially since the local newspaper, the *Modesto Bee*, published a story about his life and death on the front page. Friends and family gathered at Pete's home, stopping by to pay respects and give emotional support. They brought food and drink so his bereaved family, especially his wife, Bessie, their twin sons, and Pete's twin brother, Mike, wouldn't have to worry about cooking meals or providing for guests. In Pete and Bessie's home, as in many other Greek homes, this continued for the days leading up to the funeral. Mike again spoke into his recorder.

We drank to his memory. Many cried at his home because I was there all three nights and all three days. At Pete's home, we sat with Odell Brawley, and he said he had talked with Chester Smith, and there's one thing we all had in common—we grew up on Crows Landing Road, and it was the country boys, Chester and Odell and the Pappas brothers, who should have never succeeded in life or in business. We had that bond of poor boys from poor families becoming successful. There was a camaraderie there and a bond that we've held for years. In discussing Pete's memory, his departing us, that was the kind of talk we had around Pete's bar at the house, discussing his memories and his past, and that bond, whether we were alive or dead, will never be forgotten by those of us that grew up on the poor side of town.

The memorial for Pete began at the *Trisagion* prayer service the night before the funeral. Lasting about 20 minutes, it is a short memorial service conducted on the eve of the sacramental funeral service. After the funeral itself, the family hosts the *Mahkaria*, a funeral luncheon consisting of fish and side dishes, when relatives and friends come together for refreshment, support, and solace to remember the deceased, and to pay their respects to the family.

While most people have, or will have in their lifetimes, lost loved ones to death, the biological connection of identical twins makes the death and breadth of the loss so powerful, that often the surviving twin feels that a part of them has also died.

With Pete's sudden death, Mike became a twin without his cherished twin, alone for the first time. The family didn't expect him to live through seeing Pete in his casket for the first time, or the funeral.

Today for the first time, I will see Pete in a casket and God knows it won't be easy, and there are people in the family that don't want me to go at all, particularly my doctor, who thinks it might cause me another heart attack to see Pete in a coffin. But I cannot and will not avoid seeing my own brother in a casket for the last time.

I'll be seeing him today and I'll be seeing him Monday and Tuesday and trying to remember my brother—his facial expressions, his smile, now even when he's passed away. People will gather at the church hall and at Pete's home to drink to his memory and to discuss his life and that's as it should be—not to plant a man in the ground with one or two days' notice, a man who devoted his whole life to living, breathing, dreaming, and worrying. I believe that the Greek people have the right way to bury someone. Bury him with a going-away party, not a party of celebration, but a party of the memories of the man's life or the woman's life, who lived, and devoted something to humanity while they lived on this Earth.

How I'm going to face the next three days and seeing Pete's body, I don't know, but it will be devastating. I'll talk to him as if his spirit is in the room at the mortuary. I'll have my talk with Pete and he knows that one day, as we all know, that nothing is permanent on this Earth, that we'll see each other again.

Entering the funeral home, a collective wail of anguish came from every member of Pete's family as they saw him in the casket for the first time. Clinging to one another for strength, each family member propped their loved ones up, like massive beams supporting the vaulted ceilings of Gothic cathedrals. Collectively, they worried about Mike, who they were afraid would suffer a massive heart attack when he saw his twin brother in a casket for the first time. Pete's distraught wife, Bessie, who now faced life without her husband at the age of 46; his grieving twin sons, who not only grieved for their father, but for the first time faced the reality that they too could one day be separated from one another; his sister, Mary, and his brother, Harry, both crushed by the loss of one of their older twin brothers, another member of their nuclear family taken by death—all sobbed while leaning on one another. Noula held Mike's hand and his children gathered around and hugged him, as they gazed down upon Pete's still and lifeless body. Pete embodied Greek *kefi*, a love for life and love for living, so how could this be reality? Mike's life-loving twin brother, Pete, lay dead before them.

I finally saw him in the coffin for the first time and it was devastating. I asked everybody to leave the room so I could sit down, so that I could spend a few minutes alone with my identical twin brother, knowing that I would have only two hours before the funeral.

Over 600 people attended Pete's funeral. Attendees included family, friends, old business associates, and current employees and even advertisers. At the end of the service, the poem Mike wrote at three that morning was read. This was the last poem Mike ever wrote:

Today, dear friends and my relatives, too—we are gathered together to pay homage with you.

I speak of my twin brother, whose life has been like mine. I speak of a man who had fears—who had love.

Pete had many friends, no matter where he went. He always had a chuckle, a smile at every bend.

He was a comedian, the way he would make you smile. He would bring you joy and yes, he would make you laugh for a while.

He was an individualist, a rebel, a non-conformist they would say; he climbed his own mountain and made his own way.

But that is the way we were raised by our immigrant folks who came from a land far away.

They raised us to work in the fields and sweat in the sun, but they always told us to

"honor your name, and work hard, my sons."

No one could know how close he could be—to his identical twin brother, Mike Pappas, you see.

There is no way to explain to all of you the closeness that I felt for my brother Pete and the closeness that he felt for me. The love between us and the bond that was there cannot be put into words and said on the air.

How can I get up in the morning and have coffee today and think of going to visit my brother Pete, always an apron on he would have, ready to cook and hear a good story?

Life will never be one hundred percent for me—for fifty percent of my life is now gone to eternity.

The Lord knows I have cried and will cry even more because I will miss you.

*I will miss you each and every day when loneliness sets in and I'm in
an unhappy way.*

*You will never be forgotten, I will assure you of that, because our
children, yours and mine, will see to that.*

*They can never forget their Uncle Pete, who gave them advice and
made life so sweet.*

*You went first, my dear brother, but you lived a good life—you were
young at 48 but lived more than those who reach 108.*

*I have great memories that will keep me going until the good Lord
decides that I should rejoin you. It is now time to bid you
farewell, but before I do, I must tell you that for four days and
four nights your friends have come. They have toasted your
memory and have reminisced too of the Pete Pappas they all
once knew.*

*Goodbye, my brother Pete, whose life has been like mine. You are
going to take a new trip to a place that is divine.*

My brother Pete, until I see you again, eternal be your memory.

Pete and Mike had a great fear of the "cold, cold Earth," which was
how they had heard their mother describe burial in the ground. Consequently, between them they decided (years before Pete's death) that
when they died, they would be interred in above-ground crypts, much
as in the old country, except they would not be family-sized, but rather
individual crypts. Each couple, Mike and Noula, and also Pete and
Bessie, would have their own crypts that held a spot for each of them.

If Mike had not taken the threat of death completely seriously up
until that point, then seeing his twin brother *who looked like him identically* dead in a casket, brought that fear, coupled with the overwhelming grief of losing Pete, like a tidal wave of pain to drown him.

CHAPTER 35

1986–1989:
A Twin's Torment

WHEN PETE'S FUNERAL ENDED and everyone went home to resume their lives, the deep, heartbreaking mourning began. This is true for anyone who gets through the horrible day of a loved one's funeral. A mourning person often collapses into bed after waves of exhaustion consume them, and they fall into a dark, deep sleep. When they awake in the morning, in that place between sleep and wakefulness, for a moment, they convince themselves it was a terrible nightmare. As the sleep fades away, the agony of the loss punches them in the gut and the pain returns. The tears flow but, numbly, they try to get on with the day.

There have been countless poems and songs written about loss, usually about broken hearts from failed romances. The loss of a loved one can rarely be articulated in the same manner with two minutes of verse and music. Novels, operas, and plays have done a better job than popular songs of expressing the torment of losing a loved one to death. Weeks, months, and years pass, but the pain persists. Mike recorded his thoughts for years after his brother's passing.

Pete's death has been such a private thing, and yet, although everybody has mourned, as time goes by, they say that the healing process comes in, and I've been waiting for it. I know that three or four weeks does not seem like a long time, but I have decided ultimately that with me, there will never be a healing because: 1) we were too close as identical twins and 2) because I am not going to allow a healing. I'm not going to allow myself to forget the thousands of hours and the times that we spent together, in laughter and in tears, and in planning, and how much love we had for one another as identical twin brothers.

Had it been me to die first, Pete fully expected me to be the first one, because of the two serious heart attacks I had, he would be just as devastated as I am. Only I know what kind of devastation and hurt that I feel inside that all members of my family feel, but not to the extent that I feel it. It is too deep, it is too meaningful, it is too hurtful. He would walk around, if it was me who passed away first and say, "I wished that Mike wouldn't have lost his health" the same thing that I had said about Pete, or that "Mike worried too much"—that is the one thing he would have said over and over again: "Mike worried too much. Mike was a worrier, and I wish that he didn't worry as much, because we made all these plans to travel together, and laugh together, to see the weddings of all of our children, and the festivities that lay ahead, and still had a long life." A long life, because dying at 48 is not a long life per se, except to the extent that Pete lived it and I lived it in our travels and seeing as much of our country and the world that we had the opportunity to see, which compared to other people, was a great deal.

Mike lived in a time when few people sought help for depression in the form of therapy and/or medication. Even if other people did so, he wouldn't have sought professional help. He would have considered it a sign of weakness, something a "real man" would never do. He wasn't afraid to show his grief or to tell those around him, both family and friends, how brokenhearted he was, how he would never stop missing Pete, how he would never recover from the loss of his twin. Twins come into the world together but rarely leave it the same way. Mike was the heartbroken and incomplete twin left behind.

While his siblings, wife, children, and family tried to ease his grief and to give him as much love and understanding as they could, they could never truly know what he felt. His grief was a private misery, an agony he couldn't explain, in a life that he no longer wished to live.

How close can the blood be, how close can the family be, what kind of magic did our mother and father instill in us to cause us to be so close, so the agony and the depression is so deep, to where even one brother can imagine such a thing as suicide? It's actually a cheap way out. But, I gotta' be strong, and as I've been told by our many relatives since Pete's death, I've got to be the leader of the family and its strength, and cannot show it weakness. I can show my love, I can show my loss, Pete Pappas, but I cannot weaken now, because then my children would have no leader to follow, and Harry could become demoralized. And what of my sweet sister, Mary?

The sorrow experienced by other members of the family, who also lost Pete, was different from Mike's, but was grief nonetheless. When Pete died, everyone in the family lost someone special to them, someone who could never be replaced. For Mike, though, the loss of his twin was not only emotional and spiritual, but even physical and biological.

The inner torment, the torture, the grief, the crying, the tearing of my body is so intense, that it's very hard to describe to members of my family. I will attempt to do it no more. I've given up. I've given up trying to explain feelings that they cannot possibly understand.

The pain of loss for those who grieve, especially twins, can feel like an appendage has been severed. The loss of an identical twin is profound and dramatic. Can single humans, formed alone in the womb, their only physical connection being to their mother, ever truly know what the pain of a twin's losing a twin must feel like? What it's like to lose the only other person in the universe who was there at the same moment the spark of life created them, from one egg into two, formed together over nine months, in the same womb? And, when single babies emerge from the safe bubble of the womb, they come into this world alone, unlike twins, who burst into the world together (though one at a time). Twins, with emotional and psychic connections to one another, come into the world in a way that most of the world can never experience or understand.

Growing up, Mike's children admired the bond between Pete and Mike, each wishing they were a twin. How wonderful it must have been for their uncle and their father, and for all twins, to always have a best friend who loved and understood them completely, providing strength and support, never requiring explanations or justifications. Twins have a pure love and understanding of one another that non-twins can never know. No twin thinks, even fleetingly, they will ever be apart. Their attachment to one another is immediate, constant, and forever.

Death comes to everyone, but when it happens to twins, they are split into two, ripped apart, with one taken to the next life, and the other left behind to grieve, cope, and accept a reality without their beloved twin.

Mike's family could only try to understand, sympathize, empathize, and lend a caring shoulder to a twin whose pain seemed never-ending. Praying, they hoped they wouldn't lose their last twin alive during the days before and immediately after the funeral. They didn't realize at the time that those days were just the beginning of his painful journey of sadness.

Pete would throw his hands up and say, "I've got plenty of time." In my heart, deep down, I knew that he wasn't taking care of himself. He wasn't going to hospitals to have angiograms or angioplasties, to clean out his arteries, or to reduce the weight and the smoke, and that he did not have much more time than I.

He always thought that I would die first, and told Bessie that if I died first, there is no way that he could stand it, and that he would die very quickly after that. This may occur to me, too. I may not have long to live because I have lost half of me. I lost my right arm, I lost my greatest memory, my greatest, most cherished twin; not any more love than I have for my children, or my other brother Harry or sister Mary, or my wife Noula, but a different kind of unique love that only identical twins can respond to. And when identical twins are born into some families, they go into separate careers, and do not spend that much time relying on each other. We were together from the day of birth, relying and trusting in each other, not letting wives or family or friends or anyone or enemies separate us. The enemy of one brother was the enemy of all Pappas brothers. The friend of one brother was the friend of all the Pappas brothers. It's a beautiful sunny day as I'm driving down the freeway tape recording this, but I'm a sad man.

As the days melded into nights and the months into years, Mike's family knew that regardless of the love they showed him and how much they tried to understand, they couldn't ease his pain or bring him to a place of peaceful acceptance, because that place didn't exist for Mike in a world without his twin brother, Pete. A life without his twin was not a world Mike could live in for very long. The cherished memories of their lives together might bring him some consolation years later, but for the days and months following Pete's death, the most loving and wonderful memories of their lives lived together triggered pain and bottomless pools of tears that threatened to drown Mike in the time he had left. His life, always lived with verve and enthusiasm, became torturous—endless hours of agony spent nursing a broken heart. He continued recording his thoughts almost daily:

The death of Pete Pappas is something that has tormented my soul.

Almost six weeks after Pete's death, Mike, Bessie, and Kathy traveled to New Orleans for a National Association of Broadcasters (NAB) convention. It was a trip that Pete and Mike planned to take together.

Instead of enjoying the jazz and ambience that is uniquely New Orleans, they faced every morning's and evening's events with sorrow, hearts heavy with the unbearable weight of grief.

Kathy stayed in the room adjacent to Mike's with a connecting door, not sleeping well most nights, awakening regularly to see if her father would soon join the twin brother he loved so much. She looked for the soft rise and fall of his chest and checked to see if he was still breathing, still alive in this world, or had he left them? Was he too broken in spirit to stay on this Earth without his precious twin brother, Pete?

I woke up one morning hearing Pete's voice saying "Mike, Mike." I don't know what kind of message he was trying to convey to me. "Mike, please don't worry, please settle down, don't worry about your twin brother, don't drive yourself to an early grave, you have children to see married yet, you have my two sons and my wife Bessie to look after, you have the companies to look after, you've had heart attacks yourself, two of them." I don't know what he was trying to say to me. I don't know if I've ever believed in the spirit world, whether I have or whether I haven't, but I heard him.

Mike cried when he told Kathy of this first of many dreams he had of his dearest twin brother, Pete. His faith was constantly being tested by his decimated heart.

I do believe in an unknown superior force which has created the elements, the Earth, the thousands of planets and stars and the millions of universes. What this superior unknown force is, I don't know, but I choose to call it God. That is my belief, that is the way that I wish to believe after attending the services of many churches during my youth. I believe there is a beginning and I believe that there is an ending, and I believe there is a God, which I call a superior, unknown force, and I describe it accurately, for that superior unknown force gave me the brain to analyze for myself. I do believe in the spirit floating from the human body as I have seen some other people die.

Mike remembered one old Greek man who was a friend of his parents.

As he died, he opened his mouth and let out one last breath. Maybe that was the spirit, at least that's what my father said it was, the spirit that leaves the body. The body being the container of the soul here on Earth. But it's hard for me, because when you are one egg, you are one human being that becomes two, as identical twins, and many articles have been written about identical twins.

Mike at Pete's crypt in Modesto, 1986. After Pete's death, Mike purchased the plot next to Pete's crypt and was later laid to rest in a crypt next to his twin brother.

I feel that half of me has died, unequivocally, irrevocably, unconditionally, half of me has died. I have been told by several cardiologists in no uncertain terms that my left artery is 100% dead, my right artery is about 20% dead, but it fills up about every six months to every year, with a fatty tissue, that has to be cleaned out by an angioplasty. So, I am fighting to turn 49. Pete died at 48, some three weeks short of turning 49 years of age. The trip we had planned to New Orleans together, the trips we had planned to Hawaii, to Hong Kong, will not take place together.

And, that if had it been the other way around, as it was supposed to be, had I died first, and I was trying to talk to Pete, I would be trying to get through to Pete, like he's been trying to get through to me, for he has been trying the last forty days to relay messages to me. I have seen in the middle of the night, his face with a smile on it, looking down at me, and it has awakened me and startled me.

I have seen his face with tears on it, tears coming down from his eyes, as if he was crying for himself and his early death, as if he was crying mostly for me, not wanting to see me tortured and tormented. One night, I woke up about three o'clock in the morning. It was Pete's voice. It was clear. It was distinct. It was as if he was using every power that could be used by a spirit to talk to his identical twin brother. The only thing I can say is that no else can understand that I have seen my brother's face and I have heard his voice. I believe in God myself, but in my own way, and I hope someday that I will see my brother Pete, and my mother and my father.

Mike hoped for a spirit world and thought the chance of one existing was greater than reincarnation. He did believe in one form of reincarnation, though. As many Greek people do, Mike believed he would live on in his children. The truest form of reincarnation is that when you die, you live on through your children and grandchildren.

Oh, God, there is beauty in life and there is beauty in smelling the flowers along the way, beauty in the mountains and in the streams and in the oceans, that Pete and I and my family enjoyed! Beauty in the fog, in the sunshine, the four seasons; beauty in traveling. Beauty in the success that one can achieve in life through business, or in raising his children successfully. There is much beauty, but you also have much sadness, when you have a death in the family. And, up until now, 1986, where there could have been deaths, particularly where I was concerned, and we were fortunate compared to other families. Even though I would not consider dying at 48 years old fortunate, I can only take pleasure in the fact that he had a good life, and that I will have great memories until the day that I die, of my brother Pete. But it will never be the same, because I will get up every morning wanting to have a cup of coffee with Pete, the only one I could truly rely on, to talk about my most inner feelings, thoughts, imaginations, dreams, fears, and I was the only one he could talk to in the same manner. No matter how we expressed ourselves to our wives and our children, or to our brother Harry or to our sister Mary, never could we divulge our most inner thoughts and feelings and emotions to anyone like we could to each other.

CHAPTER 36

1986–1989:
Going Forward

THROUGH THEIR COMMITMENT AND HARD WORK, radio and television broadcasting gave Pete and Mike the opportunity to live the American dream. Their financial success allowed them to travel the United States and to visit Europe, to have beautiful homes and cars, to share their success with their parents and take care of them in their old age. Pete's and Mike's work ethic and resulting achievements gave their children a good start in life by providing them with educational and professional opportunities. They achieved every dream their own parents, John and Titika, ever had for them. For Mike, life without his brother, Pete, meant there was no future for him in this world. In his profound grief, he could only look back at the life, brotherly love, and memories they shared together.

In the immediate days following Pete's death, Mike recorded his first editorial and had it broadcast on both KTRB-AM and KHOP-FM:

This is Mike Pappas. This editorial will be the first of many to continue the tradition started by Pete, Mike, and Harry Pappas on all Pappas-associated radio and TV stations.

As you know, the editorial voice of KTRB-KHOP, the voice of Pete Pappas, is no longer with us. As his identical twin brother, I have been devastated by the loss of one so close to me. The shocking loss of a man so widely respected is a loss also to the entire broadcast industry. Pete's professionalism and strength, combined with his personal warmth, kindness, hospitality, and the friendship he showed to everyone he knew, will be missed.

Jack G of KPLA radio said about Pete, "One man can make a positive difference in this world. Pete did." The hard-hitting editorial policy of these stations will continue, only the voice will be different, for a broadcast station is more than a jukebox. It should air news, weather, sports, commentaries, and editorials.

I take this opportunity to thank our advertisers and listeners for the sorrow you have expressed and the outpouring of love you have given to the members of our family. I thank you in Pete's memory.

With Pete gone, and his own deteriorating health an everyday challenge, Mike decided to retire for good. He negotiated the sale of KTRB-AM as well as KHOP-FM. His days in the radio business would pass into history and memory.

Mike sometimes worried that the next generation of the family might forget where they had come from—the struggles of their immigrant grandparents and of their parents, who worked so hard to make life better for the following generations. He wanted them to remember the good times their family shared together and to put the heartbreak of losing Pete behind them, to focus on the joy and the love.

Think of the good memories we've had together—the motor home trips we've taken, the traveling, the dreams, the aspirations and the achievements of the first generation and what memories you, the second generation, have had with your parents, your uncles and your aunts. Stay together as cousins, continue to keep the closeness that we've enjoyed, for there is nothing else that can match the closeness of a good family, that in time of need can depend on each other and rely on each other's love and admiration.

Mike didn't need to worry, though that was his nature. His children, nieces, and nephews would never forget the wellspring of love, honor, and hope that flowed from their Cretan—and, in his children's case, Spartan—forbears. The next generation of the Pappas family would always remember and cherish the time they had with their grandparents, John and Titika, their parents, aunts, and uncles—especially those who passed away much too soon.

CHAPTER 37

1989–1990:
A Broken Heart

"If this ever happens to me again, you have to let me die."

Mike used the hospital room's telephone to call his daughter Kathy. She was told to make sure that neither her siblings or mother would be there. He needed to discuss something with Kathy because she was his firstborn and he wanted them to be alone. He knew she understood responsibility and the hard decisions he had made in his life.

Kathy knew that whatever he had to say to her, she wouldn't like it.

She had watched her father shoulder the responsibilities of the family her whole life, and now he was sick, and it was her turn to help him in any way possible. It had been a little over three years since Pete's death, and in that time Mike's health declined dramatically.

Mike reached out for his daughter as she approached his bed. He had been transferred out of intensive care into a regular recovery room, and this was his first chance to talk privately with her. He looked weak and tired. His once gleaming brown eyes looked forlorn.

"What is it, Dad? What's wrong?"

Mike's family just spent a grueling, terrifying three weeks waiting, hoping, and praying that he would survive this latest medical emergency. They took turns going in and out of his private room and in and out of the waiting room, "camping out" with other families in the same predicament as them. For the first time in three weeks, the previous night was the first in which they went to sleep without the fear, at least for one night, that Mike would not be lost before a new day began.

"You can never, ever again, spend so much money to save me."

Kathy knew he was talking about the hospital bill, but no amount of money was worth his life, of that she was certain.

"Dad, we're not going to let you die so we can save money."

He took a deep breath, his brow furrowed, and his eyes welled with tears.

"It cost us $72,000 for me to be in intensive care for three weeks, Kathy. Do you know how hard I worked, how long I worked, to earn that $72,000? Your mother is from a family of people who live long. She's going to outlive me by 30 or 40 years. What will be left for her to live on if this hospital sucks me dry and takes whatever money I've got left? What happens then? There will be nothing left."

"But Dad…"

"No 'buts.' You have to promise you won't do this again."

She looked at her father lying in his bed, pale and frail, and she knew there probably wouldn't be a next time. He had barely made it this time.

"Dad, you can't expect us not to try and save you. Don't ask me to promise that."

"I am asking you, I am *telling* you, there will be nothing left for your mother to live on. She stood with me for almost 30 years, through all the struggles and sacrifices, all the hard work, everything we gave up…." His voice choked with emotion as he squeezed her hand. "I wasn't an easy man to live with, you know that. But your mother was always there, always stood beside me, had faith in me when I didn't have faith in myself. I owe her a secure retirement. It'll be hard enough for her to be a widow."

His voice trailed off as he looked away, into a future where he saw himself dead and his wife alone. "We had so many plans. I owe it to her. I called you in here and not the other kids because I knew you could be reasonable and think this through. I'm asking you to think and not feel. Right now, just think." He tried to blink away more tears, but his cheeks were wet, nonetheless. He wiped away his tears.

Kathy had never seen the look in her father's eyes the way she saw it at that moment. He knew he was going to die; he had known it for a long time and, like the planner he was, everything had been taken care of, everything was in order, and another gargantuan hospital bill (since he had no insurance) had ruined his plans for his wife's future without him. He must be at peace when he saw his twin brother, mother, and father again and when he said goodbye to his wife, children, grandchild, sister Mary, brother Harry, and his nieces and nephews for the last time on this Earth.

His daughter held back her tears. Her heart was breaking but she wouldn't show it. He felt that she was strong, so she *would* be strong.

"Okay, Dad. We won't do anything ridiculous to save your life, I promise." He took a deep breath and let go of her hand. He asked Kathy if she had brought a notepad and pen with her. Of course she had. She knew her father would have a list in his head he needed to dictate to her, to write down for him in what he always called her "beautiful penmanship," as she had done for him since she was a child. Just as in so many previous years, he started to dictate, and Kathy wrote.

———————

John and Titika's son, Pete's twin, Mary and Harry's older brother, Noula's husband, the father of their four children Kathy, John, Dena, and Jimmy, "always a Marine," and successful local broadcaster Mike J. Pappas died five months later from congestive heart failure, passing peacefully while surrounded by the love of his family. Each family member took turns holding his hand, whispering their loving words into his ear as he transitioned from this world to the next, into the loving arms of his Lord; his father, John; his mother, Titika; and his twin brother, Pete—who no doubt said to him, "Brother, I've missed you! What took you so long?"

Author's Note

I am the family storyteller.

I am the firstborn granddaughter of Greek immigrants from the island of Crete and the daughter of a Greek immigrant mother from the village of Mistras, a short distance from the city of Sparta. I was the one chosen by my father to preserve the family's memories and stories. I am tasked to share them with the next generation, until the torch is passed to the subsequent chosen daughter to do the same.

I am connected to my parents, grandparents, and ancestors by blood and heart and spirit. Their voices, many now silent, still live within me, reminding me that their stories must be told and they must not be forgotten.

In between the years when my father nearly died at age 41 and finally succumbed at age 52 came the years when his motivated, positive vision of life became more clear and less shrouded in the mist, then the fog, that comes with an all-encompassing pursuit of success and wealth. Even after explaining to me as an eight-year-old what "bankruptcy" was (since he was obsessively talking about it all the time and I asked him about it), he added that if he or his brothers ever went bankrupt, they would do what he would do, which was to "take a gun and blow my brains out." Of course, he didn't realize that what he said shouldn't have been said to a child until many years later, when the ravages of heart disease ate away his heart muscle and destroyed his internal reality—of the ageless, fearless, indestructible Greek warrior—that defined both Pete and Mike Pappas through the decades.

After my Uncle Pete's death, my dad often sat in his recliner at home beneath a photo of Pete that was taken a few months before his death. He reminisced about him and their life together, and as he told his many stories, his sunkissed cheeks would become drenched with tears. He talked about who his brother was, the accomplishments they achieved together, the laughter they shared, and the bond that could never be severed, even by death.

Pete and Mike's lives took them from the impoverished streets of the Crows Landing Road area of Modesto to the boardrooms of corporations, some of which they created and others they were retained to save. Their financial success in broadcasting, coupled with stable home lives, changed the opinions that some of their fellow hometown Greeks and Americans previously had of them, when they predicted failure and even prison time for the twins. On the one hand, they watched their mother's tears flow when each of these insults were directed at her twin boys. On the other hand, with every tear, their anger transformed into determination to prove their detractors wrong. With every name they were called, and every prediction of failure, Pete and Mike simply embraced the labels, turning them inside out, transforming them from insults to inspiration.

In the end as in the beginning, it was always about Pete and Mike. They embodied the hopes and dreams of their immigrant Greek parents while encased in a cocoon of unconditional love and support. They grew up without money or an abundance of things—the material goods that members of my generation and those following deem to be the root of happiness. My father and his brothers had many ups and downs, facing the threat of financial ruin on several occasions, but what sustained them and fed their hope and optimism was the love they felt for each other and for their families, as well as the love they received in return.

The Greek philosopher Aristotle wrote that happiness in life came from a person's discovering and fulfilling their purpose. Pete and Mike found their purpose in life at a young age and, by that Aristotelian definition, were happy every day. With every sunrise, they got out of bed for a reason; and that reason, that purpose, sustained them in tough times. Their purpose was supported and nurtured by the loving stability of their childhood family life, their parents' and siblings' love for them, their love and devotion to one another as twins, and, later, the love and loyalty of their wives and children. Inspired by the hard lives of their Greek immigrant parents, they vowed to make them proud and to aim for stratospheric success in life.

When I read my immigrant grandfather's diary describing his first impressions of California and his journey there, I wished I could travel back in time and see our land through the eyes of Greek immigrants in the early 1900s and experience the wonder, magnificence, and grandeur of our country the way they saw it for the first time. Even though the early decades of the twentieth century were much like the Old West we read about in school—no running water or electricity in much of the country, with people still traveling mostly by foot, horseback, stagecoach, or train, often beset by lawlessness and vigilantism—still, for Greek immigrants, the United States was a far superior place than anything in the old country, and technological wonders like San Francisco's Golden Gate Bridge were unimaginable.

I think about my *papou*, John, every time I cross the Golden Gate Bridge. As I look up at its golden gables reaching skyward, sometimes disappearing into the white mist of fog, it reminds me of him, my grandmother, and my own mother. I say a silent prayer of thanks to them—poor immigrants who waited patiently in Greece to save money and obtain permission to leave Greece, then for America to give them permission to enter, who came to this country wide-eyed and innocent, seeking freedom and a better life. With courage, faith, and hope, they boarded ships and waved goodbye to their families, many of whom they would never see again. Because of their sacrifices, extreme hard work, and love of their new country, I had the privilege and blessing to be born an American.

This is a debt I can never repay.

My father once met an extremely wealthy, older man later in life who had earned vast amounts of money—more money than my father would probably ever earn. I was a teenager when we met him, and I said to Dad after meeting this fellow, "You know, Dad, if you didn't have the four of us kids, you and Mom would have had a lot less worries and a lot more money." He put his arm around me, pulled me close to him, and said, "I would give up millions and millions of dollars for each one of you kids and your mother. There is no amount of money that could've ever given me the joy all of you have. Money can buy you nice cars and homes and things and make life easier, but it can never replace the love of your family, of your wife and children. You remember that!"

Many lessons can be learned from Pete and Mike's lives, their successes in the radio and television industry, and their tragic end. Most of all, Pete and Mike weren't afraid to think and analyze life independently of the crowd or what was popular at the moment, because they had a security within themselves, rooted in their family's love, their Orthodox faith emphasized early in their childhood, a great respect for their Greek heritage, and pride in their family's honorable name and reputation.

As the firstborn sons in their family, they were the ones anointed to preserve its honor for future generations—to act as Greek warriors, blazing their way through life and growing their careers. They took that responsibility as seriously as medieval knights protecting the jewels of the crown. In so doing, they lived and died with honor. For me, my memories of our family life with my dad and Uncle Pete sustain me as I make my own way and remember life's lessons they taught us.

Truth is as we remember it, for each of us, and my memories are my truth, as were my father's, his twin brother's, and my mother's as well. My father's memories were painstakingly kept in file cabinets filled with audiotapes, files, scrapbooks of photos, news clippings, and assorted memorabilia, with lifetimes of family stories told to me in person and on an old microcassette recorder. My Uncle Pete's memories were only conveyed by the occasional anecdote. Unlike his twin brother, the past for Pete *was* in the past, so there was no need to revisit it. Life was about going forward, looking ahead, and not looking back.

My mother Noula's memories were locked away in the hope chest of her mind, memories of a childhood forgotten by choice—perhaps God's way of protecting her from childhood wartime traumas too horrible to remember in vivid detail.

Best to keep those locked away.

Consequently, I had my father, whose thoughts and feelings came spilling out, like Niagara Falls, and I had my mother, whose memories were kept in reserve and only shared with my father and her four children rarely and selectively, as she embraced us, womblike, with unconditional love throughout our lives.

As I look back upon my youth, I think affectionately of those early days in the radio business in the 1960s and 1970s—the smell of vinyl LPs newly delivered to the radio stations, rummaging through the closet of the engineer's office, and reading the labels on old reel-to-reel tapes my dad saved (one labeled "*Kathy–save*"), seeing six-packs of RC Cola stacked seven high on the right for contest winners entering the building to claim their prize for correct answers to on-air contests.

I remember the great kindness and dignity of my Greek immigrant grandparents, who lived just down the street from us, in their first brand-new home with new furniture. I remember the decency, devotion, love, and loyalty of my family, especially my parents. And I remember the fun and quirky days of our radio and, later, independent television station.

As a young child, I accepted the assignment of family historian from my father without question. I was his "little intellectual," the small girl who seemed more adult than child, and I took my job as the next family historian willingly and seriously. He loved my "beautiful penmanship" and asked me to take notes for him as soon as I learned to write in the first grade.

As I grew, my father repeatedly asked if I remembered the promise I made to him as a child—that I would keep safe his cabinets of file folders (each with a neatly typed label), stuffed full of the stories of his life and his identical twin brother's, that I would listen to the many hours of audiotapes he recorded, and that I would write their story one day so they wouldn't be forgotten.

I assured him I remembered.

———

To be forgotten was true death. My father didn't want the story of Pete and Mike, the Pappas twins, to die.

When a person of the Greek Orthodox faith passes away, mourners say in sympathy to the family, "May their memory be eternal."

Through their life story shared in the pages of this book, the memory of Pete and Mike Pappas—the Pappas twins—will live eternally.

My father used to say to me that, when I wrote the story of his life someday, it shouldn't be a story of sadness, but one of happiness and good times. Yet a good story, just like a good life, has both sadness *and* joy, and my family, as all families, had both. The joyous times paralleled a more-innocent America—one of small towns and local businesses, fresh immigrants, young descendants, patriotism, a Buick or Chevy or Ford in the driveway, backyard barbecues and potlucks, parades down Main Street for every holiday but especially for Christmas, which was still *called* "Christmas." Most parades featured members of the local VFW and AMVETS who had survived World Wars I and II and also Korea, and the Boy Scouts, Girl Scouts, and the PTA. Certainly, this more-innocent America wasn't perfect and had its problems, but working-class folks in California's San Joaquin Valley towns like Tulare, Visalia, Fresno, and Modesto all worked hard for a better life.

In the 1960s when I was growing up, *every* family was doing better than Grandma and Grandpa had done, and it was expected that you, the next generation, would do the same. The Pappas brothers were like many good sons and daughters of loving, hard-working immigrant parents. They wanted to achieve the American dream of economic success.

The path to prosperity for Pete and Mike began when they walked through the door of a radio station. The democracy in small-town America lay with people like them—cowboys and merchants whose handshakes were their word, farmers who grew the food found at the corner market, schoolteachers who were your neighbors and taught your children, doctors who made house calls, and local radio station owners like Pete and Mike Pappas, who took very seriously their responsibilities as guardians of the people's airwaves. My dad, Mike, patterned the news delivered from their locally owned radio stations after Edward R. Murrow (Dad's news idol since he was a young newsman of 24 working at KCVR-AM in Stockton). The brothers Pete, Mike, and Harry agreed that the only effective watchdogs of the government were unbiased journalism and the media, both locally and nationally, in every city and town in America.

Without accountability, there was corruption, so their duty and responsibility was to do their part to keep democracy alive in America, within the confines of the San Joaquin Valley towns their stations served. Their news stories at the top of the hour were straightforward news with both sides represented in the story—objectivity was always the goal when reporting the news. And their editorials were announced as editorials. When you listened to a Pete or Mike Pappas editorial, you knew you were getting an opinion.

The expansion of social programs, which they saw as a remedy to the guilt of the city elite, led to the creation of big government and increased taxation. Corruption by people in Washington led to laws favoring big business and international conglomerates over local business owners and domestic production. This change in government policy directly affected their locally owned radio stations, just as it affected every other family-owned business. Their editorials in favor of locally owned business and against government corruption and big business led to a faithful listening audience who believed Pete and Mike were advocates for them, when no one else listened or represented their interests.

Pete and Mike's editorials, whether aired on KGEN-AM 1370, KBOS-FM 95, KTRB-AM 860, KHOP-FM 104, or KZEL FM 96, always inspired friendly debate in local, Main Street coffee shops. On at least one occasion, my dad, Mike, was met with a hearty round of applause as he entered a Tulare, California, coffee shop for his early-morning cuppa' joe after his local station had aired an especially tough editorial.

To appease special interest groups that thought they didn't have the local media access they wanted, the Federal Communications Commission later released more AM and FM radio station licenses that ultimately favored applicants from those groups, who believed they could serve their constituency better than the local broadcasters of the period. This policy of creating too many radio stations and favoring special interest groups over experienced broadcasters forever changed the landscape of the broadcasting business, especially radio.

The negative outcome no one in Washington considered or even cared about was that, while local broadcasters served the public interest, they were also family-owned, local businesses that employed their neighbors and contributed to the area's economy. That meant they had to make money somehow, and the way they did that was to sell advertising to local businesses, of which there were a finite number, a number that was shrinking rapidly. The financial pie was limited in size, and there were more people lining up who wanted a piece. As those new stations came on the air and typically failed in short order (their owners lacking the benefit of broadcasting experience), big national companies swooped in, like birds of prey, to gobble them up.

Pete and Mike were products of small-town America. They came from the "bad" side of town with nothing but the love of their Greek immigrant parents along with a cultural and family history of honor, relentless hard work, and sacrifice. They combined that with what they learned of the can-do American spirit as young boys, along with their intrinsic need to succeed and achieve what they wanted most—material success that gave them the lifestyle they desired and the respect they craved. The twin boys who spent their early years in shacks with dirt floors and no running water wanted the best America had to offer— great or even grand houses, expensive cars, designer clothes and jewelry, and a life lived on the "good" side of town. They worked hard from a young age, and they dreamed of retiring young to travel and see the rest of the United States as well as countries they longed to visit around the world. They never planned to work until old age. Instead, Pete and Mike wanted to earn enough money to retire young and enjoy life without the stress of being local radio station operators forced to compete with wealthy, out-of-town corporate owners.

The twins couldn't retire until their amalgamation of radio stations became more profitable, despite the new competitive landscape, so that when they were ready, they would sell their stations for the most money possible.

By the time they reached their early 40s, they had everything they ever wanted. Life was good, even with the additional stress and risk of competing in the new radio marketplace. If that meant that early-morning visits to the gym and regular healthy diets were cast aside and that they smoked more out of stress, took diet pills to lose weight, and worked even harder, they would do what needed to be done. If they ever thought life was tough, they just needed to remember back to the days of their youth in poverty and recall their parents' struggles, which was enough motivation to keep them charging on to the next battle. They were great warriors waging an economic battle every day, tough and tenacious.

Until they took the proverbial bullet in the chest, the twins would never stop.

They needed to take that hill at any cost.

But, as they reached the summit, that bullet found them.

In the end, they got *everything* they ever wanted, as well as some things later in their lives that they had never wanted. That's the part of success no one speaks of out loud. The bug of ambition bites and the fever takes hold. Everything comes with a price, and the price paid is not recognizing the truth of mortality. The lie of one's invincibility, borne from great confidence and success, becomes truth. In the end, the unfathomable truths of life determined Pete and Mike's destiny.

The first and final Pappas family portrait, circa early 1970s. Standing, left to right, are Mike J. Pappas, Mike Alfieris, Mary Pappas Alfieris, Stella A. Pappas, and Harry J. Pappas. Seated, left to right, are Noula Pappas, John Pappas, the family patriarch, Katherine "Titika" Pappas, the family matriarch, Bessie Pappas, and Mike's twin brother, Pete.

Pete and Mike were our family's shooting stars.

In the memories of their families and through the pages of this book, they are immortal.

In my mind, where imagination lives and faith flourishes, I believe Pete and Mike still live in the great beyond as those two cute, dark-haired teenagers from the 1950s. I imagine them now as heavenly hosts on-the-air, with their mother, Titika; their father, John; Pete's wife, Bessie; Theo Manoli; their sister, Mary, and brother-in-law Mike Alfieris—all young and healthy, happily listening as the charismatic, handsome, and vivacious twins engage their fans. No doubt the family is sitting under the *crevatina*, arbor, around a table of Greek delicacies and pastries, as they wait for the twins to come home after their nightly broadcast to celebrate, feast, and share their love with one another.

On heavenly radio, they are spinning discs, taking requests and dedications from their devoted listeners, still behind the mic and on the phone, late into the night.

Hey there, guys and gals, do ya' wanna' hear Elvis? Or how 'bout the Platters? What about that Nat King Cole and his "Mona Lisa"?

The two of them are laughing together as they take calls from their listeners. Pete and Mike, the Pappas twins, teen radio stars, are eternally on the air.

Well, you cool cats, this is Pete…

…and this is Mike, and we're signing off for now.

Tune in tomorrow for the latest hits and the best in requests and dedications.

Good night for now, from Pete and Mike's Dance Time.

Biography of Harry J. Pappas

Twin Destinies wouldn't be complete if I didn't include information about the extraordinary life and accomplishments of my uncle, Harry J. Pappas, who was instrumental in building the Pappas family's broadcast business and his own chain of television stations throughout the United States.

1963: After graduating from high school, Harry moved to Las Vegas, Nevada, to attend the University of Las Vegas. His goal was to pursue a career as an attorney. After working for Pete and Mike for a short time at KVEG-AM, he was offered the opportunity to invest with them when they decided to buy a radio station of their own. He had $5,000 from a legal settlement for an injury he had received as a newborn. One weekend, he spent time alone to "soul-search" about the decision: Was this a good choice, to change his career trajectory and the course of his life? In the end, he joined his brothers in the broadcasting business. His $5,000 investment bought him a 10% ownership stake in their first radio station, KGEN-AM 1370, in Tulare, California.

1964–1970: KGEN-AM 1370 is purchased by Pete, Mike, and Harry Pappas. A new radio station, KBOS-FM 95, is put on the air for the first time by the three Pappas brothers.

1971: KMPH-TV channel 26 is launched by Pete, Mike, and Harry on October 11, 1971.

1974: KTRB-AM 860 and its sister FM station, located in their hometown of Modesto, California, is purchased by Pete, Mike, and Harry Pappas.

1976–1977: Harry bought out his brothers' interests and those of their shareholders in KMPH-TV 26 (Pappas Television Inc.) and formed Pappas Telecasting Inc.

1980: Harry formed Pappas Teleproductions (PTP), a television commercial and program production studio based in Fresno, California. PTP produced award-winning commercials, documentaries, and video presentations for clients, shot on location in Israel, the Middle East, Europe, Asia, and throughout the U.S.

1984 and 1986: Harry put two more television stations on the air: WHNS in Asheville, North Carolina, and KPTM in Omaha, Nebraska.

1988: Harry was contacted by executives at the Fox Network to get the Pappas stations to affiliate with their new, fourth network. KMPH was the first Pappas station to become a Fox affiliate, followed by WHNS and KPTM.

1989: Pappas Telecasting was awarded the Fox Broadcasting Outstanding Affiliate Award for Harry's idea to create the Fox Children's Network (FCN).

1995: Some of Harry's stations were the first WB Television Network affiliates nationwide, and his station in Greensboro, North Carolina, was recognized with the WB's "Froggie" award as the fastest growing WB affiliate in prime time.

2006: A number of Harry's stations became some of the first affiliates of the new CW Network, launched by Warner Brothers and CBS.

2007: KTRB-AM 860, the first radio station that fueled Pete and Mike's broadcasting dreams as schoolboys, was again purchased by Harry. With FCC approval, KTRB's transmitter was moved from Modesto, California, to serve the San Francisco Bay Area.

Prior to Harry's retirement, Pappas Telecasting Companies held more than thirty television stations across the United States.

Awards received by Harry J. Pappas:

The Ellis Island Medal of Honor from the National Ethnic Coalition of Organizations

The Hellenic Heritage Achievement Award from the American Hellenic Institute

The American Broadcast Pioneer Award from the Broadcasters' Foundation

The designation of Archon, from the Patriarch of the Greek Orthodox Church

The Theodore Saloutos Award from the American Hellenic Council of California

Inducted into Broadcasting and Cable's Hall of Fame, the industry's highest honor

Other Notable Achievements:

Invited to provide expert testimony before the subcommittee on Communications of the U.S. House of Representatives during hearings to consider regulations affecting the communications industry.

Testified before hearings of the Federal Communications Commission regarding proposals to modify the Financial Interest in Syndication Rules.

Testified before the Subcommittee on Telecommunications and the of the U.S. House of Representatives during a hearing held with regard to the Subcommittee's consideration of H.R. 3717, the "Broadcast Decency Enforcement Act of 2004."

Served as a panelist during the Federal Communications Commission's forum on localism in July, 2004.

Glossary of Greek Terms

Americani, American kids; also *Americani pethya*

aristocratia, aristocrats, weathy people

avgolemono, egg lemon soup

Baba, father (affection name)

bammyes me kota, chicken with okra

epeetah, later! (meaning "just wait")

horio, village

horyati, village peasants

kafenion, coffeehouse

kakomiri, bad fate

kale neekta, good night

kalee agoria, good sons

kefi, a love for life and love for living

kenooryo, new

mandinathes, Cretan stories recited as poems

Meeterra, mother

palikari, hero

pantalonia, pants

papou, grandfather

Paterra, father

pentozali, Cretan dance of war

philoxenia, hospitality

pilafi, rice

psomaki, a small piece of bread
teepohtah, nothing
yiayia, grandma, grandmother
zembekiko, a dance of contemplation

Greek food descriptions

baklava, honey walnut dessert in layers of filo, basted with butter and topped with honey

diples, sweet dough, deep fried, drained, dipped in honey, and sprinkled with chopped walnuts

dolmathes, seasoned beef and rice, wrapped in grape leaves, and sometimes prepared with a frothy avgolemono sauce

katlitsounia, a mixture of cheeses wrapped in a light, flaky dough and quick-fried on the stove

karydopita, honey walnut cake

kourambyethes, cookies covered in powdered white sugar

moussaka, eggplant, meat, and potato casserole

pasticho, meat and macaroni casserole covered in béchamel sauce

pilafi, rice, cooked in chicken broth, butter, and lemon juice

spanakopita, spinach pie topped with filo dough

tiropites, cheese turnovers in filo dough

Index

Acknowledgments

A heartfelt thank you to my husband, Michael C. Angelos, for his unwavering love, support, commentary, and devoted reading of every draft of this book through the years. I couldn't have completed this project without you, my partner through life, by my side.

Thank you to my mother, Noula Mehas Pappas, for her love, nurturing, and encouragement throughout my life. Your memories of the years spent with Dad infused my words with spirit. You have always been my muse.

A special thanks to my uncle and aunt Harry J. Pappas and Stella A. Pappas, for sharing your facts, thoughts, and memories of decades past spent with Pete, Mike, and your family. I am grateful for your kindness and generosity.

Many thanks to my cousin Steven E. Alfieris, Attorney-at-Law, for his legal advice, insight, and enthusiasm.

My appreciation to my brother John, who shared memories with me, and my sister Dena and brother Jimmy for their support

Grateful thanks to my daughter, Mira Angelos, and son, Evan Angelos, for all your patience and understanding whenever I've needed solitude to write. You've been my cheerleaders since you were little children.

A sincere thanks to my editor, Dana Martin, for her help and suggestions during the writing process.

Lastly, a warm thank you and much love to my late father, Mike J. Pappas, for trusting me to tell the story of the life he led with his identical twin brother, my wonderful late Uncle Pete Pappas.

I kept my promise, Dad.

About the Author

Kathy Pappas Angelos is a business writer turned author. Her career as a creative professional has included writing and editing content for online and print publications. A native Central Californian, she was on-air talent for the family's radio station as "KGEN's Kathy" at the age of three. Kathy lives with her husband and family in Central California. Learn more about Kathy at her website: KathyPappasAngelos.com.

CPSIA information can be obtained
at www.ICGtesting.com
Printed in the USA
JSHW080330210423
40255JS00002B/2

9 781610 354233